:?

Bedstead of carved oak, dated 1590. The back panels are inlaid with fruit wood. (Victoria and Albert Museum)

Antique or Fake?

The Making of Old Furniture

Charles H. Hayward

VNR VAN NOSTRAND REINHOLD COMPANY
NEW YORK   CINCINNATI   TORONTO   LONDON   MELBOURNE

First published in paperback in 1981
Copyright © 1970 by Charles H. Hayward
Library of Congress Catalog Card Number 81-50405
ISBN 0-442-26415-1

Van Nostrand Reinhold Company
135 West 50th Street, New York, NY 10020

Cloth edition published 1970
by Evans Brothers Limited and St. Martin's Press
Fifth cloth impression 1979

16 15 14 13 12 11 10 9 8 7 6 5 4 3 2 1

Contents

By the same author

English Period Furniture
Period Furniture Designs
The Complete Book of Woodwork
Cabinet Making for Beginners
Carpentry for Beginners
Furniture Repairs
Light Machines for Woodwork
Making Toys in Wood
Practical Veneering
Practical Woodwork
Staining and Polishing
Tools for Woodwork
Woodwork Joints
Woodworker's Pocket Book
Handyman's Pocket Book
The Complete Handyman
Practical Wood Carving and Gilding
(with W. Wheeler)

Introduction

In common with most subjects, the study of old furniture can be approached in several ways. The most usual is to take its main externals – its general form, timber of which it is made, decorative treatment, and so on – and consider these in relation to its historic and social background. And this is certainly an important side to the subject. There is, however, another aspect to the matter, one which is often neglected; namely the way old furniture was made.

It seems a logical conclusion that the class of men most closely connected with furniture were those who actually made it, and consideration of their work can be revealing in bringing fresh light on the evolution of woodwork. It is true that of the vast majority of these men nothing whatever is known, but the solution of their problems remains with us today in the furniture they made. Apart from this, the subject can be of tremendous interest, conjuring up visions of the lives and working conditions of people who made things in the years that have gone, shadowy anonymous figures labouring in the background, completely out of the limelight, but turning out work by methods and in conditions difficult to realize today.

In the nature of things practical considerations have necessarily had their effect on design itself. What was possible at one period may have been quite impracticable at another. Men's skill at any particular time, the tools and appliances they had, the timbers available, the invention or introduction of special processes, and the dividing up of the trade of woodworking into specialized branches – cabinet-making, chair-making, turning, carving, upholstery, finishing, box-making, and mirror-frame-making have all had their effect on the type and quality of furniture being made. It is not suggested that these practical matters have been the only influence on design, or even the chief ones, but the understanding of construction is a tremendous help in realizing how it came about that a certain type of furniture was made at a particular period.

In addition it is a subject full of interest in itself, involving research into the tools and apparatus available to craftsmen, the circumstances in which they worked, and the methods which they followed. My thoughts go back to my apprenticeship days before the First World War, when a great deal of hand work was still being done. Tradition dies hard, and the probability is that conditions and methods were but little changed from those that had been followed in a cabinet-making workshop for years, except that we did have three machines; bandsaw, planer, and spindle-moulder. Yet, even here, we were limited because, although there were about eighteen cabinet-makers and apprentices, there was only one machinist, and it was often quicker to do a thing by hand than wait until the machinist could get around to it. In any case all mortising, tenoning, dovetailing, and general jointing had to be done by hand; and it was always necessary to hand-plane surfaces even though they had been put through the machine planer first, because the latter was an early model, obsolete even by the standards of those days, leaving obvious marks across the grain, and often with gashed cutters which left their track along the length of the wood. It was only by damping the surface of the wood with hot water, leaving it to dry and then planing by hand that a good clean surface could be produced.

We were an antique shop; that is we made reproductions and fakes, repaired old pieces, and did something quite remarkable in the way of conversions. The first two had to be made in the same way that an old piece would have been made, and we had enough old furniture through our hands for repair to have gained a pretty shrewd idea of what had been usual practice in the past (though it has to be admitted that the exception did turn up from time to time). For the conversions, Victorian furniture was the chief source. Today Victorian things are coming back into popularity, but fifty years or so ago they were largely held in the contempt which most ages have for the works of their immediate predecessors. Yet it was realized that, by and large, Victorian furniture was extremely well-made and had some excellent timber in it. Furthermore it had had several years of use in a period when there were still plenty of servants to do the periodical work of polishing with wax, and consequently it had already acquired an excellent patina. From the carcases of these disdained pieces there arose some 18th century cabinets, like the phoenix, born anew. Victorian moulding sections, turnings, shapes, and handles were ruthlessly cut away and replaced by details more in keeping with the period to which the resuscitated specimen was supposed to belong. Some reconstructions were successful; others less so; and it is an interesting thought that some of them may be the treasured possession of folk happy in the thought that they possess authentic work of the golden age of cabinet-making.

However, all this is by the way, and I mention it only in passing as a memory of an experience which must have had much in common with the conditions of a cabinet workshop of the last century and earlier. All trade methods are based on the experience of what has gone before and to this extent are traditional or conservative; but fundamentally men go about things in the simplest and most obvious way because there is no virtue in creating difficulties by experimenting, quite apart from the grim necessity, half a century ago, of earning a living in a period when the rewards of toil were not great.

It is quite likely then that in our unheated workshop where we toiled from 7.00 a.m. to 6.00 p.m. in summer and from 8.00 a.m. to 7.00 p.m. in winter, we worked much as our predecessors had done for generations – except that they worked still longer hours.

And with this preamble we may turn to the furniture itself and see how practical considerations made their contribution to its evolution.

Charles H. Hayward,
St. Albans, 1970.

Fig. 1 Fine quality bureau-bookcase veneered with walnut, dating from the early 18th century. This is one of the few signed pieces of furniture. It carries the inlaid inscription 'Samuel Bennett, London Fecit'. Little is known of this cabinet-maker, but it is obvious from this bureau-bookcase that he was a most accomplished craftsman. Whether he designed it himself is not known, but if he did he must have had an excellent sense of proportion and appreciation of form as well as a thorough understanding of the principles of construction. (Victoria and Albert Museum)

Chapter 1

Why is old furniture popular?

There is probably more interest in old furniture today than at any other period. Each year seems to bring with it an increase in the number of antique shops, so that every town has its quota of them and many villages as well, all of them offering for sale items which were made, or purport to have been made, anything over a hundred years ago. It is difficult to say wherein exactly this fascination for old furniture lies. Is there any virtue in age as such? Was old furniture really made much better than anything being turned out today? Was its design superior? And is a thing really much better because somebody made it by sweat and toil with hand tools rather than the ease and simplicity that machines offer? To be honest, the answer is often no to all these points.

Is there any virtue in age as such? When a thing has been in use for a century or more things have almost inevitably happened to it. Use or abuse have left their mark in the form of broken or missing parts, scratches and bruises are practically inescapable, the structure is often rickety, wear on moving parts such as drawers is bound to have occurred, and it may have been 'improved' by additions or alterations which may or may not have been skilfully done. On the other hand when a piece of furniture has been looked after properly it acquires a patina that cannot be produced in any other way. Exposure to light also brings a mellowness of colour which cannot be entirely imitated (though some fakers get very near it). Lastly, there is a certain sentimental value in the thought of folk, long since dead, who may have used it, so that it is, as it were, a witness to history, a mute reminder of habits of bygone times (some of which, by the way, may have been repulsive to our way of thinking), and a link with an age that has gone for ever.

But was old furniture really made much better than anything being turned out today? It does not follow in the slightest that this is necessarily the case. There was shoddy construction in the past just as there is today, and the fact that a thing is old does not redeem its shoddiness. Anyone who has had much experience in repairing old woodwork knows that some of it was badly made, with a construction that was bound to fail because it was in defiance of the fact that wood is liable to shrink as moisture dries out, or indeed swell as it absorbs moisture. Fig. 2 is an example. It is typical of a cheap form of chest-of-drawers often made in pairs or half-dozens in the 19th century. Many of those that have survived have found their way into the repairer's shop where they often cost more to put right than a much more valuable, properly-made piece.

On the other hand there has been some splendid woodwork in the past, not only elaborate items made for wealthy patrons but simple, honest pieces made for everyday use in farmhouse or dwelling house which have survived probably because they were conscientiously made in the best way a craftsman knew.

So far as design is concerned this obviously remains today what it was when the piece was made (except for any subsequent alterations). Age may have given a certain softness to it but it has not altered its form, proportions, and details. There were, of course, many first-rate pieces which bear the hallmark of appreciation of form. Some of them were the work of experienced designers, but also those which owed their origin to master craftsmen frequently showed a fine quality of line and detail. This is particularly true of things made in the second half of the 18th century, often known as the golden age of cabinet-making.

At some periods there seems to have been a sense of quality or integrity in which first-rate craftsmanship was combined with artistic appreciation. To say that a cabinet-maker was an artist would be a foolish exaggeration, but when there is a high standard in a trade, the men who practise it acquire an appreciation of line and form, so that a craftsman is able to interpret into practical reality what may have existed on paper only as a sketch. The truth of this is often brought out in comparing the engravings that appear in many of the books of designs published in the 18th century. Some of the designs can be recognized in furniture that has survived, but the reality is invariably superior to the engraving. It has passed through the process imposed by practical necessity, and has been qualified and refined by a craftsman knowledgeable in the possibilities and limitations of wood as a material.

Not all furniture was of good design. Just as there have been artists of varying ability in all ages, so there have been good and mediocre craftsmen. In some cases, however, a sort of quaintness seemed to creep into furniture, especially in earlier oak woodwork which often had a certain naïve character about it which was almost childlike in its freedom and disregard or ignorance of its classical origin. This frequently gives such work a charm which is difficult to define except in a negative way.

Is a thing really much better because somebody made it by sweat and toil with hand tools? In other words, is a thing better because it was hand-made rather than machine-made? When a man makes something from beginning to end he invariably learns to select his timber for the purpose for which it is required. Whereas in mass-produced items timber may be sawn out without regard to grain direction or blemishes, a thing made individually by hand methods is invariably the result of careful selection. Furthermore it is the old story that skill to do comes of doing. A man who

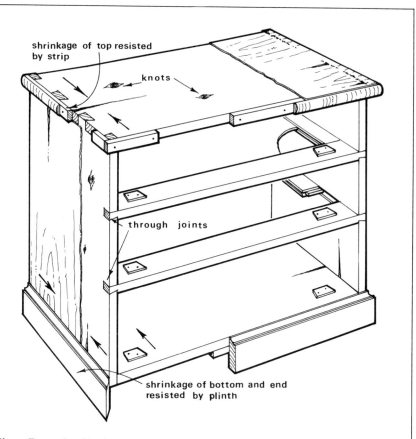

Fig. 2 Example of bad construction in a chest-of-drawers. Such chests were often turned out commercially in the 19th century. The carcase was of pine, frequently with knots. After assembling, the joints were levelled and the ends veneered. A strip was glued and nailed around the top, and lengths of cross-grained mahogany added around the strip. The top was then veneered and the rounding of the moulding completed. Finally the front edges were veneered and the plinth glued and nailed, and glue-blocked at the inside. Shrinkage from back to front was inevitable and, being resisted by the top strips and the plinth, splits in ends, top, and bottom occurred. Another weakness was that of the through joints between drawer rails and ends. Shrinkage would leave the ends of the rails slightly proud, and any racking would loosen the veneer. Lastly, knots in the groundwork were bound to show through the veneer eventually, quite apart from the possibility of resin preventing glue from adhering.

has to cut his joints with saw, chisel, and plane soon acquires an uncanny skill in using those tools. It is only in more recent years when men have found that a machine saw will cut wood not only quickly but accurately, that they have almost given up the sawing of joints by hand and have thus lost their skill in hand work.

I recall my early days in the workshop in 1912 when a cabinet-maker could saw his tenons and put his joints together with little or no fitting.

Constant practice had given him judgement and skill so that he worked accurately almost as a matter of course, no doubt spurred on by practical necessity. If he were on piece-work any delay was reflected in his pay packet; if paid by the hour he soon heard from the foreman when he took too long on a job. At the same time there was a certain pride of craftsmanship that actuated a man quite apart from more mundane considerations.

When a job required carving this would be done by the carver, a separate tradesman, and the job was invariably finished by the polisher. Apart from this, however, the cabinet-maker did everything from cleaning up the timber to the final assembling. There was consequently something personal about the things he did. The production of a good job was a matter of personal pride or conceit.

This may be contrasted with present-day practice, in which, say, veneering is done in one shop, sawing out and machining in another, assembling in a third, and the fitting-out involved in drawer and door work done in a fourth. No one man sees a job right through, and often a man doing one operation never sees the final product.

Apart from all this it has to be admitted that some operations are done better (and obviously more quickly) by machines than by hand. A circular saw, properly used, will cut a part perfectly straight and square so that only a skim with a plane is needed to finish it. No one, no matter how skilled, could do this with a hand saw. And much the same applies to other machines which have ousted hand work.

Today, when we praise (and rightly so) the skill of the men who had only the labour of their hands to do everything, we know that we would never go back to that system. Much of it, skilful as it was, was pure drudgery. Who, for instance, would want to go back to ripping out boards on the saw pit, Fig. 3? If ever there was a soulless job it must have been that, the creeping forward one eighth inch at a time, the man below in semi-darkness, a mere human machine covered with sawdust which clung to his half-naked, sweating body.

After all these largely negative criticisms we may repeat our query as to what causes people to be attracted by old furniture. Quite possibly it is primarily due to a revulsion from this machine-ruled age. People would not want to go back to the labour and tedium that is inescapable when every operation calls for human work, but they cannot but feel admiration for things that were made in that way. It is one thing to admire something; another to do it.

Then again there is the sentiment that goes with old things, calling up as it does visions of folk in costumes seen now only in pictures or in museums, and living lives far removed from those of today; and of customs completely dead. There is also the undeniable fact that cabinet-work from about 1660 and onwards did reach an extremely high standard, reaching its highest level during the second half of the 18th century.

Today we have added much Victorian furniture to the period of antiques (after having derided it for years as a thing of small worth) and, no matter what the final judgement may be, the best Victorian cabinet-

Fig. 3 A reconstruction of an old saw pit. This delightful set-up is in the St. Albans City Museum and shows the chief method of converting timber right up to the second half of the 19th century. Wind- and water-powered machine saws had been used in England to a limited extent in the late 18th century, but it was not until steam power was applied to saws in the 19th century that the saw pit began to decline. Even so it was still used in rural districts until the end of the century. It would take two men about 1½ hours to make a single cut along the log shown, for which in 1825 they would earn 6d. between them. (The Salaman Collection, St. Albans City Museum)

work was as beautifully made as that of the 18th century. In some cases it was better. Any man who has had experience in repair work knows the truth of this. This quality work, plus the fact that some really splendid timber went into its making is no doubt another reason for the preference many have for old furniture.

Lastly there is the matter of fashion. It is true that there is fashion in antiques themselves, the product of one period being preferred to all others at one particular time; but taking the subject as a whole there is almost a sort of snob value in furnishing with antiques, plus the hope that the purchase of an old piece may be in the nature of an investment. In Galsworthy's *Forsyte Saga*, Soames Forsyte says: 'That's genuine old lacquer; you can't get it nowadays. It'd do well in a sale at Jobson's'. We all hope that when we buy we buy wisely, and, although if a thing is to be in our homes we have it because it appeals to us, we still hope that it will eventually realize more than we gave for it.

Chapter 2

Construction and design

The old problem propounded by schoolboys 'which came first the chicken or the egg?' might well be asked of the title of this chapter. Certainly the two are inter-related and it is almost impossible to reach a final conclusion about the one without considering the other. All things have to be designed within the scope of what is practicable, and to the designer-craftsman this may be so obvious as to need no further discussion; yet only too often one hears of the design of furniture being regarded as a matter of external appearance only. The truth is that practical considerations have had more effect on design in the past than is generally realized. In fact, in some cases design has been the direct outcome of changes in practical possibilities. It is true, of course, that there can be almost endless variations on a given theme, hence the many and varied designs in, say, chairs of the 18th century; but it is equally true that most of such designs would have been impossible for practical reasons a hundred years earlier.

Consider as an instance of this what is happening at the present time. The manufacture of really reliable plywood, laminboard, and chipboard has made it possible to use wide unjointed panels in which all danger of shrinkage and swelling has been eliminated. This makes it feasible to design items with wide unbroken surfaces which can be fixed rigidly without risk of the splitting which would have been inevitable if solid wood were used. Thus many present-day designs are possible only because of the manufacture of these materials.

Or take another example, this time working in reverse. It would be useless today to specify in a design that, say, a table top 30 inches wide must be in solid unjointed Cuban mahogany. With luck a man might find an old Victorian table leaf which he could use; he might even be fortunate to discover an odd board in a timber yard; but to ask a timber merchant to supply such a timber as a regular line would be more like asking for the roc's egg. Little of this wood is available and what there is is almost always sliced into veneers.

These are two examples of how practical considerations are affecting design today. Much the same was true in the past, however, when what we now know as period furniture was being made. That there were designers of marked originality is undoubtedly true, but they were necessarily both limited and benefited by the circumstances of their day.

Until about the middle of the 17th century the wood used for furniture was chiefly oak. Occasionally one finds items of elm and chestnut and more rarely of softwood, but native home-grown oak was plentiful and was a durable wood which could withstand the boisterous conditions of the times. Furthermore it could· be riven easily along the lines of the radial rays. I have seen a great log of oak of 2–3 feet diameter riven open into two halves in a matter of seconds (other woods such as elm cannot be cleft in this way owing to the interlocked grain). Thus the initial conversion of wood was simplified, reducing the time consumed on the saw pit.

After about 1660 oak declined in favour as a fashionable furniture wood, though it was still used for drawer linings, interior parts, etc. and, indeed, in its entirety for some items. In fact it has been used for furniture in common with other woods ever since. However, after about 1660 and until about 1725 walnut superseded oak as the wood used by leading furniture-makers. With the exception of chair legs and backs and other shaped parts which had to be in solid wood, the walnut was invariably in veneer form. After 1725 it gave place to mahogany, until the 19th century when it again became popular for furniture.

Clearly the importation of a timber from abroad has affected the type of furniture being produced. Obviously until its import was on a reasonably large scale no serious use was possible for furniture. It is said that the first piece of mahogany ever introduced into this country was in the form of a new rudder for the *Golden Hind* after the original had been damaged during the famous voyage round the world. Another version, gleaned from *The Book of English Trades*, published in the early 19th century by G. and W. B. Whittaker of Ave Maria Lane, London, states that 'the first use to which mahogany was applied in England, was to make a box for holding candles. Dr. Gibbons, an eminent physician, at the latter end of the 17th century, had a brother, a West Indian captain, who brought over some planks of this wood as ballast . . . but the carpenters finding the wood too hard for their tools, they were laid aside as useless. Soon after, Mrs. Gibbons wanting a candle box, called on his cabinet-maker (Wollaston, of Long Acre) to make one of the same wood that lay in the garden.' It seems that the worthy doctor, no doubt prompted by his good lady, then had a bureau made, and the fine colour and polish were so pleasing that friends were called in to see it. Amongst them was the Duchess of Buckingham who persuaded the obliging doctor to part with some of his timber and had a second bureau made by the said Wollaston.

However this may be, the importation of the wood on any scale did not begin until about 1725–30. It follows then that although a few pieces in this wood may have been made earlier, the vast majority of mahogany furniture must have been made after 1725.

Towards the end of the 18th century satinwood became popular as a furniture wood, though not to the exclusion of mahogany. Early in the 19th century rosewood was used widely, in fact during the Victorian period walnut, mahogany, satinwood, oak, and rosewood were all used for furniture.

At any one time the skill of men in making things is based on the experience of the past, and as new techniques or new materials are introduced so the knowledge and ability of men are increased. At the same time it may happen that a new technique may make an old one obsolete, so that men may lose a particular skill. This is exemplified by the introduction of steam power in converting timber by machine saws. Men no longer had laboriously to cut logs on the saw pit or to cut veneers by hand.

However, in a general way the skill of craftsmen is bound up with trade practice. Up to about 1660 most furniture was made by the general wood-worker who also made various other items in wood. There were two classes of men; the highly skilled joiner who made staircases, door frames, quality panelling, etc., and the general carpenter who made more homely items such as cupboards and plain chests. Invariably the class of craftsmen is obvious from the quality of the item. As an example compare Figs. 1 and 2. Both were made in the 17th century but the skilled work in the one is in contrast with the homely character of the other.

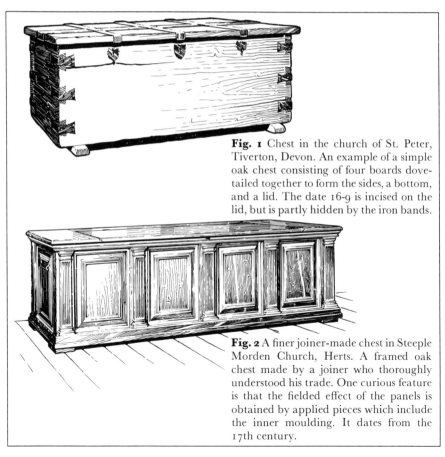

Fig. 1 Chest in the church of St. Peter, Tiverton, Devon. An example of a simple oak chest consisting of four boards dove-tailed together to form the sides, a bottom, and a lid. The date 16-9 is incised on the lid, but is partly hidden by the iron bands.

Fig. 2 A finer joiner-made chest in Steeple Morden Church, Herts. A framed oak chest made by a joiner who thoroughly understood his trade. One curious feature is that the fielded effect of the panels is obtained by applied pieces which include the inner moulding. It dates from the 17th century.

It was not until after about 1660, however, that cabinet-making became a specialized branch of woodwork. Methods of construction gradually became largely standardized; also the thicknesses of wood for this or that purpose. Furthermore, such tradesmen doing this work developed an appreciation of line, largely the result of experience. A master cabinet-maker employing several men would no doubt mark out certain parts and generally check work as it went through, but the workman would soon come to appreciate line and could be relied on to keep to a form which was standard practice. This became still more marked when chair-making became separated from cabinet-making as a trade. The understanding of the subtle lines of a chair back or the grace of a cabriole leg came only with constant practice in that branch of furniture-making.

Of course, men varied in skill then as today, and one sometimes finds work which is anything but pleasing to the eye, but generally there was an extremely high standard of workmanship in the 18th century especially in cabinets and chairs made in London or other large towns. Some items bear the stamp of having been made in country districts in that they appear to be copies, possibly from memory, of finer furniture a man may have seen in a town; or maybe they were the work of a carpenter commissioned to make a copy of a chair but who missed the spirit of the original; or possibly he had to make do with thinner timber and so lost the fineness of line. Chairs especially use a lot of wood, particularly those with compound curvature in the back.

When a man has only a limited range of tools it is clear that he can make only those things which are within the restrictions imposed by that range. A country carpenter would be equipped to do straight-forward work but it is unlikely that he would have much in the way of moulding planes, probably no carving tools, and none of the tools and apparatus for the finer branches of work. A journeyman cabinet-maker working in a town probably had his basic bench tools, but such things as moulding planes and other special tools were the property of the master cabinet-maker who would allow his men to use them as necessity arose.

Almost within my experience this was the system that used to apply before the nearly exclusive use of machinery. In the pre-1914 years of my apprenticeship one of the older cabinet-makers spoke of his father's business, that of a small master cabinet-maker, and of how one of his Saturday afternoon jobs was that of sharpening moulding, grooving, and rebate planes in readiness for the next week of work. A tedious, time-consuming operation it must have been, for most of the sharpening of moulding plane cutters had to be done with oilstone slips. The ground bevel had to be maintained and the cutting edge kept to the contour of the plane sole. It is small wonder that as much as possible of the working of mouldings was done with ordinary bench planes before the moulding plane was used.

This system was, no doubt, reflected in the fine quality work turned out by the best cabinet-making shops. Only the master man with a prosperous business could afford to have the special shapes of moulding planes needed

Fig. 3 In a chair-maker's shop. Although this photograph was taken about five years ago, it is probably typical of what a workshop would have been like in the 18th century.

in fine cabinet-work. Small shops or country woodworkers would make do with what they had, or would use simple sections that could be worked with rebate planes and possibly a round plane. For small sections they could use the scratch-stock[1], of course, but it would not be easy to work, say, a large cornice moulding with this tool.

An example of special branches of work is veneering. Until men had learnt to cut veneers and lay them, only furniture in solid wood was possible. In England it was not until the Restoration period when crafts-men from abroad settled in the country that the trick was learnt. Even then many mistakes were made at first.

Another special branch of work was carving. In some oak furniture of a date prior to the middle of the 17th century, the surface was frequently decorated with carving, usually of a conventional type and frequently it looks to be the work of the carpenter himself. There is something naïve or child-like about it which has a charm of its own although largely lacking in technical quality. Occasionally other oak pieces are of a quite different character and appear to be the work of a man whose occupation was solely that of carving. Certainly after the middle of the 17th century the carving on town-made pieces in walnut bears the stamp of professional

[1] See Glossary; also Chapter 3.

work. In fact, the start of cabinet-making as a separate trade brought with it another specialized trade, that of the furniture carver.

During the whole of the 18th century and later, carvers were not only separate tradesmen but were in themselves divided into branches. Sheraton says that there were four classes of carving: architectural work; internal decorations for furniture; chair work; and ship's work. He says: 'Having possessed a strong attachment and inclination for carving in my youth, I was necessarily induced to make attempts in this art and succeeded in some degree. I was employed in the country occasionally in it'.

The town master cabinet-maker would have easy access to carvers; if his business was large enough, he would probably employ one or more. This was yet another way in which the town tradesman had the advantage over the country woodworker. Much the same would apply to other trades such as turnery, marquetry-cutting, and upholstery. The country woodworker might have access to a lathe but he might have difficulty in calling in other tradesmen.

As the 19th century advanced things gradually changed. Transport facilities became easier with the coming of railways so that towns and villages were not so isolated as before. Machines which would convert timber and cut veneers and carry out special operations such as grooving, rebating, moulding, and so on were installed. It did not happen universally but steam power began to simplify and cheapen many operations which had been expensive and difficult before.

But it is in the wood itself that we have one of the main practical things which have influenced design. Most people admire the attractive appearance of panelling and other framed structures with highlights, shadows and, frequently, carving and moulding. Yet it owes its existence almost entirely to the fact that wood is strong along its length and weak across it, and is liable to shrink as moisture dries out or swell as it absorbs moisture. This is explained more fully in Chapter 3, but is mentioned here as yet another example of how appearance may be based on practical necessity. The proof of this is largely borne out today when modern materials have eliminated the shrinkage problem. We no longer need to use framework and panelling.

Chapter 3

The cabinet-maker's workshop

To understand why furniture was made in a certain way at a particular period it is helpful to know something of the technique of woodwork. All materials have their own peculiarities, and the method of working them and the tools needed for the purpose must obviously be based on these characteristics.

Wood is a natural substance which, so far as the scope of this book is concerned, has to be used more or less as it is cut from the tree. Although length presents little difficulty, width is restricted since a piece of wood cannot be wider than the diameter of the tree trunk. In fact, it is invariably much less than this for technical reasons into which it is unnecessary to go here. If a wider piece is essential, it has to be jointed.

Wood is strong along the direction of the grain; much less so across it. It is hygroscopic, giving up its moisture to a dry atmosphere and shrinking in the process, or absorbing it when it is drier than the air, in which case it swells. It can do this years after felling, though some woods are more liable to do so than others. It is relatively soft (though there is considerable variation), and it can be worked with steel tools.

Taking these points in order, restricted width means that any particular part can be no wider than a board that can be cut from a tree trunk and, although years ago there were trees of vast girth yielding wide boards, the average tree was much smaller. This is the reason why early oak panelling A, (Fig. 1) had relatively narrow panels, no wider than could be cut from an average tree. It was, in fact, much less because many of the oaks were riven, that is, split open with wedges, and the line of cleavage was always radial. Since it was undesirable to use the pith or centre of the log, the resulting panels were less than half the diameter of the trunk as shown in Fig. 2.

Not all woods can be riven, however. Elm, for example, has interlocked grain which will not split easily and has to be sawn. Consequently wider boards could be produced in this wood because the cuts had not necessarily to be radial. Later, when craftsmen learnt how to joint timber in its width, the panels, no matter what the wood, were wider as shown in B, Fig. 1.

In very early times man must have discovered that wood was much

Fig. 1 Contrast between narrow and wide panels in wall panelling. **A** narrow panels of about 1600; **B** wide panels of the late 17th century.

A

B

wedge

Fig. 2 How riven oak is produced.

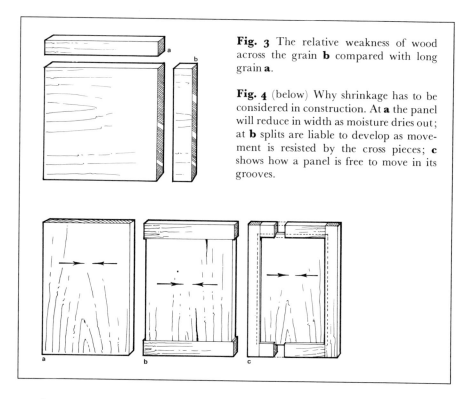

Fig. 3 The relative weakness of wood across the grain **b** compared with long grain **a**.

Fig. 4 (below) Why shrinkage has to be considered in construction. At **a** the panel will reduce in width as moisture dries out; at **b** splits are liable to develop as movement is resisted by the cross pieces; **c** shows how a panel is free to move in its grooves.

weaker across the grain than along it, and this made it important to avoid short grain which would be liable to snap under strain (see Fig. 3b). In early work craftsmen sometimes got over the difficulty by sheer bulk of material, cutting the wood extra thick or wide to resist the stress, whereas later they solved the problem in a much more scientific way, using the framework and panel. The whole thing, however, is bound up with the liability of wood to shrink or swell in its width in accordance with the atmosphere.

Nothing can stop wood from shrinking across the grain as it dries; or, conversely, swelling as it absorbs moisture. It is something that has to be accepted and, in fact, to ignore it is to ask for trouble. In many early pieces it was sometimes ignored or not realized, with the result that bad splits have since developed. It was to avoid this trouble that the framed system of construction was evolved, the framework providing strength in both length and width. The panel, which was little more than a filling, was held in grooves or rebates and, being put in without glue or other fixing, was free either to shrink or swell, without affecting the overall size or rigidity of the framework.

This is made clear in Fig. 4. At (a) is a panel which, in the event of shrinkage, would reduce in width. If the same panel were held rigidly by strips across the width as at (b) a split would be liable to occur. In addition, it might also pull in at the ends as shown. In the framed construction (c) there is no reduction in overall size though the panel may shrink along its grooves, and there is consequently no danger of splitting. It used to be standard practice in a cabinet shop before the days of plywood to send all panels to be stained at their edges before being assembled in a grooved frame. Unless this were done the panels would eventually show lines of white, unstained wood as they shrank along their grooves.

From all this it is apparent that the attractive appearance of panelling is primarily the result of purely practical considerations rather than an attempt to design something that looked pleasant. The latter was a by-product, though it was often given a decorative or lightening touch by working mouldings, chamfers, etc. (Fig. 5).

Fig. 5 Panelling decorated with mouldings or chamfers.

The relative softness of wood enables it to be cut easily with edge tools. It can be sawn into pieces, slices can be chiselled, and shavings taken off. This is in contrast with some other materials which may need to be abraided, chipped, cast, or beaten to shape. On the other hand it has a strongly pronounced grain which, although reacting kindly to correct treatment, gives endless trouble if ignored.

Hand tools have been evolved to do the main operations required to work wood; saws to cut to specific size; chisels and gouges to pare small chips or to chop; axes and the adze to reduce wood rapidly to shape or roughly smooth it; planes to reduce wood in size, to 'true', or smooth it, or, in special cases, to work mouldings or cut grooves or rebates; abraiding tools such as the rasp or file, scraping or scratching tools; and those for boring.

The way in which tools have to be used affects methods of construction, and those which have had the most marked effect on construction are those needed for working grooves and rebates, and, to a slightly lesser extent, for moulding. The essential feature of these processes is that the tool must be taken right through the entire length of the material if the tool is to be used efficiently or, indeed, at all. This is made clear in Fig. 6 which shows a plough plane in use to work a groove at the edge of wood. Clearly it could not be stopped short of the length because the straightness of the sole would not enable it to dip into the wood. The same applies to moulding planes, Fig. 7, and rebate planes. It follows then that when grooves or rebates are needed, the form of a joint has to be such that the grooving or rebate plane can be used.

In the case of mouldings there was one big drawback. A separate plane was needed for each section of moulding, and this would be expensive for

Fig. 6 An old plough plane in use working a groove. It is clear from the photograph that the tool must be taken along the complete length of the wood.

Fig. 7 An ogee moulding being worked with a moulding plane. Note the line engraved up the front showing the angle at which the plane is to be held, known as the spring.

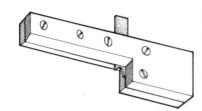

Fig. 8 The scratch-stock used to work mouldings and sometimes grooves.

Fig. 9 Working a bead with the scratch-stock. Note that it is run-out opposite the joint.

the small woodworker. Another tool was therefore devised known as the scratch-stock, which had the advantage that cutters of varying section could be fitted to it. The cutter was merely a thin piece of steel; or, for a very small section, it could be just the end of a nail filed to a reverse of the moulding. The tool was simplicity itself, consisting of two pieces of wood screwed or bolted together with a notch cut at the lower side as in Fig. 8. The side of the notch was pressed hard against the edge of the wood and the tool worked back and forth, the cutter scratching or scraping the wood, Fig. 9.

A second advantage was that the moulding could be stopped or run-out at any point; and it could be worked around a curved edge as well as a straight one. On the other hand it was laborious to use and consequently suitable for small sections only – say up to about $\frac{3}{4}$ of an inch or so. Anything bigger needed a moulding plane. However, it has remained in use right up to the coming of the machine, and is still used where hand work has survived.

There appears to be evidence that the making of moulding planes was founded as a separate trade quite early on – probably in the second half of the 17th century. Before this time all planes were rather crude affairs.

Fig. 10 Old moulding plane with hole near front to take cord or a peg.

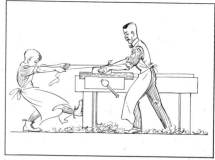

Fig. 11 This was common practice in working a large moulding. The boy had to pull slightly downwards and into the bench to keep the plane fence to the wood.

Those for large mouldings must have been extremely laborious to use – so much so that it was necessary to pass a rope through a hole or peg at the front end of the plane on which an assistant could pull while the craftsman pushed from behind and guided the plane (see Fig. 10). Even in the case of a medium-sized moulding plane the craftsman often pressed an unhappy apprentice into service, looping a cord around the back of the iron as in Fig. 11. If, after half an hour or so of such work, the boy lost most of the skin from his hands, well he was just learning his trade.

When one considers the many sections of mouldings used in furniture, especially in the 18th century, it is most unlikely that the average cabinet-maker would have much in the way of moulding planes of his own at all. He might have one or two, such as a $\frac{1}{8}$ in. bead for cocked beading, and maybe a couple of rounds, but the likelihood is that only the fashionable cabinet-maker employing many men would have anything like the full range of planes needed for all classes of work. His men would use them as required.

It is probably this that partly accounts for the finer quality of town-made furniture compared with country-made pieces. The local cabinet-maker would use whatever planes he had, or would make do by planing his rounded sections with the rebate plane, whereas the master cabinet-maker could afford to order special planes to suit whatever section was needed.

It is interesting to speculate what a cabinet workshop was like in, say, the 18th century. There are some old prints which give some idea (though many of them show either artistic licence or represent what the artist thought it was like), and many old tools have survived. It seems a reasonable supposition, however, that it was little different from any present-day workshop in which hand work is still done. One would have to make allowance for the fact that every workshop nowadays uses some basic machines – a circular saw (which not only cuts out timber but also does grooving and rebating) and possibly an edger, router, and maybe a lathe. In the old workshop there would be a selection of tools which the machines have replaced, such as a large frame-saw, betty saw for shapes,

Fig. 12 Illustration from a book published on the continent in 1574, showing chest—or cabinet-makers—at work.

plough, and many moulding planes. The basic hand tools, however, would not have been markedly different, except that in the old shop there would not have been any adjustable metal planes such as we are familiar with today; and, in fact, nearly all tools would have been of wood except for the actual cutters.

Fig. 12 is a reproduction of a woodcut appearing in a book of 1574, showing chest-makers or cabinet-makers at work. Another, Fig. 13, comes from a French book and shows an 18th century cabinet workshop. My guess is that the engraver used his imagination freely in that it is most unlikely that four men would have had so large a room to work in (there are only two benches). However, it is particularly interesting in showing

Fig. 13 A French cabinet-maker's workshop in about 1765. This is taken from the *Diderot Encyclopedie,* and is interesting as it shows tools of the time; the frame-saws (still widely used in Europe), bench holdfast, fret-saw (very like the modern coping saw), trying plane, wood square, round mallet, and the marquetry-cutter's donkey.

the tools in use and the type of work being done. Fig. 14 is another old print showing a cabinet shop in the 18th century. Again it is interesting but rather too polite for reality. Much truer to life is Fig. 15.

The Cabinet Maker.

Fig. 14 An illustration from *A Book of English Trades*, printed for G. and W. B. Whittaker, Ave Maria Lane, London.

Fig. 15 Old illustration of a cabinet-making workshop. There is considerable artist's licence. Note the rather crude single dovetail of the carcase and the impractical method of glueing the table. The legs would have been first glued to the rails in opposite pairs.

Those who can recall the colourful district of Shoreditch, the home of furniture-making in the days before 1914, probably have the best idea of what an old cabinet-maker's workshop was like. Here there were whole streets of houses built originally as dwellings but since used as workshops. In some cases every room in a house was let separately to a cabinet-maker; others were rented as a floor; and sometimes a complete house was taken by a master man who had one and sometimes two men working in every room. Such houses had plain wood staircases, the treads of which were worn away to almost paper thinness at the middle; and sometimes almost beneath this rickety staircase was an open brick recess in which a shaving blaze was prepared to heat the cauls used for veneering. In the rooms themselves it might be (and often was) necessary to open the window to enable long planks to be got in so that they could be sawn to size, though if there was a yard this might be used for the purpose in fine weather, and when there was room.

The rooms were frequently unheated even in winter except those used for polishing, though a cabinet-maker seldom did his own polishing unless he had a large business. Generally it was more economical to let the work out to a polisher who did nothing else. Lighting might be either electric or gas and here, of course, was one feature in which the 18th century workshop would have differed; there would have been nothing except candle or oil lighting; and since glue was needed on and off all day long, there must have been an oil stove of some kind, or a grate probably fed with offcuts of timber. It was also needed to warm joints before assembly to avoid chilling the glue.

The typical bench used in England during the 18th century would have been a simple affair with heavy top supported on a framework with screw vice at the head end, a series of holes in the tail leg to support long boards, a stop at the head for planing against, and a hole at the rear to receive a holdfast. On the wall would be a rack to hold tools in constant use; chisels, screwdrivers, pincers, and other small tools, but items such as saws, cramps, squares, shooting boards, etc. would be economically hung on nails driven in any convenient place or stacked around the walls. One feature, however, would have been a tool chest owned by most workmen. That this was the case appears from a note in a contemporary magazine to the effect that in 1755 a fire occurred in Chippendale's workshop in which were the chests of twenty-two workmen. In this were kept the workman's everyday tools and no doubt he kept a jealous eye on them, particularly his planes. Many of the really old planes that have survived are elaborately carved, but 18th century illustrations often show wood planes that might be illustrated in a present-day catalogue.

Looked at from outside the tool chest was a simple, utilitarian affair, usually painted or stained black. When the lid was opened, however, something very different might appear. Frequently the inside of the lid was veneered and inlaid, often in an intricate design, and the inner drawers and other fittings were neatly dovetailed together and again frequently inlaid. It was no doubt a matter of personal pride that caused the young

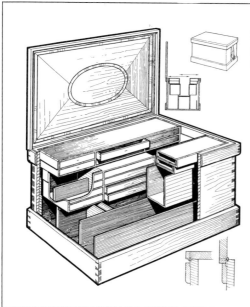

Fig. 16 Old tool chest, plain outside but with inside of lid veneered and drawer fronts inlaid.

journeyman to make such a chest. An example is given in Fig. 16.

How far the making of such delightful chests was the general rule is problematical. Certainly the practice has been dead for many years. I cannot recall having ever seen one in use when working in the trade as a boy in 1912. Every man in the shop had his own chest but in every case it was a plain affair, fitted with drawers and trays but with no attempt at embellishment.

When one considers the up-to-date equipment of the workshop in the modern trade training centre, including hand, pneumatic, and multiple-plate presses for veneering and the many machines available, it becomes a matter of wonder that the quality work of the 18th century and later could be turned out without any such aids. From the word go these old craftsmen had only their own skill and experience to help them. Their timber might have been cut into boards on the saw pit or an early form of frame saw, but after this all sawing, planing, jointing, and veneering was by hand. Of course, constant use developed skill. A man could cut his tenons so accurately that they fitted the mortises practically without any fitting – he had to be able to do so because he was paid only in accordance with the work he turned out. As a consequence the elimination of all unnecessary operations was applied to every branch of work. If then he could cut out an operation and still do a good job he unhesitatingly did so, especially on work which was commercially on a lower grade (and not all 18th century furniture was in the first class).

Thus dovetails were not marked individually with a templet or sliding bevel; the craftsman might roughly pencil in the position of the dovetails but he would then cut them freehand to the correct slope. Constant practice enabled him to do this accurately, and over the years as the tendency to cut ever finer pins with less slope on drawer dovetails developed, he gradually adapted his sawing accordingly. Furthermore, in making several drawers of the same size, he invariably fixed all the sides together in the vice and cut across all the dovetails in one sawing.

Maybe he overdid it in some respects. For instance, if any trade-made drawer, old or new, is examined it will invariably be found that the maker has taken his cutting gauge right across the dovetails (see Fig. 6, Chapter 12). Ideally this should not be done. A light gauge mark should be made, the dovetails sawn, and the gauge mark deepened locally only where the gap for the pins is to be cut. The light gauge mark is planed out later when the drawer is fitted and cleaned up. Not so the trade drawer in which the gauge mark was unblushingly left, even in a good-quality job. It cut out an operation and so saved a little time.

Apart from trueing wood and jointing, a great deal of veneering had to be done and it had to be done either with the veneering hammer or with cauls. For marquetry, of course, the latter was essential as otherwise the parts would separate. The use of the shaving blaze for heating cauls has already been mentioned (see also illustration on page 203) and, no doubt, was a job given to an apprentice. It must surely have been the cause of many a flare-up, for, apart from being close to so much wood, it had to be done near the place where the work was actually carried out as otherwise the wood caul would be chilled before it could be cramped down. Since the workshop floor invariably had its carpet of shavings, the danger is obvious.

There were some branches of work that the cabinet-maker himself never touched. Mention has already been made of marquetry. The cutting of this was always a separate trade although the cabinet-maker would lay it. Turning was another branch which belonged to another craftsman but here again the cabinet-maker assembled the turned parts. Another independent craft was that of the carver, and when one considers the quality of work turned out it is not surprising that it called for the skill and experience of a specialized trade.

Wood finishing has been a branch of its own for many years, and it is likely that it developed as a separate trade early on. There appears to be no direct evidence of this, but since a bad finish could ruin an item into which many hours had been put and for which a great deal of valuable timber had been used, it seems that specialized skill would have been essential. This was certainly true when french polishing became the usual finish in the 19th century.

It seems likely, too, that fitting became a trade of its own, at any rate in a shop employing many men. The fitter would take a job to pieces when the cabinet-maker had finished with it to enable the polisher to do his work. He would then assemble it again, trimming drawers and doors where necessary, and replace locks, handles, etc. He would also glaze doors, fit beads, and generally get the job ready for the customer.

Upholstery was another branch which developed separately, though on this score it is certain that chair-making was not undertaken as a general line by the cabinet-maker. The trade developed its own technique, especially when shaped work entered largely into it in the 18th century. Sheraton, in his *Cabinet Dictionary*, says that chair-making is a branch generally confined to itself. 'Those who work at it seldom engage to make cabinet furniture. In country manufactories it is otherwise; yet even these pay some regard to keeping their workmen constantly at the chair.'

Clockcase-making, too, developed as a separate trade. This is largely shown by the mouldings which are invariably of a quite different section from those used in the cabinet trade. No doubt there were some master-craftsmen who could turn their hands to almost any branch of work, but for the general run of workmen, trades developed as separate branches.

As I pointed out in Chapter 1, because a piece of furniture is old it is not necessarily good. There was shoddy work in the 18th century and later as well as fine-quality craftsmanship. Some furniture, then as now, often had to be made to a price, and such work was often put together in defiance of principles of construction. The consequence is only too well known to the restorer of furniture. It no doubt looked well enough when first turned out but time has found its weaknesses, and open joints, splits and cracked veneer are the consequence. An example of this is given in Fig. 2, page 13.

There must have been a demand for fairly cheap furniture in the 18th and 19th centuries and so one finds commercially-produced goods turned

Fig. 17 Small bow-front sideboard veneered with mahogany and with inlay bandings. (Mallet and Son [Antiques] Ltd.)

out as a regular line, probably several at a time. Yet time, in finding these weaknesses, has also given the furniture a certain charm, the consequence of years of polishing and use and, of course, it has the interest that goes with things old.

There is, however, another point. In the periods before mass-production came into the general practice, men really did understand how to use animal glue properly and all that this involved. I have a bow-front corner cabinet dating from the 18th century (see Fig. 5, page 226). Its construction is about as simple as it could be, the joints, apart from the coopered doors, being nothing more than plain butts put together with glue and brads. Yet the whole thing is as sound today as it ever was. The joints really did fit, and without doubt they were heated before being assembled with properly-prepared Scotch glue.

On this score Sheraton is curiously at variance with accepted modern practice. He says 'old glue is best and its goodness or strength increases by frequent boiling, if it be not burnt.' Today we are told that glue should be freshly made and on no account should be boiled, its strength deteriorating if made hotter than 140°F. How far Sheraton's opinion represented general trade practice cannot be proved, but on his title page he describes himself as a cabinet-maker and some of his instructions for practical work make it obvious that he was a practical man. If it was common practice to use old glue and frequently boil it, all one can say is that it has stood the test of time.

Chapter 4

What to look for in old furniture
The wood

There are several things to consider in the study of old furniture; its style, details, construction, timber, finish, and general appearance. Some of these can be illustrated or described; knowledge of others comes only by the constant handling of old pieces. One often hears the expression that a piece 'looks wrong', and it is difficult, if not impossible, to put into words exactly what it is that is wrong. It is constant familiarity with old pieces, plus acute observation and a knowledge of periods, that enables one to arrive at a conclusion. No man can hope to achieve this by any short cuts. Reading this or any other book will not give him this ability. All one can do is to offer a few pointers about what to look for and to advise the examination of old woodwork in museums, historic houses, and churches. However, if it takes a lifetime of constant handling to decide on the finer points connected with antiques, there are some elementary details that should become obvious to a man with a working knowledge of the subject, and the following points to look for are given in this chapter and Chapters 5, 6, and 7.

Of what wood is it made? Is the style correct for the alleged period? Is its construction true to what would have been common practice? Is its carving or inlay part of the original piece or has it been subsequently added? Is it veneered? Does it show machine marks, especially on concealed surfaces? Is it a marriage of two pieces or possibly a divorcee from a larger piece? Does it show wear marks in positions where wear would have taken place naturally? Is it badly in need of repair (remembering that good repairs can be very costly)?

Of what wood is it made?

Oak furniture The traditional timber for woodwork from earliest times up to about 1660 was oak, but it has been used intermittently ever since. Occasionally other woods such as chestnut and elm were used in the 'oak' period but by far the chief furniture wood was oak. Generally, though not invariably, it was quarter-cut so that the attractive figure

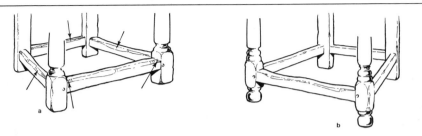

Fig. 1 Wear in old furniture. **a** Unnatural wear on chair stretcher rails. **b** Where wear would normally occur.

caused by the rays was usually present (see Chapter 3). It was, of course, always English oak. This may sound obvious but today Japanese oak is widely used and before the Second World War a great deal of American oak was in use. Clearly any item made of the last two woods could not be genuine pieces of the oak period. This is something the tradesman might identify but it is almost impossible to explain how to recognize the difference between the various oaks.

American oak is not of the same colour (it might be either of the red or the white variety) and it has not the same rich figure of English oak, but to spot any difference in colour when covered with an old finish and possibly a layer of grime is something that calls for experience. Japanese oak is milder and lighter in weight than the European variety, but any difference in weight is almost impossible to estimate in a job of any size. However, it is mentioned as a pointer that may be of value to those familiar with timbers. Cases do sometimes occur when an old table has its top so badly damaged that its owner has decided to have it replaced. Thus we may have an old framework with a new top (or one which was new perhaps fifty years or so ago).

A feature that is sometimes seen in old oak furniture is that the figure (rays) is black rather than light. In natural wood it is of a light straw colour but it turns black if coated with lead paint. Since some early furniture was occasionally painted it is often assumed that a piece with the figure turned black must be genuinely old and has at some time been stripped. This may be the case, but it does not necessarily follow because the faker can do likewise or use caustics which have the same effect.

Sometimes, too, by painting a piece of oak woodwork, say green, and subsequently stripping it, a greenish tinge is left on the surface and a deposit left in the open grain and in the interstices that occur in any carving, joints, etc. It may be pointed out as proof of age that the piece was painted originally and has been stripped leaving a rather attractive finish. And this, of course, is true, though not quite in the sense implied.

Oak furniture, being the oldest of the periods, has necessarily had more use than, say, walnut or mahogany. Furthermore, it belonged to a somewhat more boisterous age before the period of the politer drawing-room. Also, as time progressed, oak furniture was often replaced by more fashionable pieces and the oak relegated to the kitchen or servants' quarters.

Consequently, oak items invariably show more signs of wear than those of a later period, and the earlier the piece the more wear it could be expected to show. As a result stretchers of tables and chairs are often worn away where boots have scraped across or rested upon them, sharp edges and corners of table tops are rounded over, and in fact any parts, especially projecting parts, are liable to show signs of wear.

At the same time it is essential to make sure that the wear is where it would naturally occur. There is a temptation to overdo signs of wear, and it may be carried to positions where wear would not naturally take place. Take, for instance, an oak chair with stretchers. That in Fig. 1a is a faked piece; that in Fig. 1b genuine. In the latter case most of the wear is on the front rail where the feet would naturally rest and is more marked towards the middle. It scarcely reaches to the ends where the rail joins the legs because the feet would hardly reach into the corners. The turning, however, has suffered at the inner side, especially towards the front where generations have rubbed the sides of their boots. Side and back stretchers show little wear beyond the marking that is inevitable in items near the floor. In Fig. 1a the wear is artificial and occurs on side and back rails where the feet would not be placed, and the wear on the front rail has been carried right up to the corner. Of course, any good faker would not make this mistake but there are degrees in all things, and people, including fakers, do occasionally trip up.

I recall some of the faker's tools and his methods. One man had a worn-out plane iron begged from one of the cabinet-makers. This he screwed to the end of a wood shaft so that it was rather like an adze or a hatchet with the head turned sideways. This he would use to chip away the sharp edges and corners of what was supposed to be early oak woodwork. Another tool he used on oak was the wire brush with which he scraped the surface of plain and carved panels. This had the effect of scrubbing out the softer parts of the grain and gave a time-worn appearance. An old file too was used to imitate the marks and bruises that might have occurred in a natural lifetime.

Lack of wear is not necessarily a sign that the item is not old. Much depends upon its history. In Fig. 2, a chair of the 17th century, there is scarcely any wear. Even the front stretcher rail is only slightly rounded over at the top. Since, however, it is a sanctuary chair the use it has had is almost negligible, at any rate in more recent years. Incidentally such a chair was the work of a first-rate craftsman with a strong sense of design.

Sometimes things can happen in reverse, so to speak. The difficulty of doctoring wood to make it look old can be a problem. Consequently the maker of 'old' furniture uses old wood whenever possible and he retains the original surface if at all feasible. Sometimes the edge of the wood is rounded and, rather than plane away this roundness, thus removing the original patina, he uses it as it is, possibly jointing other parts to it as in the case of Fig. 3a. As a consequence the roundness continues opposite the shoulder of the joining piece as shown where it would not take place at all. Wear of this kind is quite unnatural in an old item. The wear would die

Fig. 2 Chair showing few signs of wear. Lack of wear is probably due to the chair having stood in the sanctuary of a church where it would be little used.

out at each side of the shoulder as in Fig. 3b.

Filled-in joints or recesses are worth further attention. They may indicate that the piece is a resurrection of something else. It does not necessarily indicate faking because, although wood was plentiful in the oak period, the labour of working it with hand tools must have been daunting. Consequently wood from a demolished house or from an unwanted piece of furniture may have been used again. This, however, would not be so likely in an important item.

Sometimes, in an attempt to give enhanced value to a cupboard or

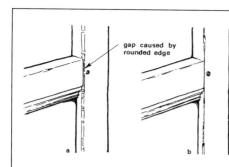

Fig. 3 Doubtful joints in old wood. **a** Gap in unnatural position at joint shoulder due to use of old wood with rounded edge. **b** Normal places showing wear, above and below the shoulder.

gap caused by rounded edge

a

b

whatever it may be, a plain surface is carved. To retain the original surface as far as possible the carving is usually of the incised type as only a minimum of wood has to be cut away. Since such incisions are invariably filled up with a concoction of dirt held together with black wax, it is often difficult to detect a fake when the carving has been well done in correct period style. As a rule, however, the carving looks new (as indeed it is) for a reason which is difficult to put into words. Edges may appear unnaturally sharp, the colour may not match up with the rest of the work or possibly it may look different from similar work in the rest of the job.

One last word about the use of oak. By naming a piece of furniture by its wood one refers to its exterior show wood. Thus in, say, the mahogany period the only parts in mahogany might be those showing at the outside and even these might be in veneer only. Inner parts such as drawer sides, backs, and bottoms might be (and usually were) of oak. In the oak period, however, the entire thing was invariably in oak throughout, including all interior parts, backs, etc.

Walnut furniture Quite apart from differences in style and detail, one of the chief ways in which walnut furniture differs from oak is that only such parts as legs and shapes, which could not be veneered are solid walnut. The rest is either in pine or oak veneered with walnut or a thin facing of walnut, as in the case of mouldings. Legs had to be in the solid because they were either turned, of the cabriole type, square-cut, or of scrolled form. Since, however, walnut was relatively scarce as compared with oak, a job veneered with walnut is sometimes found with turned legs of beech stained to match.

Walnut was indigenous to Persia and other parts of Europe, but was introduced into Italy during the early Christian era and later into Europe generally by the Romans. During Elizabethan times it was planted extensively in England and it was from these trees, which reached maturity a century or so later, that furniture of the walnut period was made.

Since veneer was used so widely advantage could be taken of the various types of grain figuring, such as butts with rich marking and burrs, both of which would be unsafe if used as solid wood. Relatively plain-grained veneer was used for parts of less importance and for cross-bandings. There was also a period when oyster-shell veneering was popular, this being usually laburnum wood branches cross-cut into thin slices and used as veneer. The pieces were either cut straight across, yielding pieces roughly circular in shape, or at an angle so that they were elliptical. Other woods such as walnut were also used for the purpose. The pieces were trimmed to rectangular shape and fitted together side by side. During the marquetry period (see Chapter 17) various woods were used for veneer; sycamore, box, holly, and sometimes fruit woods.

Fig. 4 shows a typical cabinet of the early 18th century veneered with walnut with cross-bandings and herring-bone bandings. Note that the veneers of the drawer parts are pieced together with matched grain, this effect being produced by using adjacent leaves of veneer and reversing the one against the other. The grain in the two is thus practically identical. Mouldings are cross-grained, either veneer or thin pieces of solid wood being used.

In most cases the veneer was laid on a groundwork of pine as there were objections to the use of oak for the purpose (see Chapter 16), but the latter was occasionally used. Drawer sides, backs, and bottoms were generally in oak, though rails and divisions might be of pine. Mouldings were almost always cross-grained walnut, the latter being a thin facing glued to a pine or oak ground work with the section worked in it. Flat, or the larger curved members, were often veneered.

I might mention here that when a faked piece of furniture of either the walnut or the mahogany periods was made in our workshop it always went through complete normal construction as though it was to be sold as a new piece. It was only after it had left the cabinet-maker's hands that the process of antiquing began. Little was done in the way of actual wear except for slight rounding of sharp corners, but pieces of inlay bandings were chipped off, lengths of cocked beading were broken off, and plinths and other low-lying parts were kicked or bruised. The rest of the antiquing was done by polishers who specialized in faking. And it sometimes happened that when the piece was sold from the showroom the customer wanted it repaired and the damage made good. Accordingly we had it straight back in the workshop. Thus, the customer having bought the piece at a good price as an antique, had then to pay afresh for the repairs to damage that we ourselves had inflicted only a week or two before!

This question of faking is an odd one. It never occurred to the men in the workshop that there was anything of doubtful rectitude about making these spurious pieces. In fact there was a sort of pride about making a really good job of it. Those who did the antiquing got rather better pay than the general run of polishers – about one penny an hour more – but this was because it was reckoned to be a more skilful job, not because it was pay-

Fig. 4 (opposite) Chest on stand veneered with walnut, about 1700. That veneer-cutting was a laborious process is emphasized by the patchwork used in the apron of the stand which is made up of small pieces fitted together. (Victoria and Albert Museum)

ment in any moral sense. The men themselves were just doing a job of work – cabinet-making or polishing, as the case might be – and the fact that the item was in 18th century style or whatever it might be was merely incidental. Fuller details are to be found in Chapter 19.

Mahogany furniture　It is difficult to say when this wood was first imported into this country to any extent. Odd logs probably arrived more or less accidentally in the sense that no one appreciated the virtues of the wood as a furniture timber (see Chapter 2). It was not until about 1725 that it began to be used regularly. Occasionally one comes across items which were probably made as early as the end of Queen Anne's reign, 1714, but such pieces were exceptional.

As mentioned in Chapter 2, the use of mahogany brought with it changes in construction. At first veneering was largely discontinued since the grain of the early wood was relatively plain. Drawer fronts, doors and carcase ends and tops were in solid wood, though sometimes the carcase ends were of pine with a facing of mahogany – often too thick to be called veneer. This early mahogany was the Cuban variety, dark and heavy, and, to anybody who has used it, unmistakable in its working qualities. Shavings flake and break up as they are raised, never curling up in the typical fashion of other woods. Some trees of enormous girth must have been available since unjointed furniture parts up to 3 ft. wide are sometimes found. Its suitability for furniture-making was quickly realized, for it entirely superseded walnut in a very short time. Amongst its virtues were its reliability and the fine finish of which it was capable.

Later in the second half of the 18th century a lighter mahogany was widely used, that from Honduras. It was lighter in both colour and weight and often yielded timber of magnificent figure. With it came a return to veneering, though in some cases solid wood was used. In all cases mouldings were worked lengthwise of the grain, never cross-grain as had been the practice in the walnut period (the odd exception to the rule does sometimes turn up). Today Cuban mahogany is almost unobtainable in the solid, and the Honduras variety is extremely expensive. Consequently a great deal of African mahogany and other kindred woods are used. These do not have the rich figuring of Cuban and Central American varieties and are not so reliable. Neither are they capable of so high a finish. These woods were never used in furniture of the true mahogany period, but they have often been used in reproductions and faked copies. It takes an experienced man to say with assurance that an African timber has been used in a piece once it has been polished and antiqued. Quite often the more important parts are veneered with true Honduras mahogany, leaving only turned or shaped legs to be cut in the solid from African timber.

A delightful bow-front sideboard veneered with mahogany is shown in Fig. 5. It dates from the end of the 18th century.

Satinwood furniture　Although mahogany has remained as a furniture

44

Fig. 5 Mahogany bow-front sideboard, about 1790. A fine-quality piece with drawer fronts veneered with curls. (Victoria and Albert Museum)

wood until the present time, there was a fashion for satinwood towards the end of the 18th and into the 19th century. Here again was an excellent cabinet wood, one which stood well, had fine figure, and was capable of a first-rate finish. It was perhaps even more exacting in its requirements from the cabinet-maker than mahogany because any blemishes showed up plainly. Whereas a dark line at a joint might not be badly noticeable in mahogany, it would advertise itself only too well in the light colour of satinwood. The trick usually adopted was to mix white or light yellow pigment powder with the glue but even so open joint lines or cracks do show.

Fig. 6 on page 46 shows an extremely fine satinwood commode or bookcase. The doors are built cooper-fashion and are veneered (see page 205). Note too the inlaid line which follows the outline of the shaped stand.

Fig. 6 One of a pair of Sheraton bow-front commodes, a fine piece veneered with satinwood. (M. Harris and Sons, London)

Chapter 5

The period styles

Knowledge of the period styles includes practically all the external features of furniture such as type of decoration used; sections of mouldings; general form of the furniture; shapes of legs; and so on. It is, to an extent, bound up with construction, but it is also essential to be able to recognize details that were usual at any particular period. Sometimes one gets some curious anomalies in a single piece and this calls for further investigation to find out what may have happened. To get a working knowledge of period details one should study authentic specimens as mentioned on page 37.

At the outset, however, one needs to know the type of furniture being made at any particular time. For instance, it does not call for much knowledge to realize that an Elizabethan bureau-bookcase would be an obvious absurdity, but it is clear that one needs to know when some things were first made or when they were made in a certain form. There are many text books which give this, but the following are a few pointers about the furniture used in various periods, which we may roughly divide under the headings: age of the carpenter, age of the cabinet-maker, age of the designer.

Age of the carpenter

This dates from earliest times to roughly 1660–1670. Furniture was generally oak but occasionally in elm or chestnut. Decoration was mainly carving which was invariably deep and spirited and of a naïve character, often with little evidence of fine technique. Inlay in the solid was also sometimes used. Furniture was heavily built, though with a tendency to lightness as the 17th century progressed.

Tables The early 16th century dining type was of trestle form with heavy slab end supports sawn out to decorative shape as at (A) Fig. 1, or with square or square-cut uprights in I form joined with rails and stretchers, usually keyed with wedges to enable the whole to be taken apart and stacked. The top was of boards from about 1 in. thick up to some 3 in.

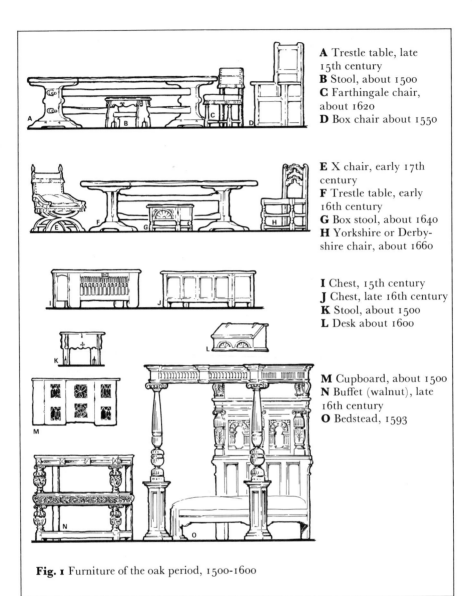

A Trestle table, late
15th century
B Stool, about 1500
C Farthingale chair,
about 1620
D Box chair about 1550

E X chair, early 17th
century
F Trestle table, early
16th century
G Box stool, about 1640
H Yorkshire or Derby-
shire chair, about 1660

I Chest, 15th century
J Chest, late 16th century
K Stool, about 1500
L Desk about 1600

M Cupboard, about 1500
N Buffet (walnut), late
16th century
O Bedstead, 1593

Fig. 1 Furniture of the oak period, 1500-1600

according to size and held together with end clamps. A later form in the
17th century was framed together with corner legs having rails and
stretchers tenoned in. The bulbous type of leg shown on page 180 was
frequently carved and was succeeded by baluster-type turnings in the
later 17th century. These were usually left plain though the rails were
often carved.

The 17th century saw the coming of many smaller forms of tables.
Some were intended normally to stand against a wall and had sloping
sides with a cupboard beneath the top. Some had a double top which
pivoted over and could be supported by a gate at the back. Also becoming

Fig. 2 Oak chest with panelled front and back. 17th century.

popular was the gate-leg table, page 146, which varied greatly in size. Usually the legs were turned and after 1660 were often twist-turned.

Chairs Early chairs were of the panelled type as Fig. 1(D). Often the seat lifted as a lid disclosing a box-like receptacle and usually the panelling at the sides was continued up beneath the arms. Later this panelling was omitted and replaced by open arms and stretchers, Fig. 2, page 122. From about 1600 onwards chairs were made in increasing numbers, often in sets, and the farthingale type (C) became popular. Note that although the back slopes the back legs are upright down to the floor. A popular type known as the Yorkshire–Derbyshire chair is shown at (H). Here again there is no rake to the back legs.

Stools were widely used in the early oak period, a chair being used only by the chief person in the household. An early 16th century trestle type is shown in Fig. 1(B). The later framed type is that at (G).

Chests By the mid 16th century the framed and panelled type of chest was common Fig. 1(J). Carving both on the framework and the panels was common, and a similar type was made well into the 17th century. Fig. 2 shows a 17th century chest which has somewhat unusual construction in that the ends are solid, not panelled. After the Commonwealth, however, the advantage of the chest-of-drawers was realized and the type Fig. 5(K) became popular, the fronts often decorated with applied mouldings mitred round into geometrical shapes and split turnings, see page 102. Fig. 3 shows a carved oak chest dated 1637.

Cupboards, sideboards, etc. An early form of food cupboard is that shown in Fig. 1(M). It is of simple planked construction with doors of solid pieces of oak. A much more advanced type is the sideboard, Fig. 1(N). Curiously enough this is in walnut and is an unusual example of the early use of this wood. Most similar sideboards were of oak. In the first half of the 17th century the court cupboard was commonly used. The turned and carved bulbous supports and panelled doors were a common feature. Fig. 4, page 112, shows a specially fine court cupboard, the maker of which

Fig. 3 Carved oak chest dated 1637. (Victoria and Albert Museum)

had an extremely good sense of proportion and design.

Bedsteads   Four-poster beds were usual in the 16th century, Fig. 1(O), and the type was continued into the following century.

Age of the cabinet-maker

This period is approximately from 1660 up to 1750. The first few years were transitional in that the trade of the furniture maker had only just begun, and early pieces retained much of the traditional methods of the general woodworker and, indeed, were often still in oak despite the growing popularity of walnut. From about 1750 onwards furniture was obviously still made by the cabinet-maker but the names of well-known cabinet-maker-designers came to be attached to furniture and this makes it a convenient method of subdividing the period.

From 1660 up to about 1725 walnut was chiefly used and from the latter date onwards mahogany became the popular wood. Practically all walnut furniture was veneered on either pine or oak, with the latter wood used for drawer sides, backs, and bottoms, and for trays, shelves, etc. The only exceptions were turned and cabriole legs and other shaped parts which were necessarily cut in solid walnut. For methods of construction see Chapter 8. Early mahogany furniture was mostly in the solid, again with drawer and other interior parts in oak.

The walnut phase   Decoration in walnut furniture relied mainly on the grain of the wood and was achieved by cross-banding, cross-veneering of rails, mouldings, etc., inlay strings and bandings and built-up panel designs such as halved and quartered patterns. When marquetry came in this in itself was highly decorative and passed through stages as outlined in Chapter 17. Carving was also used but was necessarily confined to solid parts – legs, fretted apron pieces, pediments, and to gilt and silvered cabinet stands which were often extremely elaborate and to gilt mirror frames. With the coming of the mahogany period, inlay practically disappeared and carving again became the chief means of decoration.

Tables It seems likely that the long oak dining table of Jacobean times was used right up to the end of the 17th century. At any rate there are few walnut tables of the type in existence. Presumably on special occasions a long table would be needed to accommodate a number of diners and maybe there was difficulty in obtaining walnut in large enough sizes in the solid. It was probably also felt that a veneered top was unsuitable as it would not withstand heat and would be inclined in use to lift, especially at the edges. This seems suggested by the oak table shown in Fig. 4, which, by the form of the cabriole leg with hoof foot, was probably made towards the end of the 17th century. It is about 6 ft. across and has two leaves fitted with the rule joint. The two opening legs are pivoted with a somewhat crude form of knuckle joint. Another factor may have been the growing habit of family dining in private around a small table, reserving the large oak one for special dining parties.

At any rate the gate-leg table of the oak period was continued in walnut with either twist-turned legs, plain-turned legs often of the inverted cup design and, by the turn of the century, the cabriole leg. Card tables Fig. 5(G), too, had become popular, these having a folding top, disclosing a baize top when opened and a polished surface when used as a side table. Either one or both back legs might be pivoted to support the top, or the frame might open concertina fashion. A small side table decorated with marquetry is shown in Fig. 6. It dates from the William and Mary period. Note the use of the flat serpentine stretcher.

Chairs Early walnut chairs had legs either plain-turned, twist-turned, or of scrolled form. Backs were elaborately carved with scroll work, a crude form of acanthus leafage, cupids, etc., and often had a caned panel. The

Fig. 4 Oak table with cabriole legs terminating with the hoof foot, William and Mary period. This is a quite large dining table, about 6 ft. in diameter. The leaves have the rule joint, and two legs are pivoted with a crude form of knuckle joint. Although in oak it has typical features of the walnut period.

A Chair, about 1675
B Chair, about 1690
C Chair (gilt), about 1680
D Chair, about 1700

E Wing chair, about 1700
F Table, about 1690
G Card table, about 1715
H Chair, about 1720

I Corner cupboard, early 18th century
J Stool, about 1715
K Chest of drawers, 1670-90

L Cabinet, about 1700
M Bureau, late 17th century
N Bureau cabinet, about 1725

Fig. 5 Furniture of the walnut period.

tall-back chair Fig. 5(B), was popular and was usually of somewhat poor construction in that the legs were merely pegged into a flat seat framework. Further details are given in Chapter 10.

Chests-of-drawers Oak chests were made right up to the end of the 17th century, and Fig. 8, page 106, shows the development to a cabinet-made chest-of-drawers as distinct from the earlier type made by the general woodworker. Oak was, however, fast giving way to walnut and a chest-of-drawers veneered with the latter is shown on page 105. Tallboy chests were also popular. That shown in Fig. 7 is a specially fine specimen showing typical features in the sun-ray parquetry in the bottom drawer, the canted and fluted corners to the upper chest, and the overlapping drawer fronts. It dates from about 1740.

Two other items of furniture introduced during the second half of the 17th century were the bureau or writing-cabinet and the china-cabinet. The former often had a cabinet superimposed above to hold stationery, documents, etc. Examples are shown in Fig. 5(M) and (N) and a small corner cabinet at (I). A rather delightful small bureau-bookcase is that in Fig. 8. Note the moulding beneath the lopers of the bureau. Originally the bureau was a separate writing desk with sloping top on a stand. Later it became a single item, but the moulding was frequently retained, though it eventually disappeared.

The sideboard   As we understand the term today, the sideboard did not exist in the walnut period. Commonly a side table was used. Usually it had a marble top for the same reason that dining tables with tops veneered with walnut were not made. Hot items could not be safely stood

Fig. 6 Table in walnut with marquetry decoration. William and Mary period. (M. Harris and Sons, London)

53

Fig. 7 Tallboy of the walnut period. Note the overlapping drawers, veneered and cross-grained cornice moulding. About 1740. (M. Harris and Sons, London)

Fig. 8 Small bureau-bookcase with mirror in door. The drawers are cockbeaded and have herringbone banding. About 1700 (Mallet and Sons (Antiques) Ltd., London)

on a veneered top and it has to be remembered that solid walnut was seldom used except for turned, shaped, or curved parts.

Bedsteads During the walnut period these were usually elaborate four-posters but the entire woodwork was generally covered with hangings and material tacked on.

In the years following the walnut period, which ended about 1725, the same style was continued with certain modifications but in mahogany rather than walnut, and generally in solid wood. The hooped chair back was replaced by a more or less square type and the carving of the cabriole leg took the form of a lion's mask, cabochon detail, or acanthus leafage rather than the shell-and-husk detail. One influence that affected some case furniture and side tables was that of William Kent who designed not only mansions for wealthy patrons but also the furniture for them. It was of a somewhat heavy, architectural style based on the classical, with swags of carving representing fruit and leafwork, often gilt. Side tables had marble tops with heavy underframing, again often with carved and gilt details.

Age of the designer

Several terms are applied to cover the period 1745–1850, and are usually the names of designers or cabinet-makers who have come to be chiefly associated with the furniture styles, largely because of the books of designs which they published. These books, however, were for the greater part little more than trade catalogues and mostly represent styles of furniture in general production at the time. Few pieces which have survived can be definitely traced back to the workshops of these men with the exception of items made for large mansions. Most of it must have originated in the workshops of the many cabinet-makers working in the then fashionable style. Nevertheless, the terms are convenient to give to the phases of furniture during the period under discussion.

Chippendale Invariably mahogany was used and the decoration was entirely that of carving or frets. Inlay was never used. Chairs were of the characteristic style shown in Fig. 9. Legs were of the cabriole type with carved acanthus leafage and terminating with feet of the turned club form, claw and ball, or French scrolled form; or were straight with the inner back corner chamfered and either plain square or with the toad's back moulding worked along the length. In the case of the Chinese type the legs were sometimes fretted. Backs usually had a shaped top rail of serpentine form with fretted and carved splat, the curvature of the rail flowing into that of the splat.

In some Gothic chairs the splat was fretted in the form of pointed arches but, beyond this, it had little in common with the true Gothic. Chinese

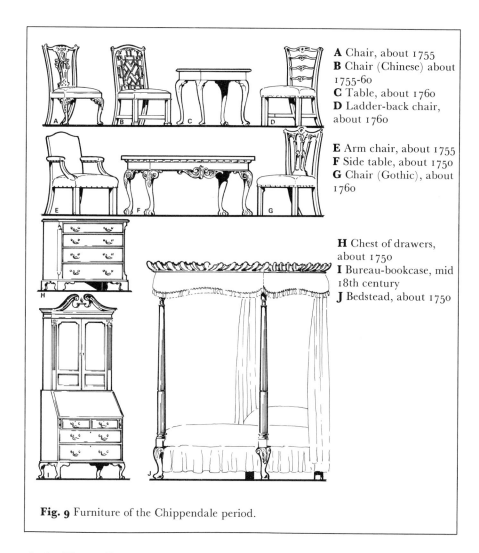

A Chair, about 1755
B Chair (Chinese) about 1755-60
C Table, about 1760
D Ladder-back chair, about 1760

E Arm chair, about 1755
F Side table, about 1750
G Chair (Gothic), about 1760

H Chest of drawers, about 1750
I Bureau-bookcase, mid 18th century
J Bedstead, about 1750

Fig. 9 Furniture of the Chippendale period.

chairs Fig. 9 (B) had a form of lattice work in the back, the detail being repeated in the arms (if any); see also Fig. 30, page 135. Ladder back chairs Fig. 9 (D) were also popular. A particularly intricate and often fragile type was the ribband-back shown on page 138.

Tables It is an odd thing that, although writing tables, side tables, toilet tables, library tables, commode tables, sideboard tables, breakfast tables, and china tables are all illustrated in Chippendale's book, not a single design for a dining table appears. However, from the few specimens of the period that have survived, dining tables were of the flap type with pivoted legs. A table of this kind might open up to 5 ft. by 4 ft. but this would not be big enough for a large dining party. The solution was to make the tables in sets which could be placed together to form a single long table. The outer leaves were of rounded shape and the others rectangular. In some cases a third table was made, this having both leaves rectangular so that it could be placed between the others.

Side tables might have cabriole or straight, square legs, and card tables were similar except for the folding top. In some cases there were two leaves, one pivoted above the other, giving a single polished top, a double baize top, or a double polished top for use as a breakfast table. A remarkably fine tea table with top of serpentine shape is given in Fig. 10. The back

Fig. 10 Tea table with hinged leaf and concertina movement of rear legs. About 1760. A measured drawing appears on page 242. (M. Harris and Sons, London)

Fig. 11 Mahogany press with fielded panels. A fine piece of cabinet work in richly figured timber. The door panels are cut in the solid. Note how the grain can be traced continuously across the fielding. Mid 18th century. (M. Harris and Sons, London)

legs open out with the concertina movement, see also page 242.

The large side table had not yet been replaced by the sideboard and was usually a marble-topped structure with cabriole, square, or scrolled and carved legs, Fig. 9(F), and frequently with boldly carved front apron rail.

Fig. 12 Mahogany cabinet, lower part with serpentine front. The lower moulded circle, which is divided when the doors open, suggests the work of William Vile. (Victoria and Albert Museum)

Chests Both single chests-of-drawers and tallboys were made. An example is given in Fig. 9(H). The canted corner was a typical feature and it might have either a quarter-pillar set in it or be decorated with an applied fret. Bracket feet were commonly used. A splendid example of a mahogany press is shown in Fig. 11. Apart from the rich figuring of the timber the carving is of an extremely high order.

Writing or library tables and bureau-bookcases were both made in the Chippendale period. A bureau-bookcase is shown in Fig. 9(I). Detail in these varied widely and could be anything from the severely plain to the highly ornamental.

Bookcases These had become a feature of most well-to-do homes and Chippendale's book includes some quite monumental examples. A cabinet of the first quality is that in Fig. 12, the style being that of William Vile, a fashionable cabinet-maker who made high-grade furniture and was employed to make many pieces for country mansions. He died in 1767.

In the bedroom the canopied type of bed continued, but the posts at the front were in mahogany with either square-cut legs or the cabriole type. In general those which have survived show more simplicity than those of the walnut period, though some of the designs in Chippendale's *Director* are extremely elaborate.

Another bedroom item in considerable use was the clothes press (see Fig. 11). It had been made in the pre-Chippendale period and continued throughout the century. Dressing or toilet tables were also widely made.

Hepplewhite This period lasted roughly from 1770 to 1790. Here again the term is a general one of convenience intended to cover furniture being made by the trade as exemplified in *The Cabinet-Maker and Upholsterer's Guide,* published in three editions from 1788 to 1794 (Hepplewhite died in 1786). He worked mostly in mahogany with inlays of satinwood and other decorative hardwoods. Typical pieces are shown in Fig. 13.

Of his chairs the best known is the shield-back (see Fig. 40, page 140). It has a greater preponderance in his book than any other type, but examples are also shown of square and elliptical form. The chairs are lighter than those of Chippendale and the carving much slighter. Legs were usually tapered, sometimes with a slight outward curve at the bottom. Others were turned and, when of the cabriole type, were taken from the French form with scrolled foot, and at the top they generally continued in a sweep with the seat rails. Those chairs with shield and oval shapes were necessarily expensive to make because of the compound curvature. For fuller details see page 139.

Side tables, sideboards, and side tables with flanking pedestals with urns all appear in Hepplewhite's book. The tables usually had four or six legs, and might be either straight or shaped in plan. Legs were usually square-tapered, sometimes moulded or recessed, and the top rail might be decorated with delicate carving or marquetry in the form of shaded fan shapes, urns, husks, etc. Generally mahogany was used, though some items

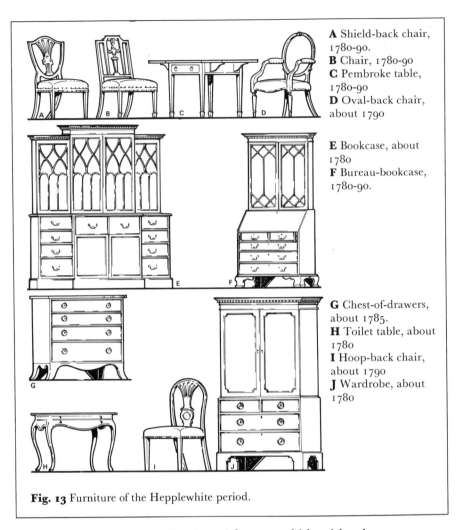

A Shield-back chair, 1780-90.
B Chair, 1780-90
C Pembroke table, 1780-90
D Oval-back chair, about 1790

E Bookcase, about 1780
F Bureau-bookcase, 1780-90.

G Chest-of-drawers, about 1785.
H Toilet table, about 1780
I Hoop-back chair, about 1790
J Wardrobe, about 1780

Fig. 13 Furniture of the Hepplewhite period.

were made in satinwood. Sideboard fronts could be either bow or serpentine shaped, or could be in reversed curves with square breaks where the two centre legs occurred.

There are many designs for small side tables with tops in various shapes in Hepplewhite's book, and the Pembroke table appears also with tops veneered in decorative patterns and with marquetry. Fig. 14 is a table of this kind. Apart from the marquetry top the legs are veneered and inlaid. The leaves are supported by brackets pivoted on knuckle joints. The pedestal library table is also illustrated. The bureau-bookcase, Fig. 13(F), features largely, the doors of the bookcase being invariably barred in a variety of patterns, and the bureau with either drawers or a cupboard. In some cases the sloping top of the bureau may be replaced by an upright fall the whole pulling forward as a secretaire, or there may be a tambour front. Usually the whole stands on bracket feet.

Both single and the tallboy chest-of-drawers were continued in the

Hepplewhite period, these having cock-beaded drawers and drawer rails crossbanded. Fronts might be bow, serpentine, shaped, or flat. Usually a chest stood on feet which curved outwards at the bottom and which were joined by a rail forming a continuous sweep and known as the French foot. It was really a form of shaped plinth cut away at the bottom in a curve Fig. 13 (G). For the construction of this see page 237. Both the toilet table and the large press, Fig. 13(J), were continued.

Large bookcases were a feature, these usually having the lowest part fitted with drawers or (and) cupboards, Fig. 13(E). Frequently the upper part was in three separate carcases, the middle one breaking forwards sometimes with broken pediment. Invariably the doors were barred in various designs.

The bedstead again was a quite monumental affair with flat, shaped, or domed canopy. The two supporting posts at the front were turned and frequently carved in delicate detail.

Fig. 14 Pembroke table with marquetry top and inlaid framing. The leaves are supported by brackets pivoted on knuckle joints. About 1780-90. (M. Harris and Sons, London)

Fig. 15 One of a pair of dining tables which fit together to form one large table. The style is that of Adam. About 1775. (Victoria and Albert Museum)

Adam Robert Adam was an architect responsible for many notable buildings, and his connection with furniture is that he designed a great deal of furniture for them. Much of this has never left the houses for which it was made, and it is unlikely that any will ever come the way of the ordinary collector. At the same time his influence as a designer came to affect the general run of furniture being made in the second half of the 18th century. Thus Fig. 15 shows a dining table made in the style of Robert Adam. It is one of a pair, the two fitting together to form a table 7 ft. 2 in. by 3 ft. 9 in. The fluted rails with carved paterae and square-tapered legs are typical Adam features.

His designs were made by notable cabinet-makers of the day, including Chippendale, and we thus have the curious anomaly that a chair might be made by Chippendale but has to be regarded as Adam rather than Chippendale. Some of the instances of this are documented in the archives of country mansions.

Adam used both marquetry inlay and delicate and refined carving as decoration. Typical motifs were the Grecian vase or urn, honeysuckle, Greek key, drapery, rams' heads, and plaques with mythological subjects. Paintings by well-known artists such as Angelica Kauffman and Wedgwood plaques were also used. Furniture legs were the square-tapered type, sometimes with the surfaces recessed and carved or fluted. Turned legs were also used, these often having a refined leaf carving cut in them. Fig. 16 shows typical items in the Adam style.

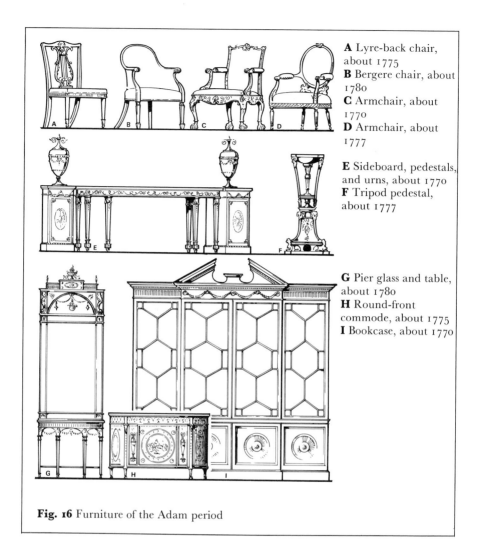

A Lyre-back chair, about 1775
B Bergere chair, about 1780
C Armchair, about 1770
D Armchair, about 1777

E Sideboard, pedestals, and urns, about 1770
F Tripod pedestal, about 1777

G Pier glass and table, about 1780
H Round-front commode, about 1775
I Bookcase, about 1770

Fig. 16 Furniture of the Adam period

Sheraton Although Sheraton was undoubtedly a practical man (if anyone doubts this he should read his description of how to work a canted cornice moulding), he does not appear ever to have had his own cabinet-making business. The attachment of his name to a furniture style is the result of his published books on the subject, and chiefly *The Cabinet-Maker and Upholsterer's Drawing Book*, published in 1791 and in later editions. It differs from books by other makers such as Chippendale's or Hepple-white's in that, whereas these latter are virtually trade catalogues of items made by those firms, Sheraton's book was intended to help the practical man in giving instructions on drawing, geometry, perspective, and in providing a large number of furniture designs with details. It is virtually impossible therefore for any pieces of furniture in existence today to have been his practical work; or at any rate there is nothing that can be

65

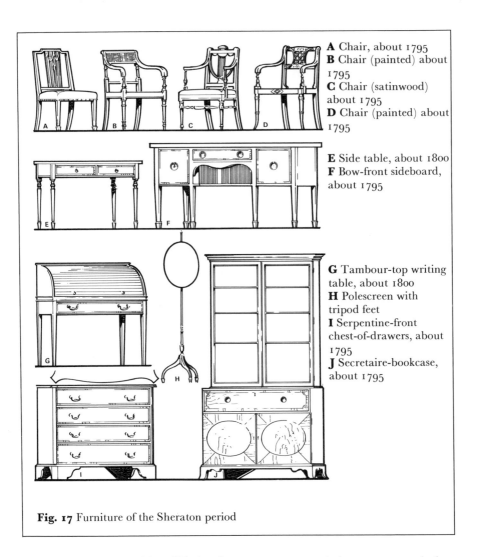

A Chair, about 1795
B Chair (painted) about 1795
C Chair (satinwood) about 1795
D Chair (painted) about 1795

E Side table, about 1800
F Bow-front sideboard, about 1795

G Tambour-top writing table, about 1800
H Polescreen with tripod feet
I Serpentine-front chest-of-drawers, about 1795
J Secretaire-bookcase, about 1795

Fig. 17 Furniture of the Sheraton period

definitely traced to him. His book was at most an influence on style but many of his designs were probably little more than representative of what was generally being made in the trade at the end of the 18th century. Many of the designs appearing in his book are almost indistinguishable from those in Hepplewhite's book with the exception of some of his chairs which bear the stamp of originality. Typical designs are given in Fig. 17.

Usually chairs were simpler than those generally in fashion in that the uprights of the backs seldom had compound curvature. They curved in side elevation only, though they might be tapered both above and below the seat rail when viewed from the front. In the case of arm chairs the arms usually joined the back in a continuous sweep, Fig. 17(B). Front legs were either square-tapered or turned. A chair showing this relative simplicity as compared with some of the elaborate Chippendale or Adam chairs is that in Fig. 18. The back legs are shaped in side elevation only

Fig. 18 Chair in mahogany, relatively simple but beautifully proportioned. Sheraton style. About 1795. (Victoria and Albert Museum)

though there is a taper towards the top and to a lesser degree beneath the seat rail when viewed from the front.

A number of tables for various purposes appear in Sheraton's book; side, writing, occasional, small flap, etc. and some have remarkable mechanical contrivances for moving parts such as stationery boxes which spring up on the release of a catch, hinged or sliding parts, tambours, and secret compartments, or drawers. Apparently there was a fashion for the toilet table to be used also for writing or reading.

The bureau-bookcase was a feature much as in Hepplewhite's book and it might stand on curved bracket feet or be supported on square-tapered or turned legs. In addition there was the writing table with small stationery nest at the back and sides of the top. Sometimes the whole top was enclosed by a tambour, Fig. 17(G). The bookcase proper followed the general style in vogue at the time, the upper carcase having barred doors in various designs which appear to have been common to all makers at the period.

In the chest-of-drawers we again have both single chest and tallboy with straight, bow, or serpentine front. Drawers were frequently cock-beaded but in some cases had inlay bandings around the edges. The Sheraton sideboard was practically as those given in the Hepplewhite book, straight, bow, serpentine, or with broken curve front.

In all Sheraton work decoration is chiefly with inlay bandings and strings, built-up veneer patterns of quarterings with oval and circular bandings, small marquetry insets of shaded shells or fans. Painted figures with decorative designs of floral and leafwork, ribbons and scroll work generally are also a feature. Mahogany was chiefly used though there are many satinwood pieces to which the name Sheraton is applied.

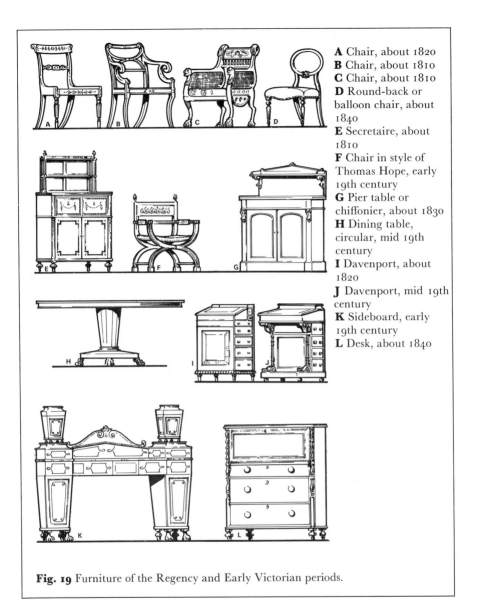

A Chair, about 1820
B Chair, about 1810
C Chair, about 1810
D Round-back or balloon chair, about 1840
E Secretaire, about 1810
F Chair in style of Thomas Hope, early 19th century
G Pier table or chiffonier, about 1830
H Dining table, circular, mid 19th century
I Davenport, about 1820
J Davenport, mid 19th century
K Sideboard, early 19th century
L Desk, about 1840

Fig. 19 Furniture of the Regency and Early Victorian periods.

The 19th century   Sheraton died in 1806, but although his late designs showed deterioration, the influence of his better work continued for a while. There were, however, other causes of change at work, and of these that of the Consulate and Empire periods of France were outstanding. Then, too, in 1807 Thomas Hope published his *Household Furniture and Interior Decoration* which went back to Greek and Roman forms. It developed into the style we now know as Regency. A table of late Regency style is shown in Fig. 20. Note the typical humps to the tops of the legs, a detail which would not have appeared in 18th century work. Other designs extending into the early Victorian period are shown in Fig. 19.

Fig. 20 Pedestal sofa table with brass marquetry decoration. About 1815. (Victoria and Albert Museum)

Chapter 6

Is construction true to period?

Prior to the mid 17th century methods of construction in furniture were largely a matter of the capability of the craftsman, the facilities he had, and the timber available to him. The joint chiefly used was the mortise-and-tenon with variations to suit its particular application. With the restoration of the monarchy came a transitional period when furniture-making was becoming a specialized craft and much of the development was due to the introduction of veneering. Some of the early work of this period shows a curious mixture of methods, the worker copying new techniques often without understanding their significance or reason. By the end of the century, however, methods of construction had largely become standardized and remained so with minor differences throughout the 18th century with modifications as experience or necessity suggested.

I have endeavoured to illustrate these features in Chapter 9 and suggest that this is consulted again for details. At the same time one cannot be dogmatic. Only too often it happens that the exception turns up. Still, it is useful to know what the general practice was in any particular period. One thing always to keep in mind is the possibility of later alterations or additions, or indeed of a later copy of an item of obviously earlier date. Sometimes the latter is revealed by the use of methods which would not have been followed at an earlier period.

Is its carving or inlay part of the original piece or has it been subsequently added? The chief reason for such an addition is usually the hope of giving the item enhanced value. When, therefore, the carving does form a special feature it is worth particular examination. Nevertheless, it has to be remembered that every age has produced its enthusiastic amateurs who find in an otherwise plain item, a ready-made subject for attention. As an example, consider the fashion after the Restoration for lacquering items in imitation of true oriental work. Indeed, there was published a book in 1688 purporting to tell its readers exactly how such work could be done. This was *A Treatise of Japanning and Varnishing* by John Stalker and George Parker. It was stated as 'Being a Compleat Discovery of those Arts' and 'The Method of Guilding, Burnishing, and Lackering'.

One assumes that the authors were satisfied that they really had 'discovered those arts' and that their readers thought that they could work in the true oriental spirit which had taken centuries to bring to perfection, and with materials and by methods which again had taken generations to discover and prove.

The result is occasionally seen in some walnut pieces which have suffered as a result of this attention. Maybe it is a tallboy or china cabinet, originally veneered and cross-banded with walnut and with mouldings cross-grained in the true style of the period, but now covered with black japan and a crude design supposed to be oriental, on a background partly raised with gesso. I once had the job of stripping off the lacquer from a cabinet to reveal the walnut veneer beneath. In a curious way it was not without a certain qualm that I did so, for the lacquer, spurious oriental as it was, had become almost an antique in itself, having been applied some 200 years previously. And of course the stripping of the lacquer removed the original patina so that we were left with a cabinet which, although undoubtedly old, looked new!

In the same way some pieces of furniture have had inlay bandings or marquetry details cut into them at a date subsequent to manufacture. It used to be possible to buy small marquetry panels of shell form, fan shapes, vases, and so on, and in my young days as an apprentice I was sometimes given the job of chopping recesses in drawer fronts and other parts to receive fan corners like those in Fig. 1a. The fall of a bureau was another favourite place to let in an oval shell pattern (b). These were often augmented with an inlay banding (c) which could be cheaply bought in 40 in. lengths and required only a groove or rebate to be scratched in to receive it.

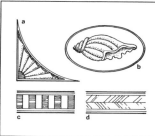

Fig. 1 Inlays used in the late 18th century. **a** Fan corner; **b** Shell; **c** Decorative banding; **d** Herringbone banding.

Presumably at that time it did give added value to the item; it must have done because no seller of antiques would have gone to the expense otherwise. But it was a wretched practice. Not only was it false, but it entailed scraping off the entire surface to make the inlay level with the groundwork, and the patina acquired by decades of patient polishing was lost. Quite frequently these inlays have risen as a consequence of faulty glueing or because they have been cleaned up without sufficient drying time for the glue. It is not suggested, of course, that all such inlay is suspect. Many old pieces had inlay bandings – in fact, it can be seen in some of the illustrated books published in the 18th century, but it is worth special

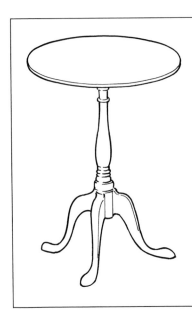

Fig. 2 Plain tripod table. Many of these were made in the late 18th century and throughout the 19th century, and they have frequently been carved subsequently to give added value.

examination. The real phase of inlay did not come in till about 1780 and then continued into the next century.

Later carved detail   It is perhaps in the field of carving that most 'improvements' have taken place and some items seem to have been the special object of attention. One of these is the small tripod table such as that in Fig. 2. At one period there were any number of these made with plain turned pillar and simple, undecorated cabriole legs. They were made for middle class folk and were cheap to make because, except for the legs, they were the product of the turner who could make them by the dozen to standard pattern.

A carved table is another matter. There is more expense involved in the carving than in the rest of the job put together, and such tables were made only for relatively wealthy people. Consequently plain tables have often been carved at a later date. It is, then, the carving of such a table that calls for special inspection. Skilfully done, it is difficult to detect but there are one or two pointers. Shallow carving can be suspect, the reason being that, in an item already turned, the whole of the carving has to be won out of what exists. When a new table is made, one in which carving is intended, the turner has to allow for this by leaving sufficient fulness where necessary. Consider Fig. 3a. The acanthus leafage turns over at the top giving the impression that the tips of the leaves droop forward. To enable this to be done the turner shapes the pillar to the contour shown at (b), thus leaving the carver material in which to carve the turn-over. When, therefore, a table is undoubtedly old and has this turn-over at the leaf tips it is generally safe to assume that the carving was done at the time the table was made – unless by a lucky chance there happened to be a member he could use for the purpose, and even then there would probably be an uneasy look about

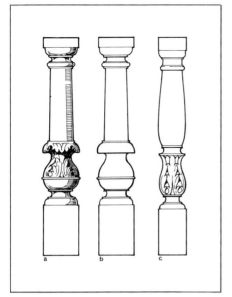

Fig. 3 The pillar of a tripod table. **a** Pillar carved at the time it was made. Note the turn-over of the leaf tips. **b** How the pillar at **a** would have been turned ready for the carver. **c** Pillar which has been subsequently carved.

Fig. 4 Pillar with turned-over leaves partly carved.

the shape. Fig. 4 shows the early stage in carving the pillar of a correct reproduction table. Note how even at this stage the turn-over of the leaf tips have a natural look about them.

In Fig. 3c no such turn-over would be possible, and the entire leafwork would have to be cut in the existing vase shape. It is not suggested that all old tables had this turn-over of leafwork at the top; some were more or less of the form given at (c) but, even so, the turner was usually required to leave enough fulness for the carver, and if the groundwork of the leafwork is cut in deeply it gives an unnatural appearance to the pillar. Consequently when an old pillar of this type is carved later the detail is usually left shallow to avoid this attenuated look.

Piecrust tables The tops of many good quality tripod tables had what is known as piecrust edging. This was a raised and shaped rim leaving the centre recessed to a depth of about $\frac{1}{2}$ in. In good work the tops were always cut in the solid. In other words, the whole of the centre had to be recessed and the edge cut by the carver. The simplest, and incidentally the best, way of doing this was to do the recessing on the lathe, the advantage being that it was possible to make the surface perfectly flat quickly and easily. It was, however, impossible to turn the edging to the finished section because of the undulat·ng shape. This is made clear in Fig. 5; (a) shows the required finished section and (b) the nearest it is possible

73

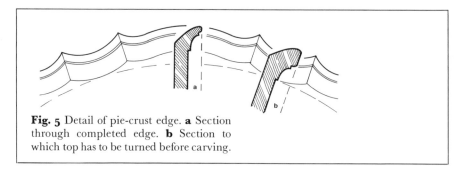

Fig. 5 Detail of pie-crust edge. **a** Section through completed edge. **b** Section to which top has to be turned before carving.

to turn the wood to it. However, even this can be a great help to the carver as it fixes the inner limit of the moulding. Having turned the entire thing to section (b) the edging is cut away with the saw to the required outline, and the moulding plotted parallel with the edge. The carver does the rest and a tricky business it can be owing to the awkward grain direction in parts. In places he has to work against the grain. It is consequently expensive to make such a top. Fig. 6 shows two stages in the carving, (a) preliminary bosting in and (b) nearly completed.

Now it is clearly impossible to cut away an existing plain top because, although the outer shape could be sawn, it would be impossible to carve the moulding since there would not be enough wood for the purpose (compare (a) and (b), Fig. 5). To get over this some makers have cut the outline to shape and planted a shaped moulding on top as in Fig. 7. This, of course, shows a joint line at the outer edge and this is a sure sign that the table is not old or, if it is, that it has had attention.

Fig. 6 Pie-crust edging in the making. **a** Early stage in carving. **b** Completed carving.

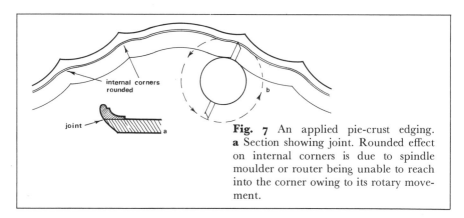

Fig. 7 An applied pie-crust edging. **a** Section showing joint. Rounded effect on internal corners is due to spindle moulder or router being unable to reach into the corner owing to its rotary movement.

Again to cheapen costs the applied moulding is often worked on the spindle moulder or high-speed router. Both these machines are rotary in their action and consequently cannot reach into an inner corner as shown at (b), Fig. 7. As a result, although the inner edge of the moulding may be acutely indented, the line of the moulding will not follow it closely in. It will thus have a wavy undulating line as shown instead of having sharp inner angles. Sometimes the faker has the grace to let the carver cut in the acute indentations afterwards, but the form in Fig. 7 is certainly a poor fake.

Another way in which such tables are sometimes 'improved' is to cut in carving on the top. At best it is a stupid idea because the whole point about a table top is that it shall be flat. If it is mere incision presumably it does not greatly affect items stood upon the top (though it makes it awkward to clean out anything spilt upon it), but there is no special value in mere incision carving. It is only when there is modelling that there is value in carving, and any top modelled in this way largely loses its function. A table top so carved calls for careful examination to see whether the carving has been won from a flat surface, in which case the surrounding area would be sloped into it.

Generally such carving is suspect because, although men in the 18th century were as capable of doing foolish things as we are today, it seems unlikely that an experienced master cabinet-maker would deliberately make a thing non-functional. There is, of course, always the possibility of an enthusiastic amateur finding an outlet for his hobby in carving such a top at a later date. A table of undoubted authenticity is that in Fig. 8. Note that the leafwork of the pillar turns over at the top, and that the acanthus leafage of the legs projects from the general surface and has not merely been won out of an existing plain leg.

Treatment of the cabriole leg During the entire period when they were popular, cabriole legs were made both plain and carved. Sometimes, however, a plain leg has received a face lift with carving to give it added value. When such carving is shallow it can be difficult to detect because there is enough wood in which to carve the detail. Take a Queen Anne leg

Fig. 8 Mahogany tripod table with pie-crust edging and pillar with birdcage movement which enables the top to be revolved and also be folded down vertically. About 1750. (Victoria and Albert Museum)

with shell-and-husk carving as in Fig. 9. Such carving would not need more than about $\frac{1}{8}$ in. depth and the leg could be recessed around it to this extent. However, at some point the recessing must flow into the general line of the leg, and the dotted line shows the minimum extent to which the leg would have to be cut back to form the background. If the latter appears to slope suddenly towards the carving as at (a) it suggests that it has been cut in a plain leg since the carver would not want to remove wood unnecessarily and with it the patina of the existing surface. In any case there would be a sort of flatness about it. The section at (b) shows how the background would have sloped slowly into the carving in a leg in which the carving was planned and done when the leg was made. Enough wood would have been left so that the carving projects from the main curve of the leg.

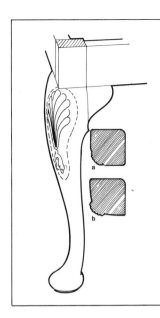

Fig. 9 Cabriole leg with carved knee. **a** Detail carved at later date. Note lack of projection. **b** Detail carved at time leg was made.

In relatively shallow carving such as this shell detail it may not be easy to detect, but anything like the deep detail involved in animal head or human mask carving could not be successfully won from the wood of an existing leg – or if it could it would reveal itself in a flatness of outline.

Maybe there is less of this added carving nowadays than formerly because it is such an expensive process. However, when it comes to mouldings it is possible to buy machine-made mouldings and these have sometimes been added to an otherwise plain piece. Generally they can be recognized, however, by an absolute regularity which no carved work could have achieved.

Is it veneered?   Here we come straightaway to period. In one case it can be wrong if it is; in another if it is not. It is safe to say that no oak period furniture was ever veneered. The veneering process was not used in England until about 1660 and any British-made item earlier than this cannot have been veneered. Oak furniture continued to be made until the end of the century (and, indeed, in the next), especially in country districts, but it was always used in the solid. Oak was plentiful and there was no reason for veneering, even in the second half of the century. Oak pieces continued to be made in traditional style with solid wood framed together.

The introduction of veneering coincided with the first use of walnut as a furniture wood, and here we have a complete reversal of things. Flat surfaces were always veneered. The only parts cut in the solid were items to be turned or shaped such as legs, chair arms, shaped rails, and parts which had to be carved. Mouldings were worked in a thin facing of solid wood, the grain of which ran crosswise, glued to a groundwork of pine or oak. Even the flat parts of these mouldings and those with large, flat curves were usually veneered. Details of how they were made are given in Chapter 15. The only exception sometimes found is in cocked beads which, being no more than ⅛ in. wide, might be in solid wood with the grain running lengthwise. Even these, however, were sometimes cross-grained (see page 161).

To find, say, a chest-of-drawers top in solid walnut is extremely rare. Occasionally a small dining table top might be in solid walnut, presumably because it was felt to be unsafe to use veneer for this purpose. As a general rule, however, it can be taken that veneer, usually with cross-banding around the border, was used for all flat surfaces during the walnut period.

Passing to mahogany, which became popular as a furniture wood about 1720, early pieces were almost always in the solid. This included table tops, door panels, drawer fronts, and so on. As mentioned in Chapter 4, early mahogany was of Cuban origin and was a dark, heavy timber, an excellent furniture wood, but not specially colour-marked in its grain because of its darkness. It was, moreover, hard and brittle and this may have been another reason why it was seldom cut into veneer. Later, when veneers were cut, it was thick, almost like a facing rather than a veneer. The probability is then that if a mahogany piece is veneered it is likely to be of later date than about 1745.

From the Chippendale period and onwards furniture might be in the solid or veneered. To an extent it would depend upon the position in a piece. Chair rails, for instance, were mostly in solid mahogany except when there was a facing of mahogany on beech. This was sometimes the case when, say, a seat rail was serpentine in shape. The mahogany facing might be only thick enough to hold up to the shape, the main strength being in the beech at the back. In any case, Cuban mahogany was a bad wood for upholstery tacks, being too brittle and liable to split. Consequently, when a chair seat was of the stuff-over type, that is the covering material was taken over the seat rails (as in Fig. 35, page 137), beech or a similar wood was used as it was not so liable to split. A chair with loose drop-in seat (as Fig. 32, page 136) would have solid mahogany rails, but the loose seat frame would usually be in beech.

To tell whether an item is veneered or not depends to an extent upon its position. When a square edge is visible it may be possible to see the thickness of the veneer, but if it is moulded or carved it may be concealed by a facing. Thus it might be assumed that a table top having a carved edging such as that in Fig. 10a, must be solid since the carving at the edge is mahogany. It is quite likely, however, that the top is of softwood with a mahogany edging tongued on as at (b) and (c), and then veneered.

If a part, such as a table rail, has its grain running crosswise, it must have been veneered because there would be no strength in it otherwise. When, however, a detail is cut away deeply in parts as is the case of Fig. 11, which is a fielded panel, and the grain of the centre part can be traced continuously from the centre part across the sloping fielding at the edge, this must be in solid wood, because if veneer had been used the grain at the fielding would be different from that on the centre part. This is exemplified

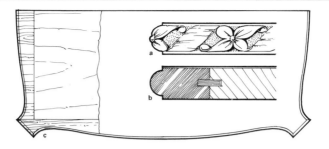

Fig. 10 Table top with carved edging. **a** Detail of carving. **b** Section through tongued-on edging. **c** Top with veneer stripped revealing edging.

well in Fig. 11, page 59, in which the grain, even in the photograph, can be followed from the main centre panel across the fielding.

In the case of marquetry, it must be veneer, except when there are small marquetry details on an otherwise plain surface, in which case they may have been chopped into solid wood. An example of this often occurs at the tops of the legs of mahogany bow-front and serpentine-front sideboards which frequently had small oval marquetry shells or fans let into the solid wood.

Another test, practicable in some circumstances, is to examine the reverse side to see whether it has corresponding grain as compared with the front. A solid panel would have at least similar grain characteristics. It can be accepted that any panel having a built-up design such as quartering or circular or oval patterns with mitred surrounds is veneered. It would not be practicable to do such work in solid wood owing to the danger of movement due to shrinkage.

Does it show machine marks? The immediately obvious point about this is that if a piece of woodwork shows marks made by a machine that had not been invented at the alleged date of the item, it is clear that something is wrong. It is true, of course, that an old piece of furniture may have been repaired with new wood or have had additions which belong to a later date, and this is certainly something to take into account. Such parts might easily show marks made by relatively modern machines. If, how-

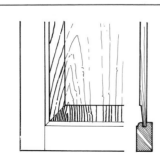

Fig. 11 Fielded panel in solid wood. The figuring of the grain can be followed across the sloping fielding.

ever, it is not a repair or addition it is clear that it should show only those marks that tools in use at the time could have made.

Saw marks   Let us compare methods of working wood that have been practised over the years. First there is the conversion of wood from the felled tree. Apart from riving (see Chapter 3), the earliest method which was still followed in some country districts right up to the end of the last century, though on an ever decreasing scale, was that of the saw pit (see page 15). The latter was either a pit in the earth with wood beams across the top on which the log to be cut was laid; or a brick or timber structure built up in place of a pit and the timber rested on this. A description of the method is given on page 14, Chapter I.

There were, however, saw mills at work at a quite early period, these being worked by wind or water power or driven by horse or human labour. On the continent of Europe and indeed in America these mills were common, whereas in England the saw pit was still the chief means of converting timber. In fact, in the mid-19th century it was often cheaper to buy converted timber from abroad than to cut it up on the saw pit.

All these early mechanical saws were of the reciprocating type, and were, in fact, a form of frame saw in which either a single saw was fixed, or a gang of about three saws which enabled three cuts to be made simultaneously. Fig. 12 shows an early form of frame saw as used in the 15th and 16th centuries. Pity the poor wretch who had to use it! It took all the energy of two men to use a pit saw making a single cut along a baulk. But here one man has to force four saws through the wood, and at each revolution of the wheel a peg in the latter has to drive against one of the

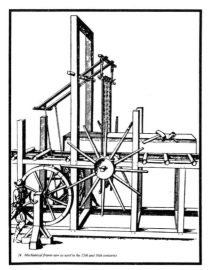

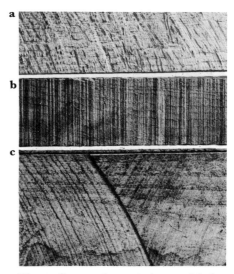

Fig. 12 Early mechanical frame saw as used in the 15th and 16th centuries.

Fig. 13 Saw marks on timber. **a** Marks made by pit saw or hand saw. **b** Marks made by machine frame saw. **c** Circular saw marks.

spars which in turn push the baulk forward. One can only assume that the artist used his imagination, and that there was in fact another man at the other side – or possibly two men at each side.

The marks made by the various types of saw are fairly easily distinguishable. Cuts made on the saw pit are not so regular as those made by the frame saw, and they are at a slight angle because the saw has to slope slightly as it is used as shown in Fig. 3, page 15. It is usually safe to say, therefore, that when somewhat irregular saw marks slope at an angle across the wood it is the result of cutting on the pit saw or with the hand saw which again is usually held at a slight angle. Such irregular marks are shown at (a), Fig. 13.

Although there certainly were saw mills on the continent in the 17th century and in Britain in the 18th century, this would scarcely apply to the final sawing of timber to required sizes, because individual cabinet shops in towns would probably not have easy access to a mill and the cost of transporting timber would be high. Fig. 13 shows at (b) the marks of wood cut in a machine frame saw.

Marks made by the circular saw are in a different category. They follow the line of an arc of a circle. It appears that Samuel Miller patented an idea for a circular saw in 1777, but it may not have been made up and was certainly not in general use. It was not until the general use of steam power in the 19th century that the practical widespread use of the circular saw became possible. Probably the greatest impetus to its development was that in connection with the manufacture of ships' blocks, a machine devised by Sir Marc Isambard Brunel (1769–1849), the father of the engineer famed for his connection with the Great Western Railway.

It follows from this that if circular saw marks are found on, say, the back of a panel, they cannot have been made in the 18th century and are unlikely to belong to the first half of the 19th century. Such marks are shown at (c), Fig. 13.

So far as veneer is concerned, this theoretically should not show saw marks at all, but if the (glued) underside was not toothed before being laid, any saw marks would be liable to show through to the surface in time owing to the glue in the interstices eventually shrinking and pulling the surface with it, revealing faint marks like a sort of dim reflection. So far as is known the first circular veneer saw was patented by Brunel in 1806. Any veneers of earlier date than this must have been cut with the frame saw, either by hand or with a machine driven by whatever power was available. It is, in fact, unlikely that veneers would have been cut on a commercial basis on such a machine until many years later. Hand methods were mostly used for veneer sawing. An illustration in *L'art du menuisier ebeniste*, Paris, 1774, shows two men cutting a log into veneers, see Fig. 2, page 201. Any marks that might eventually show through to the surface would be straight and slightly irregular.

The planer The machine-planer works on a different principle from that of the hand plane. Its cutters have a rotary action, and the entire width of a board is planed in a single pass. When the cutters are sharp and the rate of feed slow, any marks left by it can scarcely be seen after the surface has been glasspapered. When the cutters become dull, however, they have the effect of thumping on to the wood, so compressing the fibres. Such marks may be taken out by the subsequent glasspapering, but if the job is stained or oiled, the dampness releases the compression so that a series of fine regular marks appear across the grain of the wood.

If by chance the cutters are gashed, the path can be seen along the length of the wood, almost like a raised bead. So clearly was the danger of this realized in my early days in the workshop that all machine-planed surfaces were afterwards hand-planed, scraped and glasspapered. Modern machines do better than this, but if a piece of wood shows fine ripple marks across the direction of the grain it is the result of machine-planing. By ripple is meant fine actual undulations in the surface, which are not to be confused with the light and dark streaks that occur across the grain in some woods.

The first planing machine with rotary cutters was patented by Samuel Bentham (1757–1831) but it was not in anything like general use. In fact, the probability is that all wood was hand-planed (except in some specialized industries such as ship-building) until the second half of the 19th century. By comparison a machine saw was a much greater time- and labour-saver, and if the woodworking trade was slow to adopt the saw it would have been still slower to install a planer. It follows then that if planer marks are discovered in an 'old' item that part is suspect.

Mouldings The modern method of making mouldings is to use the spindle moulder, the four-cutter, or the high-speed router, all of which have a rotary action. As in the case of the planer, whether marks show is largely a matter of the condition of the cutter and the rate of feed. In the case of the high-speed router visible marks are practically eliminated as the speed is so great (it may be 26,000 r.p.m.) that marks would be so close together as to be invisible to the naked eye. When a moulding is spindle-moulded for cabinet-work the invariable practice is to dampen the surface afterwards with hot water. This releases all stresses and any consequent marks swell up and are removed when the moulding is finished with glasspaper. If this is not done the machine marks may become visible as a series of fine undulations across the moulding. These can often be seen as coarse marks in softwood mouldings to be painted. Such work is put through the machine at high speed so that the cutter makes fewer but more widely spaced and more pronounced marks. Such coarse marks are not likely to be seen in cabinet-work, but even if fine undulations are seen across the grain of a moulding-it is certain that it cannot be really old.

The old-time cabinet-maker had two chief methods of working mouldings; the moulding plane and the scratch-stock, both of which are described in Chapter 15. Regularity or the lack of it is no sure way of telling whether a moulding is old because it is possible to produce perfectly regular mouldings either way – at any rate in the smaller sections. Large

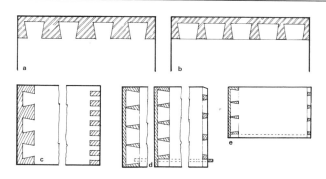

Fig. 14 Various forms of dovetails. **a** Machine-cut dovetails. The tails and pins are equal in size and are regular. **b** Hand-cut carcase dovetails. **c** Machine-cut drawer dovetails. **d** Hand-cut drawer dovetails. **e** Small drawer hand-cut dovetails.

mouldings such as cornices may be somewhat uneven if worked by hand because the various members may be worked separately or the whole may be built up.

Dovetails　It is easy to detect whether dovetails have been cut by hand or machined. The last named are always regular, the pins the same size as the tails as in Fig. 14a. In hand work the cabinet-maker invariably makes the dovetails wider than the pins as in Fig. 14 b, and the slope of the dovetail sides often varies slightly because he seldom marks them out with a bevel but saws them freehand. With constant practice he learns the correct angle but even so there is often slight variation especially in the slope in one direction compared with that of the other.

In the case of drawer dovetails those at the front in machine work again are regular with tails and pins equal in width, whereas in hand work the pins are narrow and run almost to a point. Examples of early drawer dovetails are given on pages 155-158. One last detail is that the cabinet-maker marks out his joints with the cutting gauge, and he takes this right across the wood so that it leaves a cut in line with the root of the dovetails. The purist may consider this an unsightly and unnecessary blemish, but in any professionally-made drawer I have examined, new or old, I have always found this gauge line. Thus, although it does not prove whether a joint is old or new, it does at least show that it is hand cut, because in machining no gauge line is necessary.

A dovetailing machine was patented by Bentham (1757–1831) in which the joints were cut with conical cutters, but it was not in general use and the vast majority of dovetails were cut by hand methods throughout the 19th century. One of the reasons was that it is seldom economical to set up a machine for a single job, so that it was only when mass production became common that machine dovetailing became economical.

Mortise-and-tenon joints　Here again it is necessary in hand work for

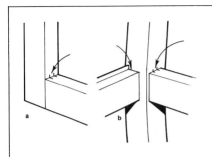

Fig. 15 Tell-tale gauge marks. When two lines can be seen the joint is usually tenoned. A single line suggests that the joint is dowelled. It does not follow, however, that any gauge marks will be visible.

the gauge to be used but it is not required for machining. It is, therefore, worth while looking to see whether there are any signs that a gauge has been used. It is true that the absence of gauge marks does not prove that the joint was machined because, when carefully done, the gauge is not taken beyond the actual joint. Men earning their living in woodwork, however, do not spend time unnecessarily on a job and it is easy to let the gauge run a trifle beyond the line. If, therefore, two parallel lines are seen at the side of the joint as in Fig. 15, it is a sign that it has been hand cut.

A further pointer occurs, however. Sometimes a single gauge line may be seen at the side of the joint. This generally indicates that the item is not a tenoned joint at all but is dowelled. The gauge mark is in line with the dowels.

On the question of mortise-and-tenon joints it is worth noting that for some work these were being replaced by dowels, especially in chair-work in the 19th century. In fact a chair-maker's kit of tools invariably included a dowel plate, this being a steel plate with holes in it of various sizes through which the chair-maker hammered pegs of wood which had been roughly chiselled to shape or even left square. This brought the wood to circular section and made a strong dowel in that the wood, being cleft, followed the line of the grain. At exactly what date this replacement of the mortise-and-tenon by dowels took place it is impossible to say, but it seems likely to have been during the second half of the 19th century. Certainly I have never come across a genuine 18th century chair with dowelled joints, and this may be a pointer in deciding whether a thing is genuinely of the age it is supposed to be.

Mortising machines were invented in the early 19th century but their use was confined to large production work and they were seldom or never found in cabinet-workshops until the second half of the 19th century and rarely then.

Fig. 16 shows a chair alleged to be of the Chippendale period but which proved to have been put together with dowels. In a sound job it is often impossible to tell from the outside whether dowels or tenons were used, but sometimes an over-run gauge line reveals it. With dowels there would be only one line (unless the dowels were staggered as might happen in thick wood), and two lines in the mortise-and-tenon as in Fig. 15, these being apart by the thickness of the tenon, usually $\frac{5}{16}$ in. in 1 in. wood.

84

Fig. 16 A chair alleged to be Chippendale but which has been put together with dowelled joints.

Chapter 7

Is it a marriage of two pieces?

The addition of one item to another is not a thing that happens often because it is clearly a lucky chance when two pieces are of suitable size to be put together. When, however, an item is useless by itself owing to an original part having been lost, it is clear that an endeavour will be made to replace the missing part, and clearly the dealer is in a better position in this respect than most others as so much material passes through his hands. Thus the stand of a cabinet may be missing and when a stand of the right type and period comes to hand the two will be mated, though it usually means altering the size or details of the stand in some way. More usually, however, it necessitates making a new stand, possibly with old wood.

Such pieces usually look wrong to the man who is familiar with old furniture. It is often difficult to say exactly what is wrong and usually knowledge of this kind comes only with experience, unless the two are grossly a misfit.

Some oak pieces seem to have gotten strange bedfellows. There was a time when some settles with panelled backs appeared on the market. These were the outcome of a piece of panelling having developed legs, and had front legs and a seat added. To fit back legs meant that one of two methods had to be followed. In the cruder of the two the legs were merely spliced on at the back as in Fig. 1a, but in better work new back uprights running the full height and having the necessary rake were made to replace the end uprights as in Fig. 1b. The front legs might be odd spindles fitted with a framing or plain square pieces, possibly chamfered or moulded.

In another way such an oddment of panelling might become glorified into the head of a bedstead complete with side rails with holes at intervals along the length through which it would be alleged that ropes supporting the bedding would have been passed. As nobody today would use such a bed without a modern mattress it was convenient to fit a box spring, pointing out frankly that this part was new! Of course, such a conversion might be quite innocently done in that someone had an oddment of panelling that was quite useless by itself but was of suitable size for turning into a bed. I myself have had several such jobs, the panelling being cut

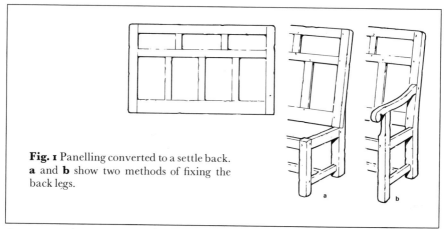

Fig. 1 Panelling converted to a settle back. **a** and **b** show two methods of fixing the back legs.

down to suit a mattress size.

An always saleable item is the small side table with turned legs and some of these started life as turned balusters from the staircase of an old demolished mansion, plus an old top and some plain rails and stretchers as in Fig. 2. The balusters of some old houses were beautifully turned and in some cases were carved. The squares at top and bottom were originally cut off at an angle to fit the sloping handrail and string of the staircase, but it is easy to cut this off square and chop mortises to take rails and stretchers. Sometimes the top and bottom squares were too short for the purpose and new squares were necessary. I have known of some surprisingly successful 'Jacobean' tables which are a reincarnation from a former staircase existence. Sometimes when the balusters were too long for conversion into tables (and this may happen in landing balusters) they became the legs of cabinet stands.

In all this work it is seldom that the whole idea is schemed out from the start. But any furniture restorer over the years collects oddments of all kinds, either because he buys such things knowing that they will eventually be usable in one way or another, or because they are left over from other jobs. At the time of acquiring them he may have no clear idea of how they will come in but eventually a use suggests itself.

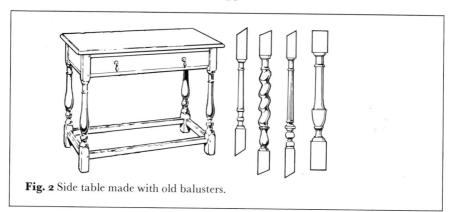

Fig. 2 Side table made with old balusters.

Fig. 3 How two saleable items may be produced from a press.

Is it a divorcee from something else?   This occurs chiefly in items which are not readily saleable in their original form. The case of the tall-boy is mentioned in Chapter 19, this being turned into two separate chests. Another item, not so readily adaptable, is the large press in two carcases with drawers in the lower one and cupboard with sliding trays above. These pieces have excellent accommodation but they are invariably too deep for most modern rooms. Furthermore the upper trays in the top carcase are too high to be practicable. It may happen that the lower chest with top carcase replaced by a moulded top will fetch more than the piece in its original state. This leaves the top cupboard, and frequently this has to be cut down in depth to make it suitable for present-day use, the trays being either correspondingly cut down or omitted. The whole is then mounted on a stand with cabriole or square legs, forming a useful ward-robe, undoubtedly old so far as the main part is concerned but of doubtful authenticity as a period wardrobe. Fig. 3 shows the idea.

What is one really after in old pieces? Many of them are of doubtful value for modern use in their original form. Is attention of this kind there-fore justifiable? Presumably from the practical angle there is no harm so long as the change is realized; the only mischief is that such adaptation may give a false idea of what period furniture was really like.

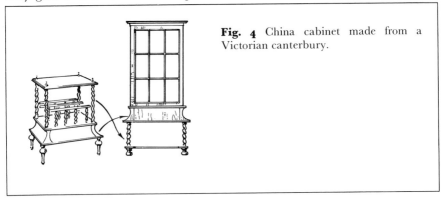

Fig. 4 China cabinet made from a Victorian canterbury.

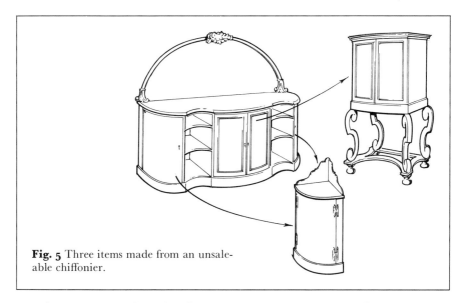

Fig. 5 Three items made from an unsaleable chiffonier.

A few years ago Victorian furniture was a treasure trove for alterations. Now that this furniture is being valued for its own sake this does not happen so much – at any rate in smaller items, especially as the cost of alterations is so high. Most of this furniture was extremely well made and was in use long enough to have acquired a good patina. Fig. 4 shows how a Victorian canterbury of little value forty to fifty years ago was converted into a tolerable china cabinet of the early walnut period. The main box with drawer was retained, the rest being stripped off. Some discarded staircase balusters were used for the legs, these being joined by a flat stretcher. For the sides of the cabinet a pair of old oak doors were slightly packed out to make the width and veneered for the sides, and a new front door made. The result was a china cabinet which, although it would not have taken in an experienced man, sold at a fair figure.

Another example was the conversion of a huge Victorian chiffonier, beautifully made in walnut. It turned up later in the form of a bow-front cabinet on scrolled legs and two walnut corner cupboards. These are shown in Fig. 5. In other cases large tomb-like sideboards have emerged as Adam sideboards, the obviously Victorian parts such as carvings and mouldings being removed and replaced by earlier details. Such alterations were rarely really successful, however; they just looked wrong.

There have been countless ways in which furniture has been altered, either to make it more saleable or to enhance its value, and when an unusual piece is found, or one having curious details, it is worth while considering whether it may originally have been something else. Fig. 6 shows how a Victorian chest-of-drawers was converted to an 18th century piece by fitting new mouldings, replacing turned wood knobs with brass handles, and fitting bracket feet. An oak chest of doubtful authenticity is shown in Fig. 7, though some of the timber is undoubtedly old and shows the original surface. Close examination shows, however, that much of the

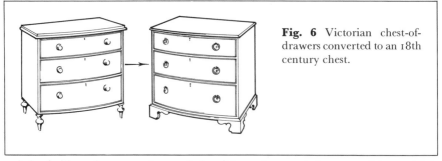

Fig. 6 Victorian chest-of-drawers converted to an 18th century chest.

oak including the carved panels is of American origin, something which would have been impossible in a chest of the alleged period.

Does it show wear marks in natural positions? The wear on drawer sides and runners is dealt with more fully in Chapter 12. The degree of wear depends upon the use the item has had plus its age. Clearly a chest-of-drawers in everyday use in the small domestic house would wear far more quickly than one in the spare room of a quiet country mansion. Thus, although some wear is bound to have taken place, the degree of wear is not a positive test of age. In any case, drawers have frequently been repaired with new slips at the bottom of the sides, and with new runners.

One point worth noting is the back of the drawer when pulled right out. The bottom invariably projects at the back to allow for its being pushed forward in the likely event of shrinkage. A favourite faker's dodge was to brush a thin coat of glue at the back as in Fig. 8, and shake dust on to it to simulate the accumulation of years. If this dust cannot be wiped off it has quite likely been glued and a close examination will reveal this.

Fig. 7 Oak chest which is a fake. Although some old wood has been used for parts, much of it is in American oak.

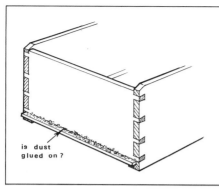

Fig. 8 The dust of ages applied in a few seconds.

is dust glued on?

It also sometimes happens that an extra deep item has been cut down in depth to make it more suitable for modern conditions. This, of course, makes it necessary to cut down any drawers correspondingly and, since it would be difficult to re-cut dovetails without taking the whole drawer to pieces, a common plan was to saw the sides to the required length, cut the pins from the back and butt it between the sides, fixing with glue and nails. It is an almost sure sign that this has happened if a drawer is dovetailed at the front and butted and nailed at the back.

Wear on stretchers of tables and chairs has already been discussed in Chapter 4. This happens mostly on oak furniture, partly because it is older, and also because habits in earlier years were not so polished. A man in Tudor or early Jacobean times might wear his heavy outdoor boots indoors, and would not hesitate to rest his feet on the stretchers of a table. As the floor might be covered with rushes which might be anything but clean, he might consider that the chief purpose of the stretchers was that of resting his feet. All items near the floor can be expected to be more worn and marked than other parts. This is partly because items are frequently dragged about rather than lifted and, in any case, things near the floor are liable to be kicked.

Oak table tops are inevitably more worn at the top edges and corners than at the middle. In the case of long tables it is sometimes possible to see the positions where diners have sat for generations by the wear at the edges where platters have been drawn back and forth as in Fig. 9. The temptation of fakers, however, is to overdo the wear, and when a top is really rounded by alleged wear it is quite possibly only the abrasion intentionally given to simulate the appearance of wear. In most oak tables, in fact, except for slight rounding of otherwise square edges and corners, and bruises and cuts across their edges, there is not usually a lot of actual wear.

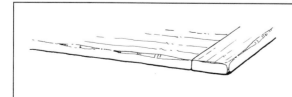

Fig. 9 Wear at the edge of a table top.

In later walnut and mahogany furniture wear is far less, and in the former is usually confined to chipped veneer, scratches, and occasional bruises. Much the same applies to mahogany items though the corners of table tops, drawers, doors and so on, have been frequently bruised or smashed. Here most signs of wear, apart from chipped veneer or inlay bandings, is in bruised or missing pieces of moulding. Quite often such parts have been repaired or replaced at some time in the past. Such repairs may or may not have been skilfully done.

On the bottoms of legs and feet of chairs which have no castors, there is usually a quite burnished appearance, the result of the chair having been moved about over carpets for years. This usually applies even to oak chairs because, although they originally stood on wood or stone floors, possibly with rushes strewn over them, they have survived through later periods when folk had got past the rushes stage. Chairs and stools show more wear and are more burnished than other items because they are more easily and more frequently moved about. A heavy table may stay in the same position for years, whereas chairs are constantly shifted.

So far as finish is concerned, the so-called rubbed antique finish is purely a flight of fancy, and belongs to the realm of poetry rather than to hard fact. So far as it goes, corners and edges with constant use and polishing tend to remain light whereas other parts accumulate dirt and become begrimed over the years, but anything like the intentionally shaded effect with light centres and dark edges of panels is not found in real old furniture. It is impossible to convey the genuine appearance photographically, and the only plan is to examine carefully the appearance of authentic items to be found in museums, private collections, old mansions, churches, etc. In carvings, corners, and interstices generally there is bound to be an accumulation of old wax and dirt and an absence of sheen since the polishing duster cannot reach into such places.

In the 18th century mahogany chair in Fig. 10 the top of the back rail, centre of splat, tops of arms, and top edge of seat rail are a medium mahogany colour, not really light since the wood is of Cuban origin, but of the characteristic reddish-brown tone seen on newly polished wood of that variety. The rest of the chair is almost black except for the extreme edges and corners which are of the reddish tone mentioned above. This, however, is not true of all chairs of the 18th century. Some which presumably have been kept in condition with wax and friction polishing retain their mahogany colour all over, except for crevices.

In all probability, the difference is due to variation in the original polishing. The finish mentioned by Sheraton in his book, that of fine brick-dust and linseed oil, would produce an eggshell gloss and would be followed by wax polishing by servants for years. It was not, however, the perfect method for keeping out dirt, and it is likely that the continued use over the years resulted in the dark or black colour mentioned above. Some chairs, however, were varnished and this would keep out dirt and retain the original colour much better. In the early years of the 19th century french polishing was introduced and this again would be an excellent means of keeping out dirt and so preserving the colour.

Is it badly in need of repair? Good class repairs can be expensive. They call for a knowledge of period styles and methods of construction when parts are missing, and they need to be carried out so that signs of repair are hidden so far as it is possible. Furthermore, a supply of the right

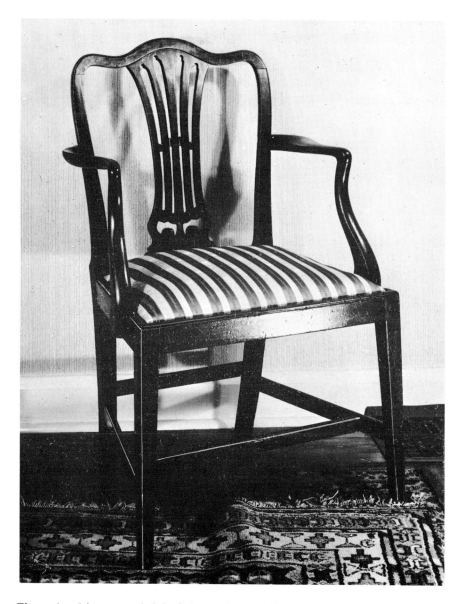

Fig. 10 An 18th century chair in Cuban mahogany. For fuller details of this chair, see the measured drawing on page 240.

kind of timber and veneers is necessary. Not many workshops are equipped for the work and for it to be undertaken by an unskilled man can be disastrous.

The importance of all this is in the price one is prepared to pay for a thing. If it needs much in the way of repair it must be allowed for. Every dealer knows this when he buys a thing. If it is in a bad way he may have to spend forty or fifty pounds in putting it right. In some cases this figure can be trebled. That is why he will not touch some items at all. In the trade these pieces are generally known as 'breakers' because the dealer would have to spend more on them than he could ever hope to recover. This point is elaborated in Chapter 19.

Structural faults are the worst, especially on veneered items. A plain oak table with fractured leg or rail may be fairly simple to put right, but if veneer extends over it as in many walnut pieces this will have to be dealt with in addition to the breakage. One of the problems, and one which often seriously affects the cost of repairs, is that of dismantling, either to replace broken parts or to insert fresh glue. It is often difficult to free a part without opening other joints which may be sound. Problems like this are dealt with in my book, *Furniture Repairs*, and, indeed, the whole subject is full of problems, no two of which are the same. They are only mentioned here to warn readers of what they might let themselves in for if they buy a wreck.

Chapter 8

The chest

It is difficult to appreciate what things were like in bygone periods of history; and the farther back one goes the more difficult it becomes. We are so used to the amenities of the 20th century that it is hard to think of life without them. Even in the 18th century, the golden age of cabinet-making, furniture of any quality at all was only for the relatively well-to-do. The vast majority of folk must have had only the simplest and crudest of necessities, most of which have gone the way of all things, either because they just were not worth keeping, or because they broke up owing to poor construction. In the early oak period only wealthy people would have had any furniture at all, and very little at that.

The story over the years, then, is one of gradually increasing types of furniture, better and more refined methods of construction and, later, changes due to the introduction of different timbers, the whole bound up with the dividing of the trade into various specialized branches; cabinet-making, clockcase-making, carving, turning, and so on.

It seems likely that the earliest item of furniture to be made was a chest of some kind. It might be needed to contain valuables, possibly to be portable; and it might be required to serve either as a table or seat. Churches would need one to hold chalices and other valuables, vestments, records, and possibly money; civic bodies would require a place in which documents, books, or again cash could be kept; and wealthier private people would feel the need for one to store their personal possessions.

The chest, then, would be an early necessity and, although it is not suggested that all furniture was evolved from it, it was the genesis of many types. It was the item with which most craftsmen were familiar, and in making other items they would draw on their experience in chest-making. It is in fact possible to trace the evolution from the early crude chest to the refined chest-of-drawers of the 18th and 19th centuries. I will therefore elaborate on the development of this humble item, not only to show the stages of its development, but because its varying construction over the ages is reflected in many other items. The man who understands the evolution of the construction of the chest will find it much easier to follow that of other pieces of furniture.

In dealing with the progress of the chest over the years it would be convenient to be able to docket the various types into periods and assume that a chest made in a certain way necessarily belonged to a definite period; but it would be a misleading simplification. It is true that there was a general progression from one type to another in the passing of time, but it happened frequently that an early form of construction was continued long after other methods had been adopted generally. As an example of this consider Figs. 1 and 2, page 19, both of which are of 17th century date. The former is a simple piece of work consisting of four boards dovetailed together, and with bottom and lid. The iron brackets are most likely a later addition. It is a purely utilitarian chest made in the most obvious way, adequate, and with no attempt at embellishment. Compare this with the fine piece of joinery in Fig. 2. The latter is of much the same date, but was made by a craftsman of ability and experience, and shows a sense of proportion and design.

One has to consider the limited facilities a man had in the old days to know what was taking place in any district other than his own; also the limitations of his own skill in following any method other than the one with which he was familiar. In this connection, too, it has to be remembered that a different construction might necessitate tools he did not possess. All this is apart from the conservatism a tradesman might feel. What was good enough for his father was good enough for him.

It appears, too, that men who made everyday furniture, including chests, were of a different class from those who made the joinery for buildings, and were generally inferior to them. Thus, to take an example, the system of framed construction put together with mortise-and-tenon joints, often with moulded and chamfered edges, and panels fitting in grooves, was used in the 15th century for panelling, etc; yet framed and panelled chests do not appear to have been made before the coming of the Renaissance in the 16th century. To cite another inconsistency, although by the 17th century framed construction had become the regular method for chests and indeed for all furniture, one comes across an occasional throw-back to an earlier method. Therefore, although, judging by the quality of the piece, the maker was a capable craftsman, the chest in Fig. 1, page 19, is of the early solid planked type with no framing whatever.

As a matter of convenience chests may be divided into six general types: solid hewn, rounded lid, clamped, solid plank, ark, and framed. They are shown grouped together for convenience in Fig. 1. These were followed by the chest-of-drawers, the types of which were: solid oak, walnut veneered, solid mahogany, and veneered mahogany and other woods.

Solid hewn chests These were formed from a solid baulk of timber, the inside literally dug out with the adze, axe, or chisel, though quite a lot may have been bored out first. Fig. 1a is an example. What it must have cost in toil and sweat can be imagined, yet, considering the labour involved, the accommodation is extremely small. This particular chest is reckoned to be of Saxon origin, but the type was made in the 13th and 14th cen-

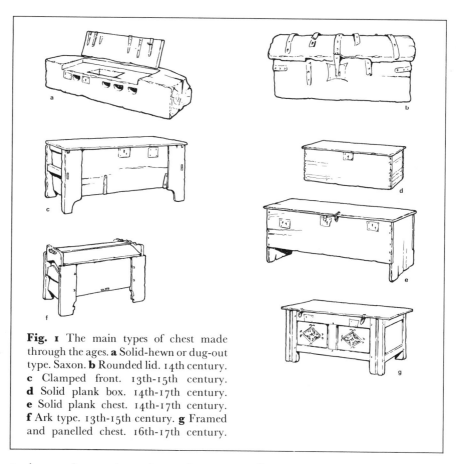

Fig. 1 The main types of chest made through the ages. **a** Solid-hewn or dug-out type. Saxon. **b** Rounded lid. 14th century. **c** Clamped front. 13th-15th century. **d** Solid plank box. 14th-17th century. **e** Solid plank chest. 14th-17th century. **f** Ark type. 13th-15th century. **g** Framed and panelled chest. 16th-17th century.

turies, and even into the 15th century. In many cases it was unsound structurally because the pith or core of the log runs through the centre and, due to the inevitable shrinkage, cracks and splits occur at the outside of the chest. In the present example the trouble is overcome to a degree by the vast thickness of the unhewn ends. In many cases, however, the end walls were much thinner, with the result that the splits caused the whole practically to fall apart. One advantage of the disproportionate size of the chest compared with its accommodation was that its tremendous weight gave additional safety since it would be extremely difficult to remove. Not many of these solid hewn chests have survived, and those that are still with us are usually in churches.

Rounded lid chest   This is another early form of chest, the lid of which is hewn from a tree trunk cut in half, Fig. 1b. The chest itself is built up from heavy planks spiked together and bound with iron at the corners. The type belongs generally to the 14th century.

Clamped front chest (Fig. 1c)   This is the earliest form of chest which is constructed rather than hewn from the solid. It was made in the 13th

97

century and continued with variations and modifications down to the early 16th century, though it is generally more typical of the 13th, 14th, and 15th centuries. It probably owes its origin to the desirability of raising the chest bottom from the floor, hence the end clamps at front and back which project downwards and so become a form of leg or foot. In that illustrated, which dates from about 1300, the front itself is fixed to them with bare-faced tenons (*see glossary*). Often such chests had the lid hinged on wood pivots. The ends might be either plain panels tenoned into the clamps but more generally there were cross-rails often tenoned right through. A fuller description of a chest of this kind is given on page 232.

Solid plank chest   There is something rather obvious about this form of chest – the sort of thing that a boy of today would put together if asked to make a box; four pieces of wood nailed together at the corners, with bottom fitted beneath, and lid hinged at the top, as in Fig. 1d. In its plainest form that was literally all it was, often with no attempt at decoration at all. The corners were usually spiked together and often strengthened with metal angle plates. It is often impossible to date such chests in the absence of any records.

It must early have become apparent, however, that it had its disadvantages in that the bottom rested directly on the floor which was often covered with rushes and was probably uneven in any case. It then occurred to someone to raise it from the floor by continuing the ends downwards to act as a form of trestle leg. The idea is shown in Fig. 1e. This in turn made it necessary for the grain of the ends to be vertical rather than horizontal, as otherwise the projecting part at the bottom would be liable to snap off, and in any case it would be difficult to obtain wood wide enough to reach from beneath the lid to the floor.

Such a construction had its weakness, however, in that the front and back might be 15 in. or more wide, and were bound to shrink on drying out. This movement would be resisted by the ends, the grain of which was upright (remember that wood shrinks in width and thickness, not length). The consequence was that splits were liable to develop in front and back, and in fact this has frequently happened. It is true that such movement could be minimised by seasoning the wood thoroughly beforehand and by using quarter-cut timber, that is wood cut radially from the log (see page 23), but even so some movement was inevitable, and it was no doubt the realization of this that prompted the change-over to framed construction in the later 16th century. However, these planked chests, made originally in the early 14th century, continued into the 17th century, although generally superseded by the framed type.

Ark type chest   Before passing to the final framed type, mention should be made of the raised-lid chest which was made in the 13th, 14th, and early 15th centuries, Fig. 1f. In general form it was of the clamped type but had the raised or ark-type lid invariably pivoted on wood pegs. Three pieces held together with shaped end members formed the lid, the centre flat

98

part being through-tenoned as shown. Apart from this characteristic lid, construction was much the same as the clamped chest.

Framed chest Some of the reasons why framed construction was not used in making chests earlier, despite its having been used in joinery, have already been suggested. From the mid-16th century, however, the method was widely used. Panels were fairly narrow to enable wood of average width to be used without jointing in width, and they were fitted dry in their grooves. According to the skill of the maker, the taste of the man who ordered the chest, or possibly the price he was prepared to pay, the chest might be quite plain or highly ornamented with carving or inlay. Even the plain ones, however, were usually enriched with mouldings or chamfers around the edges of the framing.

A man tackling framed construction for the first time sometimes got curiously involved. If he used a plough plane to make the grooves for the panels he necessarily had to take it right through the length of the wood as explained in Chapter 3. In the case of rails and muntins there was no difficulty; the grooves had to be taken right through in any case. In the legs, however, such a groove continued beneath the bottom rail would look unsightly, and the maker would be faced with the alternative of either using his plough right through and accepting this blemish, or of laboriously chopping his groove with a chisel or possibly using the scratch-stock (see Chapter 3). This latter method can be seen in some chests. In others, however, the grooves are taken right through at the bottom of some of the legs and stopped at others without there appearing to be any reason for the disparity. Maybe the carpenter himself slipped up, or possibly he told an apprentice to plough the grooves who began obligingly to run them all right through until discovered and stopped short by an exasperated master.

It is just possible in some circumstances, though unlikely, to stop a groove at a mortise and still use the plough plane. The idea is shown in Fig. 2a, and assumes that the mortise was at the far end of the work, was

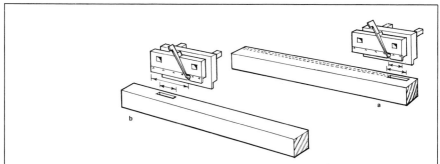

Fig. 2 Use of plough plane for grooving. This tool should preferably be taken right through the length of the wood. It could be stopped at the far end, however, if there is a mortise longer than the front of the plane sole **a**. This could not be done at **b** because the mortise is shorter than the rear of the sole.

chopped first, and that the cutter of the plough was set near the front of the tool. This would not work, however, if the plough had to be started at the mortise end as in Fig. 2b, because the sole of the plane to the rear of the cutter would be too long to drop into the mortise. It would, however, be unlikely because, although one side of any one leg could be grooved in this way, it would be impossible to plough that on the adjoining face because the leg would have to be turned the other way round.

Since the structural joint of all framed chests was the mortise-and-tenon, it is perhaps as well to understand what is involved in forming this. When there is neither groove nor moulding only a socket (the mortise) and corresponding projection (the tenon) are needed as in Fig. 3a. As these early oak pieces were usually put together without glue, a retaining peg was driven through the two as shown. Since, however, grooves to hold panels were invariably required, the effect of this was to cut away the side of the tenon, Fig. 3b, this necessitating a corresponding reduction in the

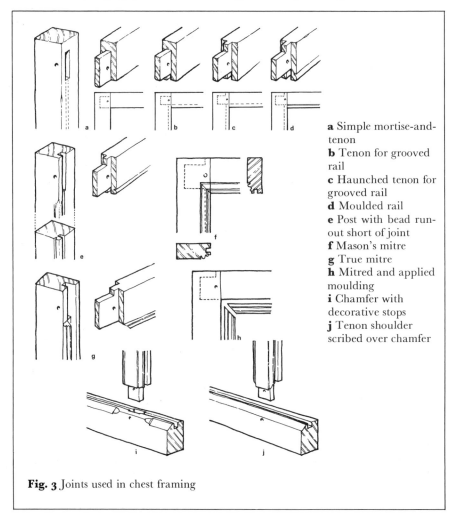

a Simple mortise-and-tenon
b Tenon for grooved rail
c Haunched tenon for grooved rail
d Moulded rail
e Post with bead run-out short of joint
f Mason's mitre
g True mitre
h Mitred and applied moulding
i Chamfer with decorative stops
j Tenon shoulder scribed over chamfer

Fig. 3 Joints used in chest framing

mortise length. As already explained, it was always simpler to take the groove right through, enabling the plough to be used, and this necessarily showed at the top of the leg. Consequently what is known as a haunch was cut at the side of the tenon as shown in Fig. 3c, thus filling in the groove in the leg.

The real complication came, however, when mouldings were required. It is obvious that the piece with the tenon could have its moulding running right through as at Fig. 3d, but clearly that with the mortise had to retain its square edge opposite the joint as otherwise it would leave a gap. If then this was to be moulded, the moulding had either to be stopped or run out short of the joint as in Fig. 3e. As explained in Chapter 3, this could only be done by using the scratch-stock (see Fig. 8, page 28) to work the mouldings, not the moulding plane. Since there was no actual intersection between the mouldings on the two pieces, they had not necessarily to be of the same section.

It must have occurred to some craftsmen that this was not always a satisfactory arrangement, and a means of forming a true intersection of similar sections was evolved, now known as the mason's mitre. It was, in fact, the mitre used in stone-work, and the probability is that the wood-worker copied the idea in wood. It is shown in Fig. 3f. In the tenoned piece the moulding was taken right through but was stopped short of the joint on that of the mortised member. The two were then assembled and the continuation of the moulding and the mitre cut with carving tools. Work of this kind, however, called for some skill in carving, quite apart from requiring tools which many carpenters did not have. It was also specially awkward in small sections as the cross grain of small members would be liable to crumble.

The obvious answer was so to design the joint that a true mitre could be cut, and the solution found was that shown in Fig. 3g in which the mortised piece was cut away at the front to form a new shoulder in line with the moulding. In this way both mouldings could be taken right through with the moulding plane, and both cut away to a straight mitre. No carving tools were needed. There were, of course, variations in detail, as will be seen in the various measured drawings of oak pieces, but the principle is the same.

Sometimes a still further simplification was found in that a plain square-edged joint was cut and the moulding worked as a separate item and mitred round after the insertion of the panel, Fig. 3h.

The woodworker copied yet another detail from the stone-mason; that of the chamfer on the top outer edge of horizontal rails. In stonework, of course, its purpose was to throw off water which might otherwise accumulate on the flat surface and seep inwards. In woodwork it obviously had no such purpose, but its decorative value was realized. It made a slight complication when there was a centre upright or muntin, and two methods were devised to overcome it. In the one the chamfer was stopped (often decoratively, Fig. 3i), leaving a square surface at the joint up to which the muntin could fit. In the other the front shoulder of the muntin was cut to a slope to fit over the chamfer, Fig. 3 j. The advantage of the latter method was that the chamfer could be taken right through with the plane without being stopped.

Usually the lid of the framed chest was also framed and panelled, though sometimes one finds an example with a solid top. Lids were usually pivoted on metal strap hinges.

Chest-of-drawers   Until the middle years of the 17th century the chest was little more than a large box. Inside there was frequently a sort of trough at one end to hold small items, but for the main part things stored in the chest had to be placed one on top of the other. During the late 16th and early 17th centuries drawers had sometimes been fitted to cabinets and cupboards and their advantage must soon have become obvious. A consequence was the inclusion of a drawer (and sometimes a second one) in the chest, and finally the whole space was given over to drawers, resulting in the chest-of-drawers as we now know it. By this time, however, the fashion of using separate mouldings mitred into various geometrical patterns, applied bosses, and split turnings had largely superseded carving as decoration, with the result that the typical chest-of-drawers shown in Fig. 4 became general. Such mouldings were worked separately and applied, of course, and frequently the drawer fronts were built out. Both these details and applied bosses made the use of glue essential. Hitherto glue had not been generally used, except for inlay, but in the second half of the 17th century its use increased, until by the last quarter glued joints were universal.

Veneering   Things were largely in the melting pot in many ways, however. Oak was disappearing as a fashionable furniture wood except for interior parts, its place being taken by walnut, both as solid wood and as veneer. And mention of the latter brings us to what is probably the greatest change in furniture-making at any period in its history. Some parts clearly have always to be in solid wood – turned or shaped legs of any kind, shaped parts of chairs – but all flat surfaces lend themselves to veneering. And it was the development of this craft that occasioned a tremendous change in construction. An entirely new system of making furniture had to be worked out.

In a panelled framework the different level of the parts brought an attractive interplay of high-lights and shadows, these being made more interesting by mouldings; and the same applied to carving. The use of walnut brought a different idea, however. The grain of walnut varied tremendously from quite plain to rich figuring, and additionally there were burrs and curls, both of delightful appearance but impossible to use in the solid owing to their unreliable nature. In veneer form, however, they could be safely used and, furthermore, once the potentialities of veneer were realized, various patterns such as quartering, halving, cross-banding, etc. were possible, and, finally, marquetry.

What in fact it largely amounted to was that the form, direction, and

Fig. 4 Oak chest-of-drawers, late 17th century. The applied mouldings are typical of the second half of the 17th century. (Victoria and Albert Museum)

Fig. 5 A contrast in construction. **a** Framed and panelled oak door. **b** Flush door veneered with walnut.

colouring of the grain was used decoratively rather than reliance being placed on high-lights and shadows, though, to an extent, these were still used. Fig. 5 explains the idea. In the oak panelled door (a) the decorative effect is due almost entirely to the shadows and high-lights of the recessed panel, the moulding, and the carving. In (b) the whole surface is level, the attractive appearance being due to the rich grain arranged in quartered form, the cross-banding, and the herring-bone inlay.

So popular was the fashion that rails, mouldings, etc. were veneered with cross-grain purely for the decorative effect. It does not take any technical knowledge to realize that structural parts could not have their grain running crosswise; they would merely snap in two. By the use of veneer, however, the grain could do so on the surface, yet run lengthwise in the solid groundwork beneath.

This fundamental change in furniture construction was largely due to the immigration of foreign craftsmen to Great Britain. Charles II returned from an exile in which he and his circle must have become familiar with the more advanced cabinet-work on the continent. William, husband of Mary, came from Holland where there were many techniques unknown in England. Later again came George I from Hanover. Each event must have encouraged craftsmen from abroad to settle in Britain, with the result that specialized new trades became established. Native workmen were quick to realize the possibilities of the new techniques and within a decade or so Anglicised versions of the new methods and ideas became established.

Marquetry A development from veneering was the cutting and laying of marquetry. It is quite likely that early marquetry was imported and was used on furniture carcases made here. Soon, however, marquetry cutters were at work in this country, and the probability is that such men took apprentices, with the result that in a few years there were British craftsmen practising the new crafts. In any case there must have been observant men who soon learnt the trick of cutting marquetry and of laying veneers.

No doubt many mistakes were made when men first began to lay veneer. The test of successful veneering is not what it looks like when first laid, but what it is like ten or twenty years later. However, within a decade or so the art had become an established technique in a cabinet-making work-shop. It is to the introduction of these two crafts – veneering and marquetry-cutting – and of walnut as a furniture timber, that we owe what is probably the greatest change that has overtaken furniture design and construction.

Fig. 6 (Left) Comparison between the framed and panelled construction of the oak period, **A, B, C, D,** and the flush form of the walnut period, **E, F, G.**

Fig. 7 (Right) Walnut chest-of-drawers, late 17th century. The whole carcase is of pine veneered with walnut. Drawer sides, backs and bottoms are of oak. For fuller details of construction, see page 238. (F. G. and C. Collins, Wheathamstead, Herts)

New methods of construction

The difference between the two methods of construction and treatment is exemplified still more fully in Fig. 6. The oak carcase at (A) is framed together with mortise-and-tenon joints, and the enclosed parts filled with panels. At (E) the carcase is of solid wood dovetailed together giving flush surfaces everywhere which were veneered. Oak drawer fronts and similar parts (B) and (C) have either applied mouldings or are carved, the decorative effect being given by the shadows thrown by the undulating surfaces. At (F) the whole thing is flush, reliance being placed on the varied direction of the grain for the effect. The same idea applies to the two doors (D) and (G). The former is framed and panelled, whereas (G) is entirely flush.

It is interesting to note that later in the 18th century, when mahogany was introduced, there was a partial reversion to the use of undulating surfaces. The probable reason was that this early mahogany was the Cuban variety, dark and often with relatively plain grain, so that the need was felt for shadows and high-lights to break up the surfaces. The truth of this is borne out by the fact that occasionally one comes across an early mahogany item from, say, about 1730, in which the mouldings are cross-grained as in the preceding walnut period. But the fact that the mouldings *are* cross-grained is scarcely apparent because the wood is dark and there is no contrasting light and dark grain. The reader will find it useful to consult Chapter 15 in which the working of both plain and cross-grained mouldings is explained.

Another way in which surfaces were broken up in this early mahogany period was by the use of fielded panels, the wide sloping chamfers giving an interesting play of light and shadow. The photograph on page 59 shows the effectiveness of fielding.

The immediate effect of these changes so far as the chest-of-drawers is concerned is well exemplified in Fig. 7, which shows a veneered chest of the late 17th century. Framing has disappeared and in its place is the

Fig. 8 Examples of chest-of-drawers construction.

a Framed oak chest with panelled ends
b Walnut-veneered chest through-dovetailed together
c Mahogany chest with separate top and runners
d Serpentine-front chest

dovetailed carcase with flush surfaces. A measured drawing of this chest is given on page 238.

Before leaving the walnut chest in Fig. 7 it should be noted that the divisions between the drawers run right through to the back as a continuous solid item.

The early cabinet-makers, however, made many mistakes largely through lack of experience. Carcases and other parts were often put together with coarsely-cut through-dovetails in the hope that the veneer would hide them. And for a while it did, but the fact that wood shrinks as it dries out was overlooked, with the consequence that eventually the form of the joints could be traced right through to the surface of the veneer. Furthermore, any racking of the carcase involved movement in the joints, and this was necessarily transferred to the veneer. Lastly, end grain of wood does not hold glue well and, since the dovetails were bound to show end grain in parts, the veneer was liable to lift, with the passing of time.

An example of the framed construction still used in the mid-17th century is given in Fig. 8a. Solid wood (oak) is used, and the mortise-and-tenon is practically the only joint used except for the drawers. There is however one difference in technique compared with earlier work. The whole is assembled with glue, whereas hitherto parts had been put together dry and the parts held together with pegs. The presence of glue is shown by the fact that there are no retaining pegs, and the idea was probably prompted by the prevailing use of applied mouldings in decorative patterns, bosses, split turnings, inlays and sometimes small marquetry panels. These had to be glued, of course, and with the general tendency to refinement of detail it may have struck craftsmen that pegging was a somewhat crude method and that the use of glue made it unnecessary.

Walnut chests The next stage, Fig. 8b, shows a big jump. The chest is designed so that all outer surfaces are flush. The whole thing is a sort of box with divisions stood up on end. The corners have coarse through-dovetails and the divisions fit in grooves. Veneer hides the corner joints and the grooves are concealed by an applied bead. Mouldings are fixed around top and bottom and the veneer over the former continues across the moulding. It should be noted that the top forms part of the actual structure. Later it was made as a separate item fixed with screws driven up from beneath. Mouldings are cross-grained in accordance with the custom of the period and the chapter on mouldings should be consulted for details. Another early walnut chest-of-drawers is shown in Fig. 9. Note that here again the top forms part of the actual structure.

When carcases of this kind were first made they no doubt appeared satisfactory but it could not have been long before the faults mentioned on page 106 began to show themselves. This eventually resulted in still other changes in construction as will be seen later.

The quality of this walnut furniture varied widely. Some of it, and especially that of the early years of the 18th century, was of much better construction and, although through-dovetails were common, they were much more finely cut.

Fig. 9 Walnut chest-of-drawers with bracket feet. Note the cross-grained flat bead fixed to the front edges of the ends and drawer divisions. About 1700 (Foster of Putney, London)

Mahogany   Fig. 8c shows the carcase of a mahogany chest-of-drawers of about 1770. Although in a general way it is similar to Fig. 8b there are several details which are different. In the first place the top proper is a separate item, this being fitted above front and back rails with widening brackets glued at the inner edges. In other chests there might be a complete false or under-top lap-dovetailed to the ends. Divisions between drawers might consist of a front rail of oak or pine about $\frac{3}{4}$ in. or $\frac{7}{8}$ in. thick lipped with mahogany at the front edge or veneered, with a thinner continuation at the back fitting in grooves in the ends. Alternatively there might be separate drawer runners fitting behind the drawer rails as in the present example, and again resting in grooves with separate dustboard also in grooves.

Fig. 10 shows a mahogany chest-of-drawers of the late 18th century in which the top proper is separate from the main carcase. It is interesting also in having the shaped French foot.

The structure Fig. 8c was the basic method of making all good-quality chests in the 18th century and later, with variations according to the particular form. Thus, in a bow-front chest, the drawer rails would be curved at the front to conform with the shape and either be faced with a thin piece of mahogany bent round and glued, or be veneered. Details of a serpentine front are given in Fig. 8d. It is much the same basically but the ends have a thicknessing piece glued into a shallow rebate at the front to enable the ends to curve outwards to give a suitable return shape at the ends. In cheaper chests, however, the ends might be flat even though the top might be curved at the ends.

In the 19th century chests were made in much the same way – in fact, best quality Victorian work was structurally as good or better than similar work of the 18th century. There was, however, another cheaper type of furniture made which was basically unsound and shoddy; unsound because it was constructed regardless of the inevitability of movement in wood across the grain; and shoddy because poor timber was frequently used. Such chests were in all probability made in groups of two or more because it was cheaper to make them in quantity. Such a chest is shown in Fig. 2, page 13, and the weakness of construction is obvious. In the better chests of the type the drawer rails were stub-tenoned or slot-dovetailed in; but in some cases two dowels were used at each side and there was little strength because the dowels could only be short. If the ends were $\frac{3}{4}$in. thick the dowels could only be a bare $\frac{1}{2}$ in. long as otherwise the point of the bit would emerge at the outside.

In another equally poor form of construction the rail was through-dovetailed in from the front. Although it certainly tied the ends together it necessarily showed end grain at the ends and either shrinkage or movement eventually caused the place to show through the veneer at the outside.

Another bad feature of many of these chests was that the drawers were frequently made independently of the carcase so that accurate fitting was difficult. It is true that the man used to making such mass-produced

Fig. 10 Simple mahogany chest-of-drawers of the late 18th century. (Foster of Putney, London)

furniture became highly skilled at it. Although unsound in design it must have looked surprisingly well when first made. Drawers were frequently made to stock size first, and when the carcase was assembled the drawers were placed in position so that the whole thing went together square and only a minimum of fitting and trimming was necessary later.

Chapter 9

Case furniture

By the term case furniture is generally understood items which are of box-like or cupboard form, rather than of framed construction such as tables, chairs, etc. It includes such pieces as bookcases, china-cabinets, bureaux, presses, and so on. In all these pieces there was a certain similarity in the way they were made, with variations according to the period, the skill of the maker, the price to be paid, and to an extent the timber being used. Possibly, too, the district of origin may have made a difference. In addition, there were modifications according to the particular type of furniture and its purpose.

Early oak work   Early oak pieces were usually of simple and frequently crude construction. They often consisted of plain boards nailed together as in Fig. 1. The sizes and proportions of such items were, to an extent, no doubt decided by the widths of boards available, because men had not then learnt the art of joining and glueing together boards side by side. Consequently, although trees of greater girth were available than can be procured today, really wide boards were usually reserved only for special parts. Thus in Fig. 1 the door is 15 in. wide and the flanking boards 12 in. It is quite likely that the maker happened to have boards of these widths available and accordingly made his cupboard to these sizes. Fig. 2 shows the construction of another larger cupboard made in much the same way.

This plain planked construction was followed by the more scientific system of framework and panels as shown in Fig. 3. Here again the common widths in which timber was available usually decided the proportions of the individual panels, but clearly the method gave much greater scope for variations in both treatment and size, since it was only necessary to add extra intermediate framing members to enable panels of less width to be used. These early framed items were invariably assembled dry (that is without glue) and held together by pegs passed through the joints. Incidentally these pegs were usually cleft, and, as in all probability the axe was used, the resulting pegs were roughly square in section. At the end to be inserted they were roughly rounded with the chisel, but quite frequently the other end was either left square or had only the

Fig. 1 Oak cupboard of simple construction, late 15th or early 16th century. (Victoria and Albert Museum)

corners chiselled off. At any rate they never had the regular roundness of the modern dowel.

The court cupboard of the 17th century was of the same framed and panelled construction but was on more refined lines. Fig. 4 shows an

Fig. 2 Oak cupboard of planked construction, the parts nailed together. The door boards must have been cut on the saw pit as they show no figure and could not have been riven. Mid 16th century.

Fig. 3 Oak cupboard of framed construction. The mortise-and-tenon joints are assembled without glue and are pegged. About 1500. (Victoria and Albert Museum)

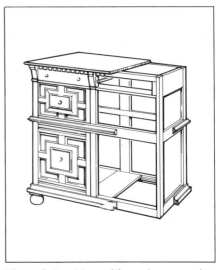

Fig. 4 Court cupboard, dated 1610. The whole is framed together. For details of door joints see page 169. (Victoria and Albert Museum)

Fig. 5 Oak cabinet of framed construction with all joints glued. The mouldings are applied and are also glued. About 1670

immense advance in the detail of the joints, the door mouldings being worked in the solid with true mitres cut at the corners (for details see Fig. 7, page 170. Usually, though not invariably, these cupboards were in two separate carcases, and the whole consisted virtually of a series of frames assembled together, except that the corner posts were common to both side and front frames, and to sides and back. Again for the most part glue was not used except for any inlay, for which of course it was essential.

As mentioned in Chapter 8, as the second half of the 17th century progressed increasing use was made of glue for the main structure. This is shown in Fig. 5 in which no pegs are used, reliance being placed entirely on glue. Another example is shown in Fig. 6 in which glue has been largely used. In fact, once the reliability of glue had proved itself, the use of pegs was largely discontinued.

Chapter 8 also explains the changes in constructional methods in the second half of the 17th century due to the introduction of veneering, the growth of furniture-making as a separate branch of woodwork, and the use of walnut as a furniture wood. Clearly all case furniture was affected by the change, even more than such items as tables and chairs which were still necessarily of framed construction. The period was altogether one of considerable development in that it saw the inception of several new case items such as the bureau and bureau-bookcase, china-cabinet, bookcase, and cabinets of various kinds.

Furniture for writing   In the earlier part of the 17th century men had been content to use an ordinary table for writing, or had a box with sloping lid which could be placed on the table. The idea is shown in Fig. 7, though the chances are that such a desk would be used largely to hold

Fig. 6 Oak cabinet with marquetry decoration. About 1670. (Victoria and Albert Museum)

books and writing equipment, the sloping top being used rather to hold a book at a convenient angle for reading. However this may be, it was clearly a portable affair, and when the idea arose of making a cabinet specially for writing (the bureau) the general form of the portable desk was copied. It was provided with a stand but the sloping top was used for writing only when opened down flat.

Such a bureau is shown in Fig. 8, and it will be seen that it has been caught up in the craze for veneering which all fashionable cabinet-makers followed at the turn of the 17th and in the 18th centuries. It is made in two separate parts, bureau and stand, and it is obvious that they are distinct since the stand is wider than the bureau. The latter is of pine put together with through-dovetails, with writing top and drawer divisions fitting in grooves. In common with the general method of the period, the veneer is taken right over the joints, a practice which was later avoided owing to the liability of the veneer to be affected should any movement occur (see Chapter 16).

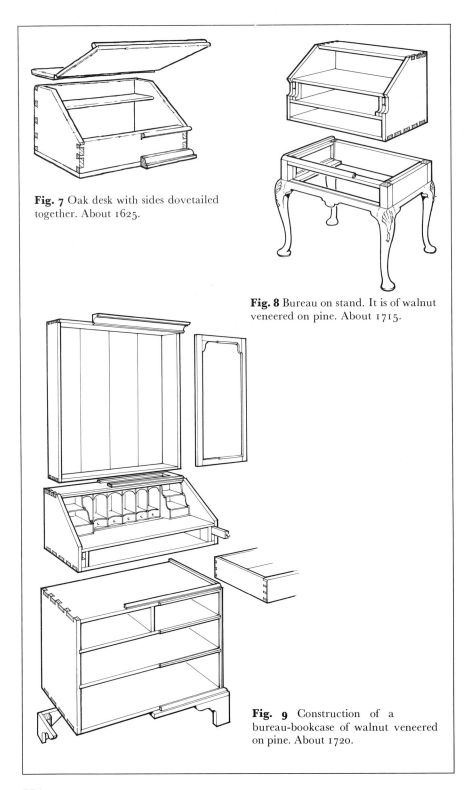

Fig. 7 Oak desk with sides dovetailed together. About 1625.

Fig. 8 Bureau on stand. It is of walnut veneered on pine. About 1715.

Fig. 9 Construction of a bureau-bookcase of walnut veneered on pine. About 1720.

It is understandable that an item such as Fig. 8 should be regarded frankly as a writing desk supported on a stand; but a good example of how tradition persists is shown in the next stage, Fig. 9. If one forgets the top bookcase, the lower part is clearly meant to be a complete bureau in itself, yet it is still made in two carcases separated by a moulding. As late as the second half of the 18th century this was still sometimes done (see Fig. 13), but generally the tendency was to make the whole bureau in one. Even then, however, a moulding was frequently added beneath the top drawer although there were not two separate carcases.

The story of old furniture is full of curious inconsistencies, however, as exemplified in Fig. 10 which is in oak and is *c.* 1700. The carcase is entirely in one. Maybe that is one of the fascinations of old furniture; the exception is always turning up, showing the folly of being dogmatic.

An example of about 1750 is shown in Fig. 12, and here the separating moulding has disappeared. The whole bureau is frankly in one. Note, too, that the drawers are separated by rails tenoned into the ends with dust-boards grooved in at the back. Compare with Fig. 9 in which the divisions pass right through to the back of the carcase. It is true that thinner wood is used towards the rear, but when the drawers are pulled right out a flush surface appears at the top since the rear part fits in a rebate in the thicker front member. Taken generally, separate rails with loose dustboards suggest a later date than those all in one.

Both Figs. 9 and 12 have bookcases above the bureau, and, although there is a similarity of construction, an interesting difference occurs in that whereas Fig. 9 has its cornice built as part of the whole, in Fig. 12 it is

Fig. 10 Oak bureau of about 1700. (W. A. Pinn, Dunstable)

Fig. 11 Walnut veneered bureau-bookcase. Queen Anne period. (Victoria and Albert Museum)

an entirely separate item. The latter is an infinitely better form of construction, but its use was not universal and it did not belong to any particular period. As a general guide, in Queen Anne furniture the cornice was in one with the main carcase, but from about 1725 onwards it might be either, depending largely on the quality of the piece.

Perhaps it is as well at this stage to explain why the separate cornice was the better method. It was shown in Chapter 3 that wood is liable to shrink across the grain as it dries out, and, if prevented from doing so by another part fixed across it, a split is liable to develop. This is exactly what happens in a fixed cornice. The wood of the moulding is at right angles with that of the carcase side, and resists any shrinkage tendency. Of course it was minimized largely because the Cuban mahogany of which most furniture was made from about 1725 onwards was a stable wood. Furthermore people in those days were not in such a hurry, and wood was given a chance to season properly before being used. Another point was that a bookcase was comparatively shallow. Its ends would not normally be more than about 10 in. deep, and shrinkage over this distance in dry wood would be slight. Such items as presses were much deeper, however; the ends

Fig. 13 Mahogany bureau, about 1780. For measured drawings and details see page 228. (F. G. and C. Collins, Wheathampstead, Herts.)

might be 18–20 in. deep, and risk of shrinkage over this distance would be considerably greater. Still, many items were made with a fixed cornice, and indeed it is quite common to find that either a split has occurred in the ends, or a joint has opened.

As shown in Fig. 12 the bookcase portion was put together with lapped dovetails. This joint had in fact become more or less standard for case furniture, its advantage being that it was entirely concealed at the sides. The dovetails were exposed only at top and bottom where they were not seen. In the case of the bureau portion the same joint could be used at the top when there was to be a bookcase above because the latter hid the joints. This, however, was not possible when there was no bookcase, and the cabinet-maker then cut a double-lapped dovetail in which a lap was left on both joining parts. In this the joint was entirely concealed except for a narrow line of end grain at the sides (this was the lap). For details of the joint see page 246.

The bracket feet in Fig. 12 are worth noting because they were such a common feature of 18th century furniture. At the front the two pieces were joined with a plain mitred joint, and strengthened with a large glue block rubbed into the internal angle. The foot was screwed as a whole beneath the carcase and again glue-blocked. At the rear, however, the back, usually of a cheaper softwood, was cut off to a sloping line and lap-dovetailed to the fretted side pieces (see Fig. 9).

Fashionable cabinet-makers must have carried good stocks of prime mahogany, and it is almost with envy that one thinks of the fine solid timber often used in unjointed widths of anything up to 30 in. or so. The best figured timber of this kind was reserved for such parts as table tops, bureau falls, etc., but even the ends of bureaux, bookcases, and so on were often of solid wood. Sometimes, however, they were veneered, and in this case the front edges were given a lipping of mahogany. This applied also to the drawer rails which were frequently of softwood or oak with either a facing of mahogany about $\frac{1}{8}$ in. to $\frac{1}{4}$ in. thick, or were veneered.

There is one respect in which 18th century furniture is sometimes disappointing – the backs. These were frequently nothing more than plain boards of pine and, occasionally oak, nailed on. Sometimes the edges were

Fig. 14 Satinwood secretaire bookcase, about 1780. (Mallet and Son (Antiques) Ltd., London)

rebated so that they fitted together without a gap showing, but sometimes there was not even this. In the case of a bookcase or china-cabinet the inside faces would be planed to a good finish, but for a bureau or chest-of-drawers where they were hidden the surface was frequently left from the saw or with an adzed finish. Such boards were probably the outside cuts from a baulk which had been roughly dressed with the adze. Of course, it has to be realized that the hand labour of cleaning up timber from the rough was colossal, and when a thing was not seen it must have seemed a waste to spend time and labour in planing it. It was not merely a matter of planing out saw or adze marks; it would have to be thicknessed as well, and there might be quite considerable variation in boards cut on the pit saw.

This is not true of all 18th century pieces. The best work often had panelled backs, especially display cabinets in which the back was visible, though here the inner face might be covered with silk or other material, and then it might consist of plain boards only. In comparison, Victorian furniture was frequently better in this respect. Backs were often framed and panelled and finished neatly. This would not apply to cheap commercial furniture, but it was generally true of good-class work.

However, to revert to case furniture generally, a magnificent example of a combined writing cabinet and bookcase, which dates from about 1780, is shown in Fig. 14. It is in satinwood with tulipwood and kingwood inlay bandings. The lower centre part has a writing top which is pulled forward when in use, and the whole is enclosed by a tambour. There are

Fig. 15 Mahogany bookcase with veneered and barred doors. About 1780. (Mallet and Son (Antiques) Ltd., London)

also tambour-enclosed recesses at each side. A particularly interesting feature is that the flush doors of the lower portion are shaped at the lower edge and project downwards in front of the cupboard bottoms.

Another fine specimen is that in Fig. 15. The bookcase doors are specially interesting in that the tracery bars are not moulded, but are flat with the front veneered, the grain running crosswise, with a satinwood inlay line at each edge. A quality piece of this kind has a panelled back.

An interesting display wall cabinet is shown in Fig. 16. It dates from the following century, about 1810–20, and has both carved and inlaid decoration. It is worth noting that here much of the tracery detail of the door is applied over the face of the glass. In earlier traceried doors the whole was designed so that separate panes could be fitted in from the back, and the pattern had to be fairly straightforward as otherwise the glass could not be cut to fit into awkward corners and angles. It will be realized that in Fig. 16 it would be impossible to cut glass to fit round, say, the arrow heads and feathers, and other acutely shaped parts. In this case the glass is all in one in the main centre pane, and the tracery applied over it. To many the use of separate panes gives the more attractive result in that much of the early glass was not entirely flat, and the reflected light on the undulations and on the different levels in the separate panes had a charm of its own.

Fig. 16 Wall display cabinet in mahogany with inlay and carved decoration. About 1810-20. (Victoria and Albert Museum)

Chapter 10

Chairs

It has already been noted that cabinet-making as distinct from general woodworking became established as a separate craft during the second half of the 17th century. There had, however, been another break away in the earlier years of the century; that of the chair-maker. When one looks at chairs of that period one is struck by a certain family likeness in the various types. They differed in detail but there was a certain general over-all similarity in style and method of construction. Generally, too, work-manship was of a higher order than hitherto, and once turning was introduced, the chair-makers were quick to exploit it fully, first in plain then in twist turning. There was more scope for turning in chair work than in other pieces of furniture, largely because a chair in its nature consists mainly of a series of framing pieces tenoned together.

The installation of a lathe in a chair-making workshop was, no doubt, an early necessity. Indeed at one period there was a fashion for chairs made entirely from turned spindles except for the seat. It is no doubt the wide experience a chair-maker would have in turning that accounts for the generally high quality of chair work – plus the fact that the items to be turned were seldom more than could be won from 2 in. squares, whereas a table, say, might have legs of bulbous form up to 9 or 10 in. diameter. So large a size would be more difficult to turn and would certainly call for help in working the lathe.

Early chairs Up to this period chairs had much in common with joiner-constructed furniture. Thus the chair in Fig. 1 is little more than a series of panelled frames. The portion beneath the seat might in some cases be a cupboard, the front opening as a door or the seat acting as a lid. In this sense it could be regarded as a small chest with back and sides continued upwards. In the 17th century the box was replaced by an open arrangement of legs and rails, the former usually turned. The panelling at the sides was also omitted leaving open sides and arms. Fig. 2 shows a somewhat crude chair of the open-arm type, the whole put together dry with pegged mortise-and-tenon joints. It is interesting to note that the top rail of the back rests above the uprights as a sort of cresting, this being

Fig. 1 Arm or box chair in oak dated 1574. Note that the sides are panelled from the floor to beneath the arms. (Victoria and Albert Museum)

Fig. 2 Oak chair, one of a pair in the chancel of the church of St. Mary and St. Clement, Clavering, Essex. 17th century.

the tendency in arm-chairs of the early 17th century. Hitherto it had invariably been contained between them as in Fig. 1. Fig. 3 shows the construction of the chair. Quite often this top rail developed into rather an elaborate cresting and usually ear pieces were fitted beneath its projecting ends as in Fig. 4e.

Until the early years of the 17th century chairs had been relatively rare.

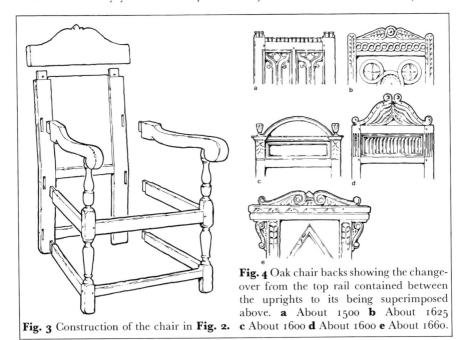

Fig. 3 Construction of the chair in **Fig. 2.**

Fig. 4 Oak chair backs showing the change-over from the top rail contained between the uprights to its being superimposed above. **a** About 1500 **b** About 1625 **c** About 1600 **d** About 1600 **e** About 1660.

Fig. 5 Farthingale chair with chamfered square legs, about 1620. (Victoria and Albert Museum)

Fig. 6 Early upholstered arm-chair. Mid 17th century. (Victoria and Albert Museum)

In a mansion the lord and his lady might use chairs at meal times, but lesser folk had to be content with forms, stools, or even chests. As the 17th century progressed they became more common and, although the heavy arm-chairs of the type shown in Fig. 2 were still made, the tendency was to a lighter type, and single chairs without arms, often in sets, were also made. It was in this period that the craft of chair-making as a separate trade was developed. Fig. 5 shows a farthingale chair, a type made in large quantities in the first half of the 17th century. It is interesting in showing early attempts at upholstery. There was, of course, no springing (this did not come until the 19th century) but the seat is webbed and the covering taken right over the frame – it is in fact the first stuff-over seat. In some cases a loose cushion was fitted.

The application to an arm-chair is seen in Fig. 6, and it shows a marked difference in the standard of comfort being demanded when compared with Fig. 2 which is only a few years earlier in date. Another early form of upholstered chair dating from the early 17th century was the X chair in Fig. 7. It is sometimes known as the Knole chair because of the number of them made specially in honour of a visit paid by James I to Knole Park, Kent.

The Yorkshire and Derbyshire type in Fig. 8 also became popular in the middle years of the 17th century. The arcaded top rail of the back is typical, though in some patterns both back rails were of single arcaded form. In all these chairs the joints are invariably pegged but, since a chair had necessarily to withstand a good deal of strain, the tendency was also to glue them, especially in view of the growing lightness of the members.

Fig. 7 X chair and footstool entirely covered with upholstery. Early 17th century. (Victoria and Albert Museum)

Fig. 8 Oak chair of the Yorkshire and Derbyshire type. Mid 17th century. (Victoria and Albert Museum)

We shall see that the pegs themselves were omitted eventually, especially when the change-over to walnut came.

Early oak chairs had no rake to the back legs Fig. 9b. Occasionally there was not even a slope to the back, Fig. 9a. Presumably it was felt that the chair was heavy enough to resist any tendency to tilt backwards. Some-

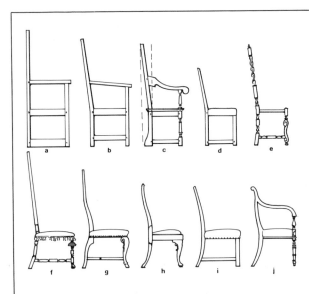

a 16th century
b Late 16th century
c About 1600
d Early and mid 17th century
e About 1675
f About 1690
g Early 18th century
h About 1715
i About 1760
j About 1810

Fig. 9 How the rake of chair backs developed, later with curves:

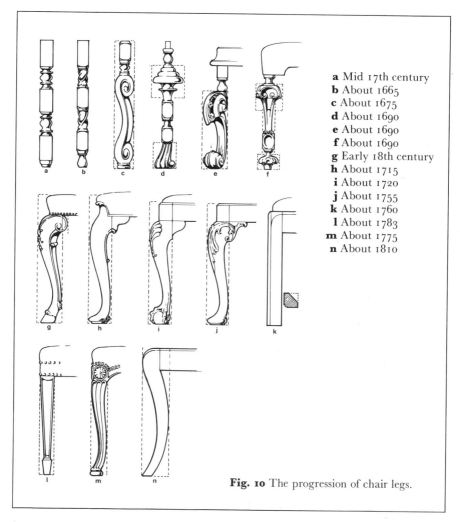

Fig. 10 The progression of chair legs.

body must have realized the danger, however, and sought to combat it by leaving a thickness at the bottom which projected backwards Fig. 9c. It did not take any extra width of wood as shown by the dotted line, unless the maker planned the two immediately adjacent to each other. It was not until towards the end of the century that the idea came of giving the back legs a backward rake. At first the early idea of having just the foot with backward projection was copied, Fig. 9e, but later the entire leg sloped, Fig. 9f.

Combination of turning and shaping   Most early turned front legs were so arranged that their turned part came within the substance of the squares from which they were turned. This is shown in Fig. 10a. The same applied to twist-turned legs (Fig. 10b). It was usually only in large tables and court cupboards that bulbous turnings were used. In these the centre turned part needed a much larger section than the square which formed

125

Fig. 11 Preliminary turning of chair leg at **Fig. 10c** before the centre shaping is cut.

the core (for an example see page 180). From about 1670 onwards, however, the custom arose of combining shaping with turning as in example Fig. 10c, and this obviously needed much more wood than was required for either the top square or the turning. In this case the wood was cut wide enough to include the widest part, and the turned parts completed as in Fig. 11. Afterwards the shape would have been sawn out and the whole finished with spokeshave and carving tools.

Turners at this period were experimenting in their craft considerably and were fast becoming highly skilled, and it was not long before they found the trick of turning the back legs as well as the front ones. The idea is shown in Fig. 12, the work being turned from different centres. It could be a frightening experience to someone not used to it to see one of these chair back uprights being turned. At the end being turned the wood merely revolved in its own thickness, but the other would fly round in a circle of over two feet diameter, and heaven help anyone who came within its range. With an arrangement so badly out of balance a counterweight was needed as at both (a) and (b), but even so there was considerable vibration. Occasionally either the wood snapped or the wedged metal strap holding the wood worked loose, and the whole would then fly across the workshop, again with unfortunate consequences for anyone in the way.

Twist legs   Twist turning was a combination of plain turning, carving, rasp and file work, and scraping. The square was first turned to the overall shape (usually a cylinder with turned members), and the spiral marked out with a strip of card wrapped around the cylinder. There might be a single or double twist (single-bine or double-bine).

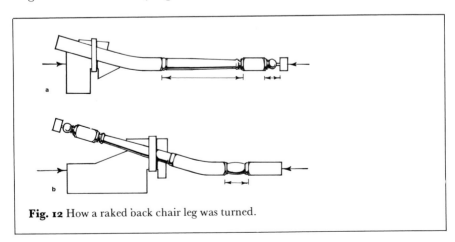

Fig. 12 How a raked back chair leg was turned.

Fig. 13 The carving of a double-bine twist leg after preliminary turning.

That in Fig. 13 is a double-bine and shows the next stage, that of carving away the hollows between the bines. This would be followed by rasping and filing, and finished by scraping. Some of the later twists were beautifully finished, and in some light table legs the spaces between the bines were cut completely through so that there were two independent and intertwined open bines. An example is given in Fig. 9, page 185. This, however, was not done on chair legs as they would not be strong enough.

Another type of leg which was a combination of turning and carving was that at Fig. 10d. Clearly here to make the leg from a square of wood big enough to hold up to the largest part would have required wood of extremely large section and it would have involved a lot of work in cutting away the unwanted parts. The method adopted was then to use a square or core equal in size to the parts to which the rails had to be jointed, and to glue on thicknessing pieces locally where the wide part of the turning occurred and at the scrolled foot. This is shown by the dotted lines in Fig. 10d. It will be realized that the method carried another advantage in that the true surfaces of the centre square were preserved at the points where the rails were jointed. To cut away a piece of wood of large section to form squares of reduced size in accurate alignment with each other would be awkward since the plane could not be used conveniently across them.

Fig. 14 How the centre square of a leg was thicknessed locally to include the wide parts of the leg at **Fig. 10f**. The leg is also shown partly carved in **Fig. 15.**

The leg in Fig. 10f is interesting in that it appears to be an attempt to disguise the fact that it was basically a turned leg. Here again it was thicknessed locally to cut down cost in both labour and material, and then turned to the overall pattern. Fig. 14 shows the leg on the lathe with one of the large squares turned down to cylindrical form as a preliminary to the main shaping. The turning completed, the carving was marked out and cut as partly completed in Fig. 15. Note the line of the joints, particularly in the foot. Such a leg would be expensive to make in view of the amount of carving in it but the cost is reduced by the preliminary turning. The chair with the completed turned and carved leg is shown in Fig. 24.

The cabriole leg Towards the end of the 17th century the fashion of turned legs largely died out, to be replaced by the cabriole leg which in various patterns remained popular for the next seventy years or so. A well-designed cabriole leg is a joy to behold: a poor one can be really ugly. At its best the English type has never been bettered and seldom equalled. It was dignified and graceful. Essential features of a good shape are: a high knee, gradual taper from knee to ankle, flat curves free from bandiness, and avoidance of overdone, fussy carving. Over the years it changed its form and detail as shown in Fig. 10g, h, i, and j, but the dates given for each should not be regarded as exclusive to each. For instance both the turned club foot (h) and the claw and ball (i) were used at any time from about 1700 up to 1760 or so. On the other hand the hoof foot (g) generally belongs to the late 17th or very early 18th centuries, and the shell and husk carving on the knee (i) was seldom used after 1720. Acanthus detail such as that at (j) belongs more to the middle years of the 18th century.

In view of this popularity of the cabriole leg over a long period it is worth while considering the practical work involved in making it. In all the examples given it will be seen that they were cut from squares of timber, and that the whole of the shape was contrived within the limits of that square, with the exception of the ear pieces which were glued on. The method then was to decide the size of square needed to contain the shape and draw in the curves within these limits. A templet of thin wood or card was made to enable as many legs as might be required to be marked out alike. In a chair-maker's workshop the walls were invariably covered with these templets tied together in bundles. Thus for, say, a Queen Anne arm-chair a bundle would contain templets for front and back legs, arms and their supports, splat, top rail, and seat rails. A square, having been planed true, would be marked out on two adjacent faces as in Fig. 16. If it was to have the club foot (Fig. 10h) this detail would then be turned.

Main sawing out was done with the chair-maker's frame saw and both curves on one face would be sawn as in Fig. 17. This, of course, removed the outline of the shape on the adjacent side, but the waste pieces were replaced temporarily, and the square turned over so that this face was uppermost, enabling the second shape to be sawn out. This produced a square-cut leg such as that in Fig. 18. At this stage the mortises at the top

Fig. 16 The curves of a cabriole leg marked out on the square of timber, the foot already turned.

Fig. 17 The shape of the leg cut on one face.

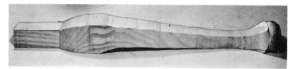

Fig. 15 The partly finished leg shown completed at **Fig. 10f** and partly turned in **Fig. 14.**

Fig. 18 Shapes cut on both faces giving a square-cut leg.

were cut and wood for the ear pieces glued on.

From now on the work consisted of rounding and shaping with spokeshave, rasp and file and that invaluable tool, the chair-maker's scraperspokeshave. This was somewhat like a spokeshave in appearance but had a purely scraping action, the edge being turned similarly to a cabinet scraper. These tools were made in various shapes; flat, rounded, hollow, etc., to suit the particular work in hand. Fig. 19 shows a leg being cleaned up with the spokeshave.

Of course when the leg was required to have carved detail enough wood for it had to be left in the original cutting out – in fact, a fake can sometimes be spotted through lack of this. Perhaps an old chair had plain cabriole legs and, in an attempt to add to its value, the knee has been carved. But since the carving had to be won out of the existing surface it looks recessed

Fig. 19 Cleaning up the leg with the spokeshave.

Fig. 20 Walnut tall-back chair of about 1690. (Victoria and Albert Museum)

Fig. 21 Tall-back chair of about 1680.

Fig. 22 Tall-back arm-chair with scrolled arms. About 1690.

instead of appearing, as it should, to be raised from the knee. This is explained more fully in Chapter 6.

To return to the end of the 17th century, chair-makers were now working largely in walnut, and were beginning to understand the art of compound curvature, that is shapes which curve in both front and side elevation, or in elevation and plan. Hitherto shapes had been simple or non-existent. In any chair during the oak period, the only concession to curvature was in the shape of the back or in the arms. Even in Fig. 20, dating from about 1690 the back is shaped in side elevation only. Compare this with Fig. 25 which was made only a few years later. The back is raked and it is shaped also in front elevation. Only the man who has worked in such compound curves can realize how additionally complicated it can become. It is not only that joints can be tricky, but that a compound curve may look satisfactory when viewed from one direction but may appear completely distorted and unsatisfactory when looked at from another. Later in the 18th century some amazing curved designs were worked out, especially in chair backs, as we shall see later. Some curved parts were shaped in front elevation, side elevation, and also in plan.

This, however, is anticipating things somewhat and for the moment we may turn back to Fig. 20, which, however attractive it may look, shows a deterioration in construction. The seat is simply a thin frame with the front legs merely dowelled into it and at the back it has only the lightest of tenoning into the legs. In this particular chair the legs have a backward rake but in many chairs of the period they were vertical. With the best of treatment a chair has to withstand considerable strain; but many men have the habit of tilting a chair backwards, and the additional strain this

Fig. 23 Arm-chair with carved and gilt show wood. About 1680.(Victoria and Albert Museum)

Fig. 24 Walnut chair having shaped stretcher of X form. About 1690. (Victoria and Albert Museum)

involves is obvious. The tall back increases the leverage that can be exerted and the wonder of it is that so many of these chairs have survived. However, the close of the century saw a better construction.

Craftsmen must have become much more satisfied with their ability to cut really good joints because, in addition to making chairs which were much lighter than in the oak period, they now proceeded to eliminate any form of stretcher between the legs. It was one thing merely to glue joints. Even a badly cut joint will hold together for a while, but the essential feature of a good joint is that it resists stress in itself apart from the glue. A bad one soon fails, especially in an item such as a chair which in its nature has to resist considerable strain.

Fig. 21 shows a typical chair of about 1680 date in which there are side stretchers tied together by a centre stretcher in H form. In addition there is a fretted and carved front stretcher. In Fig. 24 a lighter and less strong arrangement has been substituted, less strong because there is inevitably a good deal of short grain in the curves. In Fig. 26 there are no stretchers at all. It may have been felt that these did not go happily with cabriole legs, though in some chairs of about 1700 they are retained as in Fig. 25.

Fig. 26 shows a chair with the characteristic features of the early years of the 18th century, notably in the fiddle-shaped back with compound curvature, vase-shaped splat, shaped seat plan, shell and husk carving on knee and cresting, and the use of walnut cross-veneer on back uprights and seat rails.

This plan-shaping of the seat had, in some cases, a marked consequence

Fig. 25 Walnut chair having cabriole legs with hoof feet, about 1700. (Victoria and Albert Museum)

Fig. 26 Walnut chair with seat rails and back uprights veneered. About 1720. (Victoria and Albert Museum)

in construction. In most chairs the seat rails are fixed to the legs with mortise-and-tenon joints, and in a square-shaped chair it is only necessary to chop the mortises square in to the legs, Fig. 27a. They do, in fact, meet in the thickness of the wood. When, however, the front of the chair is wider than the back the side rails have to slope and the mortises have therefore to be chopped at an angle as in Fig. 27b. This is far more satisfactory than cutting the mortises square and sawing the tenons at an angle because the grain of the latter would slope and would be weak. The chair-maker used to fix the wood to be mortised on a sloping block so that when he chopped the mortise the chisel was held upright.

It is apparent, however, that when the seat was of the plan shape shown at (f) things were not quite so simple. Since each front corner was rounded, the top square of the legs would necessarily have been cut away considerably, and to have chopped mortises in it would have weakened it still further. Some makers used to do this and overcome the weakness by glueing and screwing a thick shaped block to the inside as at Fig. 28a. It must have appeared as an awkward construction, however, and in most cases chair-makers adopted an entirely different method as in Fig. 28b. The front and side seat rails were first joined together at the corners as a whole with a halving joint, and the plan shape sawn out and cleaned up. The top square of the leg was let into this either in the form of a tenon, or cut to dovetail section, and inserted into a slot cut in the outside of the

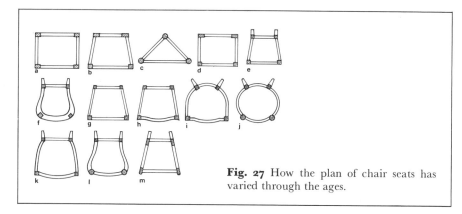

Fig. 27 How the plan of chair seats has varied through the ages.

made-up frame. Since the whole of the outside was veneered the joints did not show. Where a cross-grained moulding was needed at the top to form a rebate for the loose seat, a rebate was cut around the shaped edge and pieces of cross-grained walnut glued in as at Fig. 28c.

A feature common to some of these walnut chairs was that the whole of the back was veneered on the front surface. This may seem a somewhat surprising feature in that the back was necessarily subjected to quite a lot of rubbing and wear, but in fact the condition of the veneer is invariably

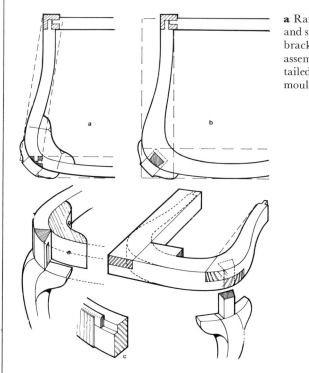

a Rails tenoned into the legs and strengthened with heavy brackets. **b** Seat framing assembled and leg dovetailed into it. **c** Cross-grained moulding glued into rebate.

Fig. 28 Chair seat construction in the walnut period.

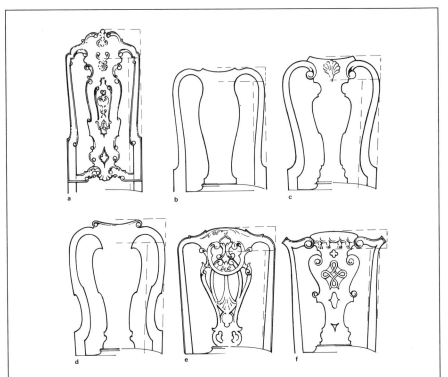

Fig. 29 Shapes of chair backs from about 1700 up to 1730 **a** About 1700 **b** About 1710 **c** About 1720 **d** About 1725 **e** About 1730 **f** About 1730

quite good except sometimes at the joint between the top of the splat and the top rail where a certain amount of movement has taken place causing stress marks in the veneer. The surface of splat and uprights was, of course, flat or only slightly hollowed.

The growing use of mahogany from about 1720 and onwards necessarily affected chair-making, and the dark Cuban variety was used, always in the solid, not veneered on the face. The shell decoration was still used occasionally on the knees of cabriole legs, but more usually the carving was a lion's mask, satyr mask, acanthus leafage and, later, the cabochon detail. In the case of the lion's head the leg usually terminated with the paw foot. Perhaps the greatest change, however, was in the shape of the back, the hooped or fiddle shape being replaced by straighter uprights which at first joined the flatter top rail in a curve as before but which eventually curved outwards to form a projecting corner. The slat too was invariably pierced. The progression of these back shapes is shown in Fig. 29. It is rare to find cabriole legs with stretchers in this period – and indeed at any subsequent period, but straight square legs were sometimes used and these were usually tied with stretchers. An example is that in Fig. 32.

A typical chair of the Chippendale period is given in Fig. 33 and as this particular piece is such a perfect specimen it is given in detail in Fig. 34.

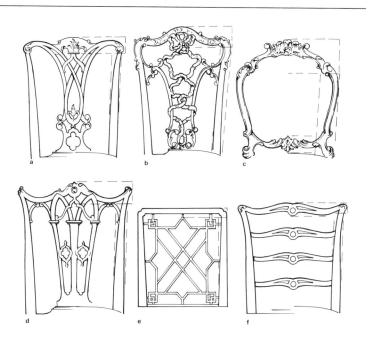

Fig. 30 Chair backs of the Chippendale period. **a** About 1760 **b** Ribband back, about 1755 **c** French padded back, about 1760 **d** Gothic back, about 1765 **e** Chinese back, about 1760 **f** Ladder back, about 1760

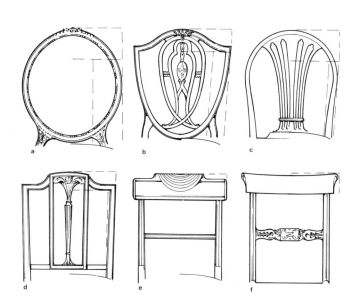

Fig. 31 Chair backs of the later 18th century and early 19th century. **a** Adam period, about 1775 **b** Hepplewhite, about 1775 **c** Hoop back, about 1775 **d** Hepplewhite, about 1790 **e** Regency, about 1810 **f** Late Regency, about 1820

Fig. 32 Ladder-back chair, mahogany about 1760.

Fig. 33 Chippendale period chair, about 1755. (Victoria and Albert Museum)

The back is almost an exact replica of one appearing in Chippendale's *Director*, but the shape of the seat is different; also the pattern of the cabriole legs. And here is an odd note. Although the turned club foot (as given in Fig. 33) and the claw and ball foot are both associated with Chippendale (even though both had been used at an earlier period), there is not a single illustration of a chair with either type of foot in the *Director*. Nearly all the cabriole legs terminate with the French scrolled foot or a free interpretation of it, with an occasional lion's paw detail.

It is worth while considering this chair, Fig. 33, in detail, because, although it would be an expensive chair to make, there is a remarkable economy in its setting out and, indeed, it is a delightful example of how effectively a beautiful shape is associated with and derived from the practical technicalities of the chair-maker's craft. The back legs have a subtle curvature which at first sight appears to be complicated, but on analysis it becomes obvious that the whole can be worked from timber no more than $4\frac{1}{2}$ in. wide by $1\frac{3}{4}$ in. thick – in fact if the two are cut adjacent to each other the wood for the two need be only 7 in. wide. This effect is achieved largely by sloping the legs towards each other as in Fig. 34.

It is an interesting speculation on how far the designer started off on what to him was an ideal shape and then selected timber to suit; or began with timber of a certain size and planned his shapes to come within it. In

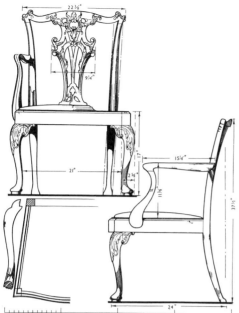

Fig. 34 Detailed drawing of the chair shown in **Fig. 33.**

Fig. 35 Mahogany chair with fretted splat which follows closely one of the engravings in *Chippendale's Director*. About 1755. (Victoria and Albert Museum)

all probability the truth lies somewhere between the two in that there is invariably ample length in timber but only restricted width; also strength in length but relative weakness across the grain. It follows then that the technique of woodwork generally demands flat curves as compared with other crafts – ironwork, for example, which can be bent to any shape without loss of strength. Thus, quite apart from cost, economy in width is desirable in curves, and so design becomes associated with the technique of a craft. Much the same applies to the cabriole legs which need squares of $2\frac{5}{8}$ in. only.

Other popular patterns of chair backs during the Chippendale period were the ladder back (Fig. 30f), Chippendale Gothic (d), ribband back (b) and the Chinese type (e). Apart from the cabriole type (with all its variations) front chair legs were usually straight and square (see Fig. 10k), often moulded or rounded at the outer corner, ogee moulded, or decorated with frets in either Chinese or Gothic style. Fig. 35 shows a well-proportioned chair of about 1755, with serpentine front seat rail and typical fretted back splat. Square legs of this type were clearly cheaper to make than the cabriole type and were no doubt made for less wealthy customers. The chair makes an interesting comparison with that in Fig. 36 which would cost considerably more to make owing to the amount of carving. Many people would, however, prefer the simple chair, Fig. 35.

Fig. 36 Ribband-back chair in mahogany. The back is very like one appearing in *Chippendale's Director*. About 1755. (Victoria and Albert Museum)

Fig. 37 Mahogany open, arm-chair with carved cabriole legs terminating with claw-and-ball feet. About 1760. (M. Harris and Sons, London)

Construction was much the same in all chairs except for variations in detail to suit the design. Seat rails were tenoned into the legs, the tenons in alignment with the slope, mortises at an angle to suit; top back rails were above the uprights and were mortised to receive the tenons and grooved to take the splat. In most cases the back seat rail was raised at the centre (often it was an applied piece) to receive the bottom of the splat, though there were exceptions in Gothic and Chinese chairs and in stuff-over chairs. The raised part is often termed a shoe.

A chair with open arms of about 1760 date is shown in Fig. 37. The front legs are carved with typical acanthus leafage, but an unusual feature is the shell detail on the knee which suggests an earlier period. There is something dignified about the whole form that makes it obviously the work of a first-class chair-maker. Another example of much the same period is the closed arm-chair in Fig. 38. The majority of its cost was put into the upholstery since the show parts of the frame are entirely plain. It is a good instance of how fine proportions and form combined with simplicity have produced an extremely attractive chair.

From about 1760 on until nearly the end of the 18th century a growing style was that now known as Hepplewhite, though in fact it was a style followed by fashionable cabinet-makers generally. It was of a delicate and refined type with more restraint in carving than had been shown in some earlier chairs and often with quite daring curvature. Typical back patterns were the shield with fretted splat, Fig. 31b, square type with vertical bars, oval with 'spokes', or triple feathers, round head, Fig. 31c, and a form of

Fig. 38 Fully upholstered arm-chair with scrolled arms and winged back. About 1760. (Fosters of Putney, London)

Fig. 39 Oval-back arm-chair of the Hepplewhite period, about 1790.

ladder back. Legs were usually straight, square tapered, Fig. 10 l, or turned. The cabriole leg was seldom used and when it was it was of the French form. A chair with this latter type of leg is shown in Fig. 39.

Shield and oval backs were costly to produce, partly because the compound curvature cut into a lot of timber, but also because it took a lot of experience and skill to make a really shapely chair. Compound curvature can be a tricky thing. A shape drawn out in front elevation on the flat may look very different when it is curved in plan and additionally shaped in side elevation. A really first-quality chair would almost certainly need to have a preliminary mock-up made to ensure that the final result would look well. Fig. 40 shows a fine specimen of a shield-back chair.

Fig. 41 shows the quantity of timber needed for the uprights of a shield-back chair. Most of the elevation curving would be sawn before assembling, but even here extra fulness would have to be allowed because the plan shaping necessitates the front being dished. Note, too, that the rail beneath the splat has to be fitted with a mitred-shoulder mortise-and-tenon joint as in Fig. 42, because otherwise the short grain would be liable to crumble. It is clear that in work of this kind it is not enough merely for the shoulders to be tight. The tenons must fit properly throughout their length if they are to resist the stress, and it is certainly due to this fine hidden craftsmanship that these chairs are sound after nearly two hundred years of use.

Another extremely expensive chair to make and one calling for the highest craftsmanship, was the oval back of Hepplewhite and Adam

Fig. 40 Shield-back chair in mahogany of the Hepplewhite period, about 1780. (Victoria and Albert Museum)

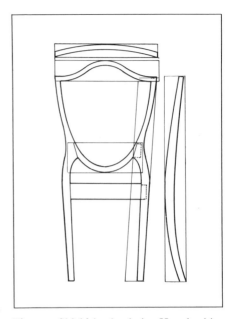

Fig. 41 Shield-back chair, Hepplewhite period, showing timber required.

design. An Adam example is given in Fig. 43. Such chairs were roughly D shaped in seat plan, Fig. 44, and this necessitated the back legs being contained between the seat rails rather than being at the corners. Owing

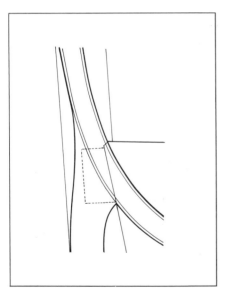

Fig. 42 Detail of joint of mid-back rail in the shield-back.

Fig. 43 Adam oval-back gilt chair, about 1777. Note the three-dimensional shaping of the back. Apart from the oval front elevation it is additionally curved in both side elevation and plan.

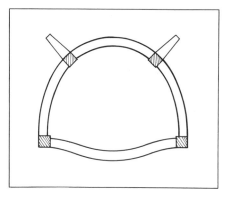

Fig. 44 Why back legs splay outwards in a chair with D seat.

Fig. 45 Sheraton period chair, about 1800.

to the rake the legs necessarily splay outwards towards the floor as shown. In most chairs they either remain parallel or converge.

The man who is used to straight cabinet-work only may care to pause and reflect on the problems involved in making an oval back chair of this kind. Few joints are square and many of the sizes and shoulder angles cannot be obtained by direct measurement. Today the matter is largely simplified by the use of dowels. These enable the parts to be cut off and fitted together to a dead fit by trial and error. Thus the ends of the parts after cutting to the required angle could be offered together and a shaving taken off where needed to make a perfect fit, and the holes for the dowels then bored. When there is a projecting tenon this cannot be done. The parts can only be fitted after both mortise-and-tenon have been cut and there is little room for adjustment because the tenon has to fit properly.

In the Sheraton period, belonging to the last decade of the 18th century and the early years of the 19th century, chairs were simpler in that the backs seldom had compound curvature. The uprights were parallel, though they might be tapered both above and below the seat rails as in Fig. 45. Arms, however, were often compound, having flat serpentine curvature in plan in addition to elevation shaping. Seats might be of the simple tapered type or the side rails might be flat, rounded, or of serpentine shape. They were usually either of stuff-over form or caned, occasionally with loose cushions. Plain square tapered legs, often with spade foot, or turned, were usual. Many Sheraton period chairs had inlay decoration but there was also a vogue for painting. In some cases the entire chair was painted, in which event the wood was usually beech, but both mahogany and satinwood was used in such chairs. The painting was just an enrichment of floral and leafwork patterns or of classical ornament.

Lightness was the keynote of Sheraton chairs, widths and thicknesses

Fig. 46 Regency chair with sabre legs, about 1810.

Fig. 47 Regency chair in mahogany, about 1810. (David Tron, London)

being cut to a minimum and, considering that stretchers were omitted, they were amazingly strong. Of course, the chair-maker's trade had been established for well over a century and craftsmen had learnt their cunning and had a long tradition behind them. It makes an interesting contrast, that of a 17th century oak chair with one of the late 18th century, but if the progress from the one to the other had been long and slow it was also continuous. Men had learnt their skill of working in curves and had found the trick of accurately jointing shaped members. Of course, the habits and conditions of people who ordered chairs had changed. The polite drawing-room of the late 18th century was quite different from a room in, say, Cromwellian times, though that in its turn had been an advance on the Tudor period.

A point that soon strikes one about many Sheraton chairs compared with the Hepplewhite and Adam designs is that the back rails are regarded frankly as separate items. In Fig. 45, for example, both back rails are taken square across and are tenoned in.

Compare this with say the oval, hoop, or shield back of a few years earlier. It is difficult to see just where the rails join the uprights because the curvature is continous. Another feature is that the backs were usually lower.

With the coming of the Regency period (1810-20) compound curvature largely disappeared, though there was often marked curvature in one plane. Backs were often of pronounced serpentine curvature with arms boldly scrolled (see Fig. 9j). A feature of many of them was that the back

Fig. 48 Reproduction Regency chair, about 1815. See also page 241.

Fig. 49 Stage in the assembly of the Regency chair in **Fig. 48**.

Fig. 50 How mid-back rail is turned from four centres.

uprights were often in the same plane as the sloping sides instead of being set square, and one result of this was that the lower ends of the legs converged appreciably as in Fig. 27m, instead of remaining parallel or sloping outwards as in many previous models. Front legs might be of the sabre pattern, Fig. 10n, turned, or sometimes of scrolled form terminating with paw feet at the bottom and grotesque or animal heads at the top. At this period too brass inlays in the form of lines or conventional designs of leaf work in Greek style became popular.

Two Regency chairs having much in common are shown in Figs. 46 and 47. Both have sabre legs which curve into the side rails in a continuous sweep, and in both the side rails meet the back in a hollow curve. Of rather different form is the chair in Fig. 48. This is a close copy of an original chair, and some idea of the construction is given in Fig. 49. The twist rail of the back needs to be turned from four centres, and Fig. 50 shows how this was done. A counter-weight must be screwed temporarily to one side to give balance. The measured drawing on page 241 gives the chair in greater detail.

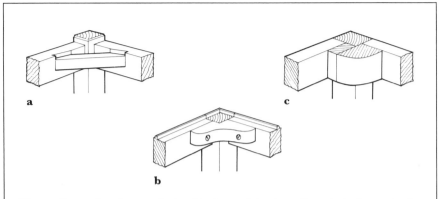

Fig. 51 Struts, brackets, and glue blocks used to strengthen chair frames in the 18th century and later.

Since the beginning of chair-making men must have realized the strain to which a chair was subjected, and they sought to combat it by fitting struts between the rails. In the case of stuff-over chairs these struts were let into notches cut in from the top as at Fig. 51a, where they were hidden later by the upholstery. Quite frequently the makers were not particular about stopping the saw at the bottom of the notches but callously took it straight down almost across the entire width of the rail. A later and more satisfactory method was to fit corner brackets as at (b). This was more usually associated with loose-seat chairs, the brackets being level with the rebate in the rails where they gave additional support to the seat. A still later development often found in light chairs of the Sheraton period and later were glue blocks (c). One narrow piece (left) was glued in first. After the glue had set a shaving was taken off to make it level with the leg, and a second block (right) glued in. Finally the outer surface was rounded over to a neat curve.

This abridged story of chair-making has nevertheless been a long one but there is more traceable sequence about it than in many other pieces of furniture, the probable reason being that it so early became and remained a separate trade of its own. It is extremely doubtful whether the average cabinet-maker could ever have tackled chair-making – at any rate the more elaborate patterns.

There is a certain convention about trades; knowledge is handed on and a man from progressive experience is able to calculate sizes, work out angles and above all cut shapes which look well from all viewpoints. The man not used to such work would not know where to leave extra thicknesses or widths to allow for this. In many respects chair-making is one of the most highly skilled trades, involving as it does odd angles, both simple and compound curvature, a good eye for line, and the cutting of first-rate joints at all sorts of odd angles, sometimes without any square surfaces to work from; and all this despite the fact that a chair in its nature has to resist more strain than most other items of furniture.

Chapter 11

Tables

Early oak tables were invariably of the trestle type, consisting of heavy end members or trestles, generally cut to a decorative outline and joined by rails which passed right through and held with wedges driven through holes cut at the outside as in Fig. 1. The top, which might be 2–3 in. thick, rested loosely on the trestles, and the whole could thus be taken apart and stacked to one side if necessary (it would take several men to do this because of the great weight). Sometimes in place of the shaped trestles there might be stout squares of timber tenoned into cross-pieces as in Fig. 2. Such tables belong generally to the 16th century and earlier.

The table with turned or square-cut legs and underframing such as that in Fig. 3 originated in the early 16th century, but became specially popular later in the same century and in the first fifty or sixty years of the next. Round about 1600 such tables often had great bulbous legs such as that in Fig. 2, page 180, and were thicknessed locally as described in Chapter 14. The rails and stretchers were tenoned into the legs, and in the

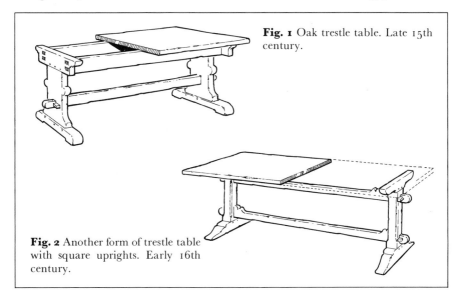

Fig. 1 Oak trestle table. Late 15th century.

Fig. 2 Another form of trestle table with square uprights. Early 16th century.

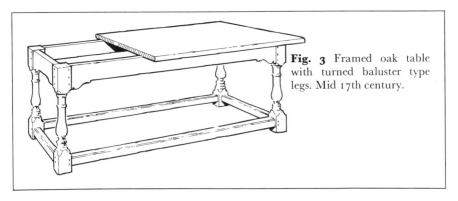

Fig. 3 Framed oak table with turned baluster type legs. Mid 17th century.

case of extra long tables there might be six legs. Sometimes the rails were tenoned into the centre legs, but in other tables the top rails were in one length and the centre leg tenoned up into it.

When, in the 17th century, it became the custom for people to take their meals privately as a small family group instead of in the great hall with the entire household, the necessity arose for small tables. These were frequently of the folding-leaf pattern and a popular type was the gate-leg table shown in Fig. 4. Here the same framed construction was used, the tenons pegged and seldom glued. Fig. 5 shows the way they were made, and a detail that strikes us today as being rather odd was the frequent omission of a rail above the drawer. The top itself served to keep the drawer from dropping as it was opened, but it is clear that any warping of the top across the grain would affect the running of the drawer.

Frequently the tops of these tables were of elliptical shape, and a rather delightful detail used in many of them was the rule joint between the main top and the leaf shown at Fig. 5a. This necessitated a special form of hinge (b) which had one flange wider than the other to bridge across the hollow of the leaf, and also countersinking of the screw holes on the reverse side to that of the knuckle.

These tables varied tremendously in quality. Some were of the simplest possible character with plain rails of slat-like form; others had beautifully turned legs, sometimes of twist form. Those of the first half of the 17th century were usually of oak, but from about 1660 onwards walnut was generally used. A comparison of Figs. 4 and 6 demonstrates the tremen-

Fig. 4 Gate-leg table in oak. Mid 17th century. (Victoria and Albert Museum)

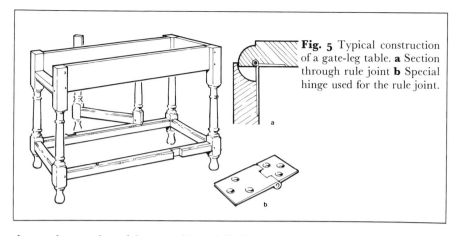

Fig. 5 Typical construction of a gate-leg table. **a** Section through rule joint **b** Special hinge used for the rule joint.

dous advance in cabinet-making skill that occurred in a short time in the 17th century. That in Fig. 4 is a perfectly sound piece of work, but is the sort of job that any competent carpenter could tackle. In Fig. 6, however, new techniques were involved, quite apart from the twist-turning. The latter would not have been done by the cabinet-maker in any case. The whole thing is veneered, much of it with marquetry, and the moulding of the top is cross-grained. Note, too, the flat stretcher shaped in plan and veneered. Such a table was clearly made by a man experienced in the new techniques that were being introduced, though it is only fair to point out that tables of this kind were intended for the polite drawing-room or dining-room. They could not have withstood the more exacting treatment that was inevitable in the farmhouse or general dwelling house.

Another type of leaf table that became popular from the late 17th century onwards was the card table, and a delightful example from the early years of the 18th century is given in Fig. 7. Here the development of cabinet-making techniques is still more obvious. The whole thing, except for the cabriole legs, is veneered, but in addition the rails are shaped in plan to follow the outline of the top. Furthermore the top in the open position is supported by swing legs which are pivoted on knuckle joints. In some cases the moving legs had what is known as the concertina movement, and moved backwards similarly to the bellows of a concertina. A measured drawing of a table with this movement is given on page 242.

Fig. 6 Table veneered with walnut and marquetry. Charles II period. (Victoria and Albert Museum)

147

Fig. 7 Walnut card table. Note the crosswise direction of the grain on the rails, and the herring-bone bandings. Queen Anne period. (M. Harris & Sons, London)

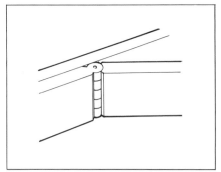

Fig. 7a Knuckle joint used for the swing leg of many tables in the 18th century.

It is of later date but the action is the same.

Incidentally, the knuckle joint (see Fig. 7a) mentioned above is difficult to put right once it has become badly worn. To work properly the joining faces of the overlapping parts must make a close fit, and the centre metal pin on which pivoting takes place must fit without slackness. This may involve fitting an oversize pin and packing out the faces of the projections with pieces of veneer. Yet another complication is that the rails were frequently made of beech, and both this and the walnut of which tables of the period were made are particularly liable to attack from the furniture beetle. In bad cases the replacement of the rails with new wood having new joints cut in it is the only answer.

A detail of the table in Fig. 7 that must have caused the cabinet-maker to think furiously was the form of joint needed between the front legs and rails. The straight, flat part to be found at the top of an ordinary cabriole leg was not practicable owing to the rounded plan shape; and it was necessary to start off with a square of timber of considerably greater section than was normally needed for the leg. The idea is shown in Fig. 8. Note also from this illustration how the rails are thicknessed locally at the ends to enable the shape to be worked.

Writing tables or desks as distinct from the bureau or secretaire were popular features of the 18th century library, and a fine example of about 1750 is given in Fig. 9. Such quality pieces were, of course, only for wealthy patrons. This particular piece is attributed to William Vile, cabinet-maker to George III.

There must have been a considerable market in the mid-18th century for what is often referred to today as the architect's table. Ince and Mayhew in their *Universal System* call them writing or reading tables. Some had a top which could be set at an angle; others remained flat but could be folded back to reveal a writing top. A feature common to all, however, was that the front legs were divided, and could pull forward, thus increasing the working area. An example is given in Fig. 10. It seems a reasonable assumption that such a table would have been used by the steward of a

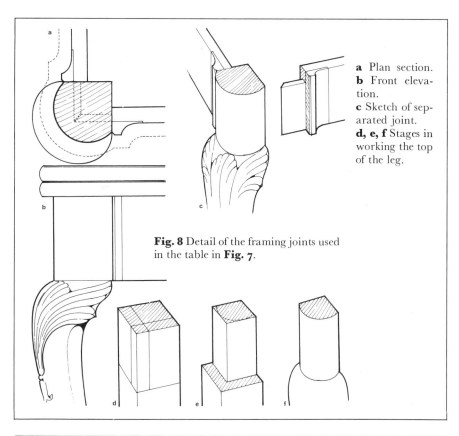

a Plan section.
b Front elevation.
c Sketch of separated joint.
d, e, f Stages in working the top of the leg.

Fig. 8 Detail of the framing joints used in the table in **Fig. 7**.

Fig. 9 Mahogany library desk attributed to William Vile. 1740-50. (Victoria and Albert Museum)

Fig. 10 Reading or writing table in mahogany. About 1760.

Fig. 11 Tripod table, with piecrust edging and bird cage movement.
(Mallet and Son [Antiques] Ltd.)

country mansion for his business of paying wages, receiving rents, and conducting the affairs of the house generally.

The need for small occasional tables increased as the 18th century progressed, and a popular type was the small tripod table, generally with circular top with pie-crust edging as in Fig. 11. Usually the top was made to revolve by means of the 'bird cage' arrangement, this having four small turned pillars fitting into a square block. The top was also free to tilt to enable it to stand close up to a wall when not in use.

A card table of about 1780 is shown in Fig. 12 and is of special interest because of the slender form of cabriole leg which flows into the rails in a continuous sweep. It is based on the French form of cabriole leg, but is an Anglicised version in the relative flatness of the curves. The honeysuckle detail at the top was widely used. As the rails are of serpentine shape, following the line of the top it is clear that wood thick enough to contain the entire curve was needed. Fig. 13 shows how this was arranged. The rails would have been of rectangular section in the first place as at (a) as this would simplify considerably the marking out and cutting of the joints. Before the joints were glued, however, the legs would have been cut to shape and carved, and the rails worked to the serpentine curve with slight fulness at the ends to allow for final trimming and levelling after assembling. Lastly the whole was veneered, in this case with curl mahogany.

A form of dining table popular towards the end of the 18th century was the pillar-and-claw type in Fig. 14. Some had four claws or legs; others three. These were dovetailed into the pillar and strengthened with a metal plate screwed on beneath. It will be realized that several combinations in size of table top were possible, since, apart from the three units, there were two loose leaves which were held in place with metal clips inserted at the edges.

150

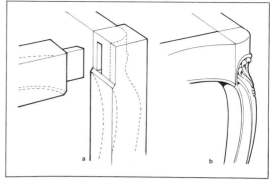

Fig. 12 Card table in mahogany with French type cabriole legs. About 1780. (Mallet and Son [Antiques] Ltd.)

Fig. 13 Detail of joint and amount of timber required for the table shown in **Fig. 12**.

Small occasional tables were a feature of the second half of the 18th century and the following century. The Pembroke type is shown in Fig. 15. Tops were of many shapes; rectangular (usually with rounded corners), elliptical, bowed, and, as in the present case, of serpentine form. The flaps were invariably supported by brackets pivoted on knuckle joints. Toilet tables too were popular and an interesting example made by Gillows, Lancaster is shown in Fig. 16. It has the maker's name stamped on it. Another similar type is that in Fig. 17.

Other popular tables were the drum type, Fig. 18, generally leather lined. There were usually four drawers, with dummy fronts in between. In the 19th century the games table became popular, and an example is given in Fig. 19. Note the curious humps on the legs which show the 19th century origin. Such a detail would never have appeared in the 18th century.

Fig. 14 Pillar dining table with two extra leaves on quadruple supports. Late 18th century. (M. Harris & Sons, London)

Fig. 16 Toilet table in mahogany by Gillows, Lancaster. About 1800. (Foster of Putney, London)

Fig. 15 Pembroke table with top of serpentine shape. About 1790. (David Tron, Chelsea, London)

Fig. 18 Drum table in mahogany. Early 19th century. (M. Harris & Sons, London)

Fig. 17 Toilet table, about 1800. (David Tron, Chelsea, London)

Fig. 19 (Left) Games table fitted for backgammon. About 1820. (Foster of Putney, London)

Fig. 20 (Above) Sofa table in kingwood with brass mounts. About 1820 (Fosters of Putney, London)

Fig. 21 Circular dining table with brass mounts on monopodium base. Regency period. (M. Harris & Sons, London)

At the close of the 18th century the sofa table became a feature of the drawing-room, a long type usually with flap extensions at the ends. It was intended for use at a sofa. Its development in the Regency period is shown in Fig. 20. The use of metal mounts and inlays was a feature of the period, and was the counterpart of the French Empire style.

The last example, Fig. 21 shows a magnificent circular dining table of the Regency period. It was the forerunner of the type which became extremely popular in Victorian days. The workmanship involved in making such a piece was of the highest order. Beneath the top was an under-framing which kept it rigid, yet made allowance for possible shrinkage. The lower part was made up of heavy timbers arranged in + form with stout uprights tenoned at the top. Over this the pyramid-like mid-section was fixed.

The telescopic table with screw extension belongs to the Victorian period. The making of these, was a specialized trade, and amazing pieces of work many of them were. Some were made about 6 ft. long when closed but could open out to 13 ft. or more, loose leaves being added as required. They were beautifully made, perfectly firm and rigid in use. Sometimes a fifth leg could be added at the middle to give extra support but it was not essential. The rails were usually of birch or teak, a greasy wood, and they slid one along the other with tongues fitting in grooves, and to avoid sagging they were slightly cambered (about $\frac{3}{8}$ in. in a length of about 3 ft.). I recall the upset caused in the workshop when one of these tables came in for repair. It was invariably necessary to shift several benches to enable the table to be opened.

Chapter 12

Furniture construction
Drawers

The earliest form of drawer suspension in Great Britain appears to have involved fairly thick sides with central grooves which engaged with runners fixed between the front and back of the cabinet. Frequently the drawer itself was of the most primitive construction with simple lapped joints at the front, the whole being merely nailed together as in Fig. 1. Sometimes rather coarse, crude dovetails were used as in Fig. 2, the groove contained within the dovetail. When the drawer was quite shallow (Fig. 3) the centre runner was sometimes omitted. Often the bottom was nailed up beneath the sides and back, though the front was usually rebated to receive it. There was no standardized method of construction, however, each carpenter following what seemed to be the most convenient way in accordance with the wood available and the limitations of his skill.

Occasionally when the front had to project beyond the sides, plain grooved joints were cut as in Fig. 4. In this particular case the front is bow-shaped in section and has to mitre with corresponding shaped members at the sides, hence the necessity for the projecting ends. The bow shape is an applied facing and probably conceals nails driven through into the sides. It is interesting to note that in this particular drawer the grain of the bottom runs from side to side, which is most unusual as in the majority of early drawers it ran from front to back. Possibly the maker happened to have suitable size of wood available, or it may have been a later replacement.

With the use of walnut rather than oak, furniture went through a transitional stage in which the cabinet-maker developed as a specialized tradesman, and a neater form of construction was evolved. Veneering became an essential part of furniture-making, and the older and often crude methods of construction were certainly not suitable. At first, and especially in country-made pieces, coarse dovetails were cut, these being taken right through the front of the drawer as in Fig. 5. It must soon have become apparent, however, that the method was largely unsound because any movement in the joint necessarily affected the veneer. It is true that early veneers were thicker than the knife-cut veneers we are accustomed to today, but even so they would not withstand much racking and, in any

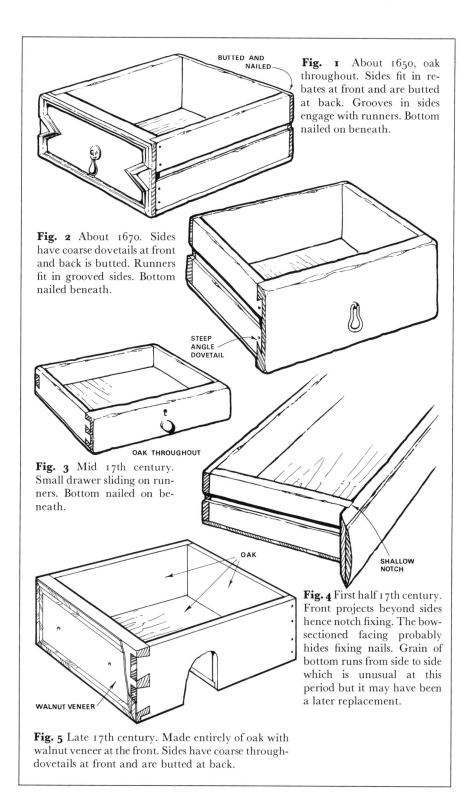

Fig. 1 About 1650, oak throughout. Sides fit in rebates at front and are butted at back. Grooves in sides engage with runners. Bottom nailed on beneath.

BUTTED AND NAILED

Fig. 2 About 1670. Sides have coarse dovetails at front and back is butted. Runners fit in grooved sides. Bottom nailed beneath.

STEEP ANGLE DOVETAIL

OAK THROUGHOUT

Fig. 3 Mid 17th century. Small drawer sliding on runners. Bottom nailed on beneath.

SHALLOW NOTCH

Fig. 4 First half 17th century. Front projects beyond sides hence notch fixing. The bow-sectioned facing probably hides fixing nails. Grain of bottom runs from side to side which is unusual at this period but it may have been a later replacement.

OAK

WALNUT VENEER

Fig. 5 Late 17th century. Made entirely of oak with walnut veneer at the front. Sides have coarse through-dovetails at front and are butted at back.

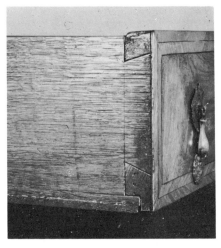

Fig. 6 About 1700. Single coarse through-dovetails are cut at both front and back. The front is veneered with walnut right over the ends of the dovetails.

case, the end grain of the dovetails was not ideal for glueing.

The drawer in Fig. 5 is of special interest as it shows that the craftsman had found a better method of fixing the bottom. Not only was the front rebated to hold it but the sides were rebated as well. Note how the bottom front corner of the side was cut to fill in the end of the rebate. One weakness of the method, however, was that the rebate depth was only that of the thickness of the bottom. Consequently the latter scraped on the bottom rail of the carcase as it was opened.

A further development to avoid this was to increase the rebate depth in the front to about double the thickness of the bottom and to add strips beneath the sides as in Fig. 6. Note how the bottom and the strip beneath fill in the end of the rebate in the front. This photograph shows the rather crude side through-dovetail cut in both front and back. The applied strips beneath the sides are also visible but it is likely that the drawer has been repaired (possibly more than once), during its life of over 250 years, and the present strips no doubt replace the original ones. It may be, too, that the sides were originally rebated as well as the front to receive the bottom and strips, but this was largely worn away at the back and completely disappeared during the repair.

Fig. 7 shows another improvement in the use of lap-dovetails rather than through-dovetails. Any movement in the joint would not affect the veneer on the front. In this case the sides as well as the front are rebated to hold the bottom and the strips. However, one finds various alternative methods used at the same period, and it was in fact quite common practice merely to plane the sides level with the rebate and fix both bottom and fillets beneath as at (A). Since the grain of the bottom invariably ran from front to back, both it and fillets appeared at the sides merely as joints to make up width.

This system of construction became common practice during the second

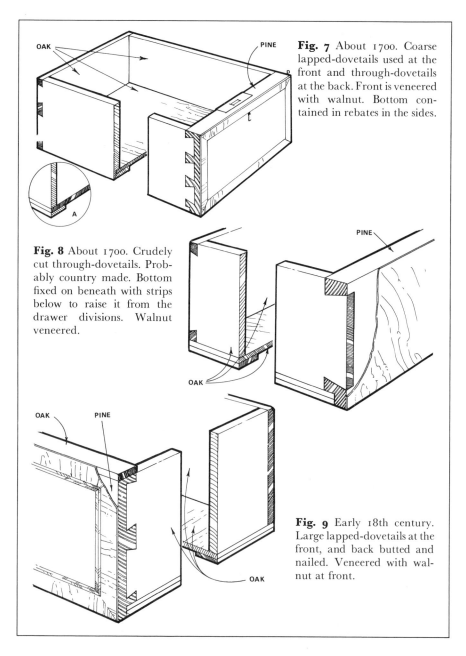

Fig. 7 About 1700. Coarse lapped-dovetails used at the front and through-dovetails at the back. Front is veneered with walnut. Bottom contained in rebates in the sides.

Fig. 8 About 1700. Crudely cut through-dovetails. Probably country made. Bottom fixed on beneath with strips below to raise it from the drawer divisions. Walnut veneered.

Fig. 9 Early 18th century. Large lapped-dovetails at the front, and back butted and nailed. Veneered with walnut at front.

half of the 17th century when walnut superseded oak as a furniture wood, though there were variations. Drawer bottoms were generally of oak and continued to have the grain running from front to back. Sides too were usually of oak, though fronts might be of oak or pine, the latter being a better glueing wood for the veneer. In the early pieces the dovetails were invariably coarse, whether through or lapped, and sometimes were only partially of dovetail form. Alternative types are shown in Figs. 7 and 8.

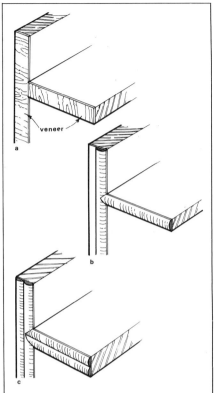

Fig. 10 Early 18th century. Rather crudely-cut lapped-dovetails. Oak sides, pine front veneered with walnut.

Fig. 11 Treatment of edges of cabinet ends and drawer divisions.
a veneered **b** single bead **c** double bead.

In better town-made pieces dovetails were finer and more cleanly cut.

Fig. 10 shows a rather coarsely made drawer with pine front veneered with walnut, and oak sides. Here again both bottom and lower strips are fixed directly beneath the sides. It is interesting to compare this photograph with that of a much later piece, Fig. 20, page 166. Note the much finer dovetails of the latter with pins running almost to a point.

At this stage it is necessary to take into account another detail which, although not actually part of drawer construction, affected its development. When walnut was first used in veneer form the advantage of using its grain decoratively was quickly realized, hence the use of cross-bandings and inlay bandings, and of mouldings made up of a thin facing of walnut glued with its grain running crosswise to a groundwork of pine or oak. Thus cabinets, chests-of-drawers, etc. had their drawer rails veneered at the front with walnut as in Fig. 11a. To give added interest the veneer was replaced by a flat bead, this again being cross-grained Fig. 11b. This flatness of section was not entirely a matter of design, however. It has already been mentioned in Chapter 3 that wood inevitably shrinks across the grain as it dries out. In the case of veneer this was not important because, owing to its thinness, it was elastic enough to give. Much the same applied to mouldings. The cross-grained walnut facing was kept to minimum thickness so that it could adapt itself to the inevitable movement without splitting or seriously opening at the joints. Rather later pieces sometimes had a double bead as in Fig. 11c, but by the end of the century all three were used contemporaneously.

A walnut cabinet with single flat bead on the face of the ends and drawer rails is shown in Fig. 12.

Lipped drawers In the early years of the 18th century, however, another detail became popular, that of the lipped drawer, in which the drawer front was rebated and moulded and projected beyond the carcase to which it was fitted. It had the advantage of making the drawer more dust-proof, and, as it overlapped the drawer rails, it concealed any gap which might develop due to possible shrinkage of the front. Apart from

Fig. 12 Walnut, veneered cabinet of about 1690. Note the flat round bead facing the edges of the ends and drawer rails. (Mallet and Son [Antiques] Ltd., London)

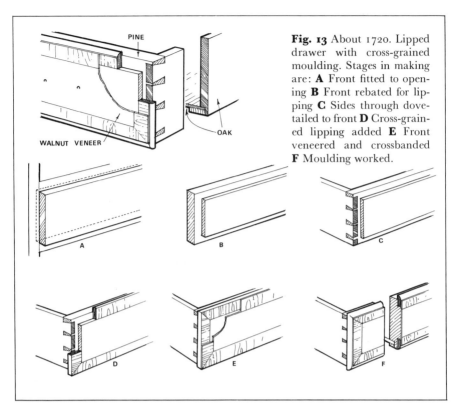

Fig. 13 About 1720. Lipped drawer with cross-grained moulding. Stages in making are: **A** Front fitted to opening **B** Front rebated for lipping **C** Sides through dovetailed to front **D** Cross-grained lipping added **E** Front veneered and crossbanded **F** Moulding worked.

this, however, it was an attractive feature in itself and enabled the cabinet-maker to exploit the practice of using cross-grained mouldings. An example is given in Fig. 13. Sometimes the lipping projected at the top and sides only, the bottom finishing flush, though there appears to be no definite rule about this. This same illustration shows the stages in which the work would have been done. The front would first be fitted to its opening as in normal drawer-making as at (A) and a rebate worked around the front edges (B). Through-dovetails for the sides were next cut, and the whole drawer glued up as at (C). In the rebate strips of walnut were glued, the grain running crosswise (D) and the corners mitred. After levelling the whole the front would be veneered, and, before the glue had set, a cutting gauge would be used around the edges to cut away the surplus veneer where the crossbanding was required. This would be laid (E) and finally the moulding worked as at (F) after the glue had set. It will be realized that it would not be practicable to work the moulding before veneering as the squeezed-out glue caused by the latter would run over the moulding. Sometimes the dovetails were lapped rather than taken right through, this having the advantage of giving a better glueing surface for the cross-grained wood of the moulding (end grain does not hold glue well).

Incidentally this lipping was not without its disadvantages, as any furniture repairer knows. As the drawer was closed the lipping acted as a

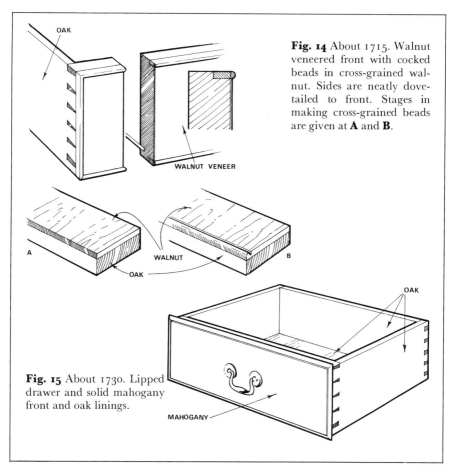

Fig. 14 About 1715. Walnut veneered front with cocked beads in cross-grained walnut. Sides are neatly dovetailed to front. Stages in making cross-grained beads are given at **A** and **B**.

Fig. 15 About 1730. Lipped drawer and solid mahogany front and oak linings.

stop, and continued closing over the years has resulted in the lipping being forced out. Since the veneer passed right over the lipping this in turn has suffered, and the repair of drawers badly damaged in this way can be very expensive.

Another way of dealing with drawer fronts in the walnut period was the use of cocked beads, and the rage for cross-grained mouldings was sometimes extended even to these as in Fig. 14. As it would have been difficult to handle long, thin strips of wood with the grain running crosswise, the method followed was to glue the cross-grained wood to strips of walnut or oak, the grain of which ran lengthwise as at (a). The bead would then be worked and sawn away as at (b) and applied to the rebate of the drawer front as a whole.

About 1720 Cuban mahogany began to supersede walnut as a furniture wood and, although an excellent cabinet wood, was dark and not particularly marked in the grain as was the lighter walnut. Consequently it became apparent that there was no advantage in cross-graining the mouldings (though pieces are occasionally found with cross-grain) as it would not show sufficiently. Drawer fronts were made of solid mahogany and the lipped effect obtained by working rebate and moulding in this as in Fig. 15. This is just another case of how practical considerations influenced design.

Drawer construction seems to have become largely standardized during the entire 18th century, though the tendency by the middle of the century or a few years before was to fit the bottom with the grain running lengthwise from side to side rather than from front to back as had been the earlier practice. When the drawer was extra long a centre muntin was fitted, this being grooved at each side to receive the bottom (see A, Fig. 16). It is sometimes suggested that drawers with the grain of the bottom running from side to side were not used before about 1730 but, although this is generally true, it is unwise to be dogmatic as exceptions do turn up from time to time. In any case pieces of later date than, say, 1750 are occasionally found with the grain running from front to back, though these are the exception rather than the rule.

So far as jointing was concerned, craftsmen had learnt the art of cutting neat dovetails as the 18th century progressed, and the tendency to cut finer joints is apparent – at any rate in town-made pieces. It seems to have been a matter of personal pride to cut really clean joints. In practically every case the sides were lap-dovetailed to the fronts, specially narrow pins being used, sometimes actually pointed. This seems to have been particularly the case with some trades – for instance, men who made toilet-mirror frames and small boxes, etc. The pins were not only pointed but the angle was so flat that the pins were little more than slivers of wood. Of course, these drawers were small and took little weight so that the lack of strength did not matter and presumably the fine pin was just a conceit on the part of the maker, or possibly a trade convention. To an extent, however, the flatness of angle was followed in ordinary furniture-making. Apart from neat joints, the whole drawer became a much more refined structure with sides and back no more than $\frac{5}{16}$ in. or $\frac{3}{8}$ in. thick, or in the case of a really small drawer, as thin as $\frac{1}{8}$ in.

Fig. 17 shows the usual jointing for drawers that would be fitted to chests, writing tables, presses, and so on. The inner surface of the front might be grooved to receive the bottom as in Fig. 17A, in which case the groove was contained within the bottom dovetail. Alternatively the front might be rebated to hold the bottom as in Fig. 17C, and a square member cut at the lower corner of the side to fill in the gap caused by the rebate. In both cases the sides were usually rebated to hold the bottom, and a fillet fixed beneath which served not only to retain the bottom but also provided a wider bearing surface, and lifted the bottom so that it did not scrape beneath. In all cases the back stood above the bottom.

The weakness of this system was that, if the fillet were glued, it resisted any shrinkage of the bottom and cracks or open joints were the result. In fact this has happened in many cases and it was no doubt on account of this that the method of fitting the bottom in grooves was thought out, Fig. 17D. The bottom, being put in dry, could move along its grooves freely in the event of shrinkage or swelling. Merely to groove the sides, however,

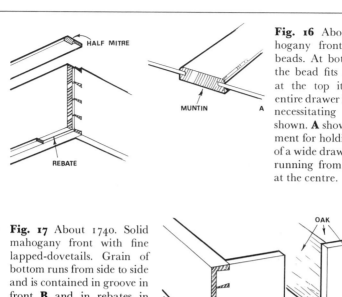

Fig. 16 About 1775. Mahogany front with cocked beads. At bottom and sides the bead fits in rebates but at the top it occupies the entire drawer front thickness, necessitating the half-mitre shown. **A** shows the arrangement for holding the bottom of a wide drawer, the muntin running from front to back at the centre.

Fig. 17 About 1740. Solid mahogany front with fine lapped-dovetails. Grain of bottom runs from side to side and is contained in groove in front **B** and in rebates in sides with strips beneath to widen the bearing surfaces and to prevent the bottom from scraping. **E** shows the dovetails on a small stationery nest drawer and **D** the method sometimes used in the late 18th century to hold the bottom. This latter method has been continued ever since.

would have weakened them unduly and the idea of grooved slips evolved, these being glued to the inner surface of the sides. The front itself was grooved as before because it was thick enough not to be weakened and the back stood above the bottom as previously.

This last system of construction appeared occasionally towards the close of the 18th century, though the rebated method also continued, and has been maintained up to the present day. A slightly different section of slip is sometimes used nowadays giving a flush effect at the inside. Generally the grooved slip method (D), Fig. 17, belongs to the 19th century. In the case of very small drawers such as would be fitted to, say, a stationery nest, the bottom was invariably flush with the bottom edges, and fitted in rebates in sides and front and butted beneath the back as at (E), Fig. 17.

Cocked beads have already been mentioned as being fitted in walnut furniture of the early 18th century. They have been used frequently in furniture ever since, though they are invariably cut with the grain running lengthwise, not crosswise. They fit at the sides in rebates in the drawer front, the lap of the dovetails being made wide enough to give a reasonable seating for them, Fig. 16. A corresponding rebate was worked at the

163

bottom edge also, but usually the top edge was planed away entirely to enable the bead to cover it completely, thus avoiding a joint along the edge. The top bead has to be cut with a half-mitre as shown. There are exceptions, however, in which the top edge is rebated in the same way as side and bottom edges.

Shaped drawers   The idea of furniture with shaped front or ends must have been a quite bold step for the cabinet-maker who had hitherto been used to straight work only. Ideally wood is suitable essentially for work with flat, straight surfaces because of its marked grain direction. Being much weaker across the grain there is a potential weakness when shapes are cut in it. Furthermore the end grain of the wood is largely exposed and this can result in some curious complications, quite apart from its being expensive because of the large amount of timber the process necessarily cuts into. However, with the coming of veneering it was realized that cabinets with shaped fronts were a possibility.

At first little was done about it. One occasionally comes across items with parts curved as in the case of the writing cabinet in Fig. 18, which dates from the early years of the 18th century, in which the pedestals are hollow-shaped. Sometimes, too, small items – desks or toilet-mirrors have

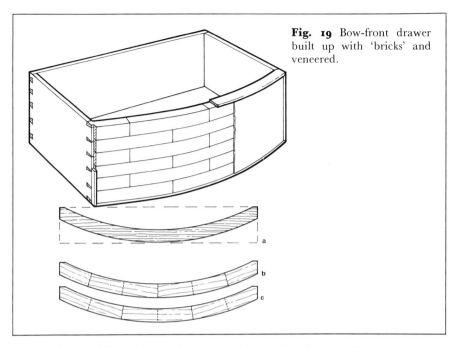

Fig. 19 Bow-front drawer built up with 'bricks' and veneered.

shaped fronts. The idea of pieces with the entire front and sometimes the ends cut to a shape did not come until the middle of the 18th century. In Chippendale's *Gentlemen and Cabinet-maker's Director, 1754,* are illustrations of pieces with bow, serpentine, hollow, and other shapes, and the making of these must have set quite a problem for the man tackling such a job for the first time. However, a system of construction was soon evolved and furniture with shaped fronts became quite commonplace during the second half of the 18th century and onwards. Bow-front and, to a somewhat lesser extent, serpentine-front chests-of-drawers were widely made.

The problem then was to produce a drawer front which was sufficiently strong, did not show a lot of end grain on the surface, and did not involve undue wastage. The craftsmen solved it by the 'brick' system, the entire thing being made up of relatively narrow and thin pieces glued together brick fashion with the vertical joints staggered as in Fig. 19. A comparison between (a) and (b) shows how the method largely overcomes the difficulties. The minimum thickness of timber that would be needed to enable the front to be cut in the solid is shown by the dotted line at (a) and it is clear that considerable end grain would be exposed towards the ends. This does not hold glue well and, in the case of more acute curvature, would be weak. By building up the front with 'bricks' the grain direction follows the curve as at (b) and there is little end grain exposed. The 'bricks' would cut into the minimum of wood and would not need a large block of wood but could be cut from relatively small narrow pieces, always an advantage. Loss of strength at the vertical joint was ensured by staggering them (c) so that no two joints were opposite each other in the adjacent layers. Serpentine and other shapes were made in the same way.

Fig. 20 Fine dovetails cut in a bow-front drawer.

Fig. 20 shows part of a bow-front drawer made in this way and is of interest in showing the fine dovetails being cut in the later 18th century. There is only one fault. The craftsman has let his saw run in too far at the second dovetail. Probably he had his knuckles rapped by the master cabinet-maker – he may even have been fined.

Occasionally small bow-front drawers were made from three thicknesses bent to shape and glued together over a former. An example of this is the small drawer of the table shown on page 243.

Chapter 13

Furniture construction
Doors

There is something rather obvious about the early form of door that carpenters used to fit to their furniture – a single slab of wood without any joints, either quite plain or decorated with carving or crude moulding, and pivoted with wrought-iron hinges. Invariably it was in a single piece, and it is reasonable to assume that the item for which it was made was schemed so that the opening for the door was no wider than the width of wood available. Sometimes such doors were as much as 15 in. wide but more usually they were nearer 12 in. or less. The wood was quite thick – at least 1 in. – and often thicker, and since much of it was quarter-cut it has frequently kept remarkably flat. No doubt much of it was riven. This, however, was not an invariable rule. There is a 15th century door in St. Albans Abbey made from planks which have no figure and must have been sawn through-and-through from the log. The same thing applies to the doors in Fig. 1, which are not quarter-cut and could not have been riven.

To pivot the door the usual method was to use long iron strap hinges, these having the advantage of serving to strengthen the door across the grain. In the best examples these hinges were made a feature in themselves, being wrought to a decorative shape with chamfered edges and sometimes engraving. In some cases, however, simple butterfly hinges were used, these sometimes being of the crudest type made by the local blacksmith.

The crudity and weakness of such a door must soon have become obvious, especially when, as often happened, the door was pierced right through, either to afford ventilation or to give a decorative effect. The piercing virtually reduced the strength by as much as 50 per cent in parts and, although in quarter-cut timber the door might still be strong enough for the purpose, it would be a dangerous weakness in slash-sawn wood because the line of cleavage runs parallel with the rays which would be more or less at right angles with the surface.

Fig. 1 shows a cupboard with these solid doors dating from about 1500 and is typical of much of this early work. Another similar type is that in Fig. 2, but here there is no through piercing, the wood being thick enough to enable the deep carving to be cut in it. It would be a mistake to assume

Fig. 1 Cupboard with doors in a solid piece. About 1500. (Victoria and Albert Museum)

Fig. 2 Solid plank door with deep carving not pierced right through. Early 16th century. (Victoria and Albert Museum)

that a more satisfactory system of panelling was not known, however. In large house and church doors the usual early method was a form of lamination, the outside consisting of a series of vertical boards with horizontal boards inside, the whole nailed together. From this came an inner framework, with intermediate members halved together, again with tongued vertical boards nailed to it. As a development of this came the idea of grooved mullions to hold the boards, with horizontal rails at the back halved over them. Finally the fully framed and panelled method was evolved by the latter part of the 15th century. It seems, however, that men who made the general run of furniture lagged behind the more skilful and advanced joiners, and so one finds this survival of crude construction at the same time as the finer work made for the more important buildings.

Framed doors Still, the advantage of the framed-and-panelled system must soon have become obvious. The framework provided strength in both height and width, the panels being held in grooves and acting rather as a filling. They were thus free to shrink in their grooves without affecting the stability of the door and without any consequent reduction in the overall width. Equally important, the size of opening was no longer restricted by the width of board available for the door, and could be literally any width within reason. Even the width of wood available for

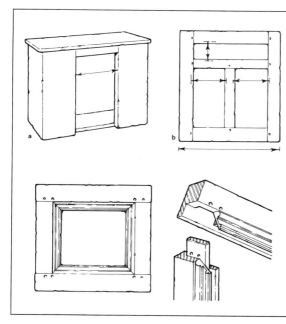

Fig. 3 Diagram illustrating advantages of the framed system.
a Simple cupboard with door opening restricted in width by the width of wood available for a solid-plank door. **b** Framed and panelled door. There is little or no shrinkage in overall width and the panels can be relatively narrow.

Fig. 4 Framed door in which the stiles are tenoned into the rails. Dated 1610.

Fig. 5 Detail of the joint used in **Fig. 4**.

the panels did not affect the issue because it was only necessary to introduce a muntin or intermediate grooved member and the panels could be relatively narrow without affecting the overall door width. These details are made clear in Fig. 3.

This panelled construction was used by furniture-makers throughout the 17th century, though occasionally one finds the solid door used, especially for small openings. A panelled example is that in Fig. 4 and it has the rather unusual feature that the rails run right through from side to side with stiles or uprights tenoned into them, though in the same cabinet the lower doors have the more conventional system of the stiles running right through. The complete cabinet is shown on page 112. An interesting feature is that the moulding is worked in the solid, this being shown by the fact that the inner retaining peg is right opposite the moulding. If it were applied the peg would have to be opposite the flat portion since the width of the tenon would be limited to this. The exact detail of the joint is shown in Fig. 5 and the immense advance in joinery skill compared with Fig. 1 is obvious. The same form of joint is used in the door in Fig. 6 in which the rails are tenoned into the stiles. An enlarged view of the joint is given in Fig. 7.

The moulding of the door in Fig. 6 is mitred at the corners, and this brings us straightway to an interesting point. It is doubtful whether the ordinary mitre with the moulding cut away at the ends at 45 deg. (in a square frame) was used much before the middle of the 16th century. Previously one of four other methods were used, sometimes more than one in the same item. These were: the mason's mitre, scribing, running out or stopping the moulding short of the joint, and butting. Of these the first was no doubt a copy by the carpenter of what was common practice in

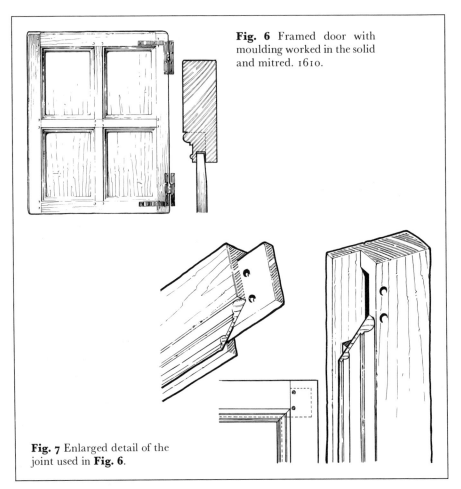

Fig. 6 Framed door with moulding worked in the solid and mitred. 1610.

Fig. 7 Enlarged detail of the joint used in **Fig. 6**.

stone masonry. When a man uses a moulding plane he obviously has to take it right through the length of the wood. He cannot stop the moulding locally as the sole of the plane prevents it. This will become clearer in Chapter 15 on mouldings (see Fig. 1, page 191). In the mason's mitre the plane cannot be used, at any rate on the mortised piece, though it could be used on that with the tenon. This means that the moulding has to be worked with the scratch-stock and stopped short of the joint as at (a), Fig. 8. It has then to be finished with carving tools as at (b). For the stone mason this would be a normal procedure since obviously no sort of moulding plane could be used, the whole moulding having to be carved from beginning to end.

It was no doubt the difference in the technique of woodwork compared with that of stone that led the woodworker to find another method which would enable him to use his moulding planes. The simplest way out of the difficulty was to run the moulding along the tenoned piece, and either to leave that with the mortise square, or to work a moulding with the scratch-stock and either let it run out or stop it short of the joint as shown in Fig. 9a.

In this there is, of course, no true intersection, and the moulding on the one could be of quite different section from that on the other (as it frequently was) as at Fig. 9b. In fact a chamfer could have been used just as easily.

And this brings us to an interesting point. We have already seen how the woodworker owed much to the stone mason for his ideas. Here is something else he borrowed. Many openings in buildings such as windows had the lower edge bevelled to enable water to drain away easily and the joiner, perhaps struck by the attractive appearance, or merely copying a detail, followed the same idea, chamfering the top edge of the bottom rail as at Fig. 9d, where the chamfer is stopped each side of the joint. That this was not merely accidental is shown by the fact that it was invariably the bottom rail that was chamfered, seldom the uprights or top rail.

It was soon realized that the idea carried a second advantage with it; the chamfer need not be stopped even when there was a centre upright or muntin. By cutting the shoulder of the muntin at an angle to suit the chamfer rather than square, it could fit without a gap, including any moulding at the edges. It was in fact a scribing over the chamfer as at Fig. 9e.

Here again there was no true intersection since the joining parts were dissimilar. The joiners, however, had already learnt another trick, that of scribing two mouldings together, the one being cut to a reverse of the moulding section at the shoulder, the appearance being almost the same as when they are mitred. There was, in fact, a slight difference in that at

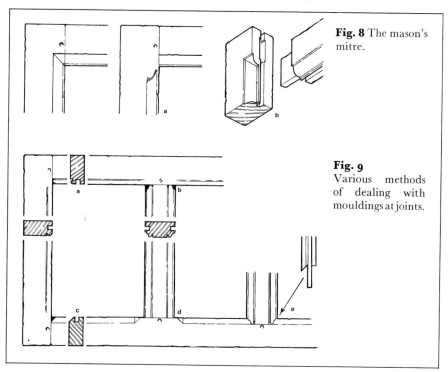

Fig. 8 The mason's mitre.

Fig. 9
Various methods of dealing with mouldings at joints.

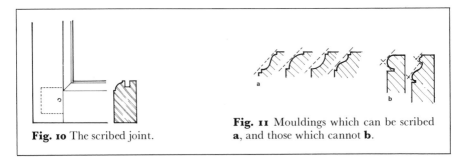

Fig. 10 The scribed joint.

Fig. 11 Mouldings which can be scribed
a, and those which cannot **b**.

the square member the mitre line did not run straight across but followed
the line of the moulding as in Fig. 10. The reason is that the scribe necessarily cuts away any wood parallel with the surface but there is no gap.

One wonders what complications and unexpected results the early
joiner may have had in scribing. Possibly his first effort was on a simple
moulding and was successful, but later he would find that some elaborate
sections just would not work out. Anyone who spends half an hour or so in
experimenting in scribing will find that not all sections can be scribed.
The rule is that the moulding must fall away continuously from the general
surface as shown by the dotted lines in section (a), Fig. 11, all of which
could be scribed. If, however, the line runs outwards in any part as in
section (b) the scribing is impossible. For such sections, apart from the
true mitre, the mason's mitre was the only answer. In any case salient or
external joints must be mitred. They cannot be scribed.

Curiously enough, although joiners used the scribe freely at all periods,
the men who made furniture during the later 16th and the 17th centuries
invariably cut the plain mitre, except where they let the mould run out or
stop, or when they scribed over a plain chamfer. There are few cases of two
mouldings being scribed together.

Fig. 12 shows a selection of 17th century doors of typical design and
with various forms of joints. In all of them mouldings play an important
part and it will be noted that a channelled moulding on the face of the
framing often occurs in addition to that at the edges. In some instances it
is taken right through in both stiles and rails (d) whereas in others it has
been stopped on the stiles and cut in by hand to meet that on the rails as
in (e). That at (f) is interesting in that the moulding, which is of bolection
form, is applied. The tendency to elaboration in mouldings increased in
the second half of the 17th century. They were usually applied and were
mitred in an intricate arrangement as at (g).

The use of applied mouldings and inlay probably suggested another
change in procedure in that, whereas most doors had been put together
dry, that is without glue, and were pegged, it now became customary to
glue the joints and omit the pegs. Thus this late oak furniture anticipated
a method which was used in walnut items when the use of veneer was
practically universal and/or where pegs obviously could not be used, and
which has been the cabinet-maker's system ever since.

Various kinds of hinges were used, the commonest being the face-

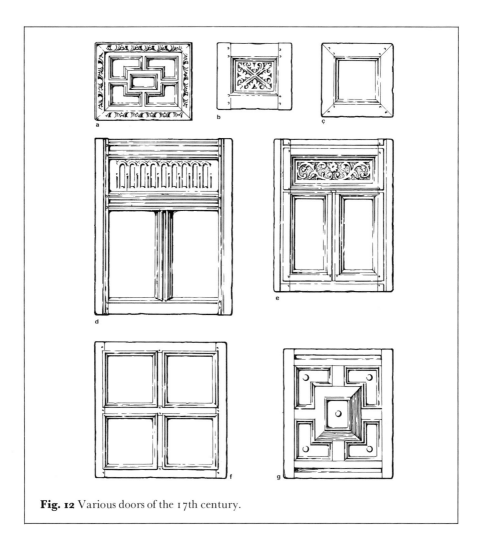

Fig. 12 Various doors of the 17th century.

applied strap or butterfly type, but the use of both these and centre hinges often occurs on the same job. Butt hinges are less common but they were used in some cases, usually recessed equally into both door and cupboard.

Veneered doors It has been mentioned in Chapter 3 that it became customary to make use of the grain of wood decoratively once veneering was introduced in the second half of the 17th century. Hitherto any value of attraction it may have had seems to have been more or less accidental – in fact, there is reason to believe that some early oak furniture was painted. However this may be, once veneering with walnut became general, the grain value was realized and the practice of cross-veneering became common. Fig. 13 helps to explain the change-over in method. At Fig. 13a is the traditional method with the moulding worked in the solid and run out in the stiles opposite the joints so that square edges are retained. Grooves hold the panels and the joints are pegged.

173

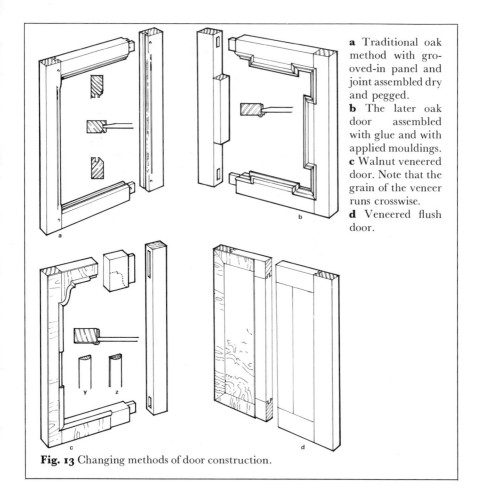

a Traditional oak method with grooved-in panel and joint assembled dry and pegged.
b The later oak door assembled with glue and with applied mouldings.
c Walnut veneered door. Note that the grain of the veneer runs crosswise.
d Veneered flush door.

Fig. 13 Changing methods of door construction.

In Fig. 13b the moulding was applied and formed a decorative pattern, blocks of wood being glued locally for the purpose. The framework was tenoned, the joints being glued, and there were no pegs. Lastly in Fig. 13c the same glued joints were used but the entire front surface was veneered, the grain running crosswise, and a flat rounded bead planted on to give a finish and, incidentally, form a rebate for the panel. In some cases the bead had its grain running crosswise (z). In this case it was common practice first to veneer the back of the wood from which the bead was cut as shown, as this gave strength, and was specially helpful when the bead was being worked. For fuller details see Chapter 15 on mouldings. Note that at the corners (c) the grain of the veneer is butted in line with the joint. This was frequently done though some cabinet-makers preferred to use a mitre.

There were many variations in the design of doors in the walnut period, some of which are given in Fig. 14. Fig. 14a is similar to that in Fig. 13c, but has a shaped heading. The rather unusual method has been followed of taking the top rail right through and tenoning the stiles into it. Fig. 14b is a variation in that the top corners and moulding is separate. In a case like this it was common to make the top rail wide enough to include the shape and cut the latter after assembly. Note that the moulding is cross-grained and, following the general practice, is of flat section, the purpose being to keep the cross-grain wood as thin as possible as there was then enough give in it to avoid splitting as a result of shrinkage, though it was essential to dry the wood as much as possible beforehand.

Fig. 14c is a door with shaped corners and to form these the stiles were made extra wide at the top as shown, though in some similar doors the corners were separate applied blocks.

It was in this walnut period that the flush door was first made Fig. 14d. In this particular case it consists simply of a clamped panel of solid wood veneered with a decorative pattern both sides. The inevitable has happened. The main panel has shrunk and has pulled in from the ends, with consequent stress marks in the veneer. In some cases there was a stout

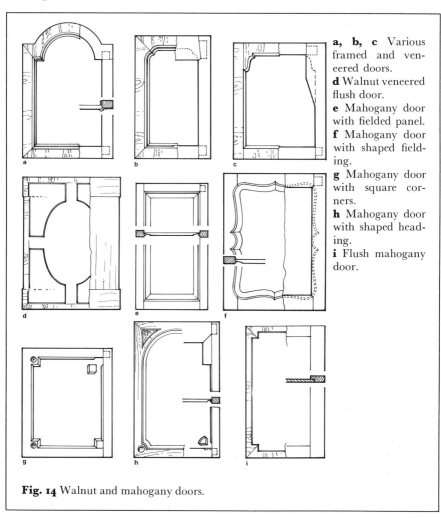

a, b, c Various framed and veneered doors.
d Walnut veneered flush door.
e Mahogany door with fielded panel.
f Mahogany door with shaped fielding.
g Mahogany door with square corners.
h Mahogany door with shaped heading.
i Flush mahogany door.

Fig. 14 Walnut and mahogany doors.

framework with flush panel grooved in but, even here, in a door of any size there was bound to be shrinkage, and in fact in many of these old pieces the line of the construction of the framework shows right through the veneer. Quite often shrinkage has resulted in splits in the panel.

Mahogany doors After the introduction of mahogany as a furniture wood there was a reversion to solid construction. As suggested in Chapter 3, this may have been because this early mahogany was Cuban which was dark in colour, and though a splendid furniture wood, did not show the strongly marked variety of grain that the lighter walnut had done. Thus a moulding of mahogany with its grain running crosswise would scarcely show the grain direction (though one does occasionally come across a mahogany piece with cross-grained mouldings). This was probably the reason for the use of the fielded panel Fig. 14e in which the panel had a sloping rebate all round, often with small inner hollow moulding. It broke up what would otherwise have been a wide expanse of plain surface. There was, however, nothing new about it. It had been widely used in joinery in the 17th century, particularly in panelling of the Wren period.

A more decorative variation of the fielded panel is that at (f) which is of about 1740 date. The inner edges of the framework are shaped and the fielding of the panel follows the line. To work such a shaping today would be comparatively simple, as it could be largely done on the spindle or high-speed router, except for the inner corners which would have to be finished by the carver. At the period of which we are talking it would have to be worked with the scratch-stock, again except for the corners which would have been the wood-carver's job. Such a door would be made in the form of a plain square frame and the inner shape sawn and rebated and moulded afterwards.

A type of door frequently used in the mid-18th century and later was that at (g). This would have the corners made as separate items and added after the assembly of the main framework. Here the latter would be rebated and moulded but at the joints the mouldings would be cut short without any attempt to mitre that of the stile to that of the rail. The moulding would then be cut to a mitre at each side to align with mitres to be cut in the applied square blocks.

That at (h) is similar but the lower corners are curved and could, in fact, be turned and afterwards cut to the quarter shape. The method of forming the top shaping is shown. Here again the entire moulding would be worked with the scratch-stock.

The last example (i) is a flush door. It has a rather unusual construction in that the panel fits in a rebate in a frame and is glued in. The face veneer is taken right over the framework and panel, and some well-seasoned stuff must have been used for there is no sign of any movement having taken place. Other flush doors were made with strips edge-glued together and veneered both sides.

Barred doors Sometimes known as traceried doors, they were made

a Oak. Second half 17th century. **b** Walnut period door. The remainder were used in the second half of the 18th century by cabinet makers generally, though **h** and **i** are more usually associated with Hepplewhite, **g** with Ince and Mayhew and **k** with Sheraton. Sections through the mouldings and bars of traceried doors are given at **e**.

Fig. 15 Examples of traceried doors.

in a wide variety of designs throughout the 18th century and later. They owed their origin to the difficulty and expense of procuring large sheets of glass, but their decorative value was soon realized, hence their popularity. An early form had been made in the second half of the 17th century but it was of relatively heavy construction with stout bars, more like those one associates with sash windows, and the design was invariably rectangular. An example is Fig. 15a, which shows a bookcase door from Dyrham, dating from 1675. It is of oak and the bars have an unusual construction in that the section appears to be built up of a main rectangular bar ¾ in. wide, either halved or tenoned together, with a half-round member planted on top forming an astragal mould, the intersections mitred.

However, the barred door of the cabinet-maker as distinct from that of the joiner was a lighter affair, and early examples belong to the walnut period. These mostly consisted of rectangular panes, the section usually of flat half-round shape, generally cross-grained. The construction is shown in Fig. 16a. To stiffen the moulding and to form a rebate for the

177

glass a bar was fitted at the back, this being recessed into notches cut in the main framework. It will be realized that to work and handle cross-grained moulding no more than $\frac{3}{8}$ in. wide by bare $\frac{3}{16}$ in. thick would be difficult or impossible, especially as some of the lengths needed were considerable. The method adopted therefore was to veneer the back, the grain running lengthwise. (See Chapter 13.) The glass was usually puttied in.

Fig. 15 shows some of the many designs of barred doors of the 18th century. Those with straight mouldings were the simplest to make and the method followed was to cut a panel to fit closely into the rebate, and draw on it the exact positions of mouldings as in Fig. 17, giving also centre lines. The last named were of importance because all mitre lines had to intersect on them. On these lines the lengths of moulding were assembled, the mitres being lightly glued. The glue having set, the panel was removed and the door turned over to enable the back bars to be added. These were let into notches in the framework and halved at the intersections. Tape glued into the angles made strong joints (see Fig. 16b).

Those doors with shaped mouldings were more awkward to make. Usually the bars were laminated in two thicknesses, these being bent and glued around a former of the required curvature. In some cases, however, they were cut in the solid, especially when the curvature was flat. Mouldings were mostly cut in the solid and worked with the scratch-stock (see page 194). Sheraton in his *Cabinet-Maker and Upholsterer's Drawing Book* gives full instructions for making a door with curved mouldings and, curiously enough, says that both bars and mouldings were to be laminated, the former in two thicknesses and the moulding in five. Whether this was a theory of his own it is difficult to say. I have never come across a piece in which the curved mouldings were laminated, though the bars may have been. Still, one never knows with antiques; one may turn up at any time.

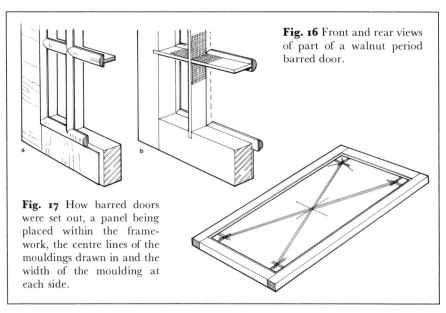

Fig. 16 Front and rear views of part of a walnut period barred door.

Fig. 17 How barred doors were set out, a panel being placed within the framework, the centre lines of the mouldings drawn in and the width of the moulding at each side.

Chapter 14

Furniture construction – Legs

When judging the value or interest of an old piece of furniture it is of considerable help to have at least a working knowledge of the work that went into its making. It enables one to see why a certain detail was expensive to make, either in time or material, or why some apparently elaborate features were in reality fairly simple to produce. Of all the parts that go into the making of furniture probably the commonest are those of legs and feet. They occur on so many items: chairs, stools, tables, cabinet-stands, sideboards, dressers, and so on. And so far as types and designs are concerned, their name is legion, for they are many. Perhaps, therefore, the reader will bear with me if I go into the subject in some detail giving the main types and explaining the work that went to their making.

Since turning developed as a separate craft fairly early on and remained so throughout the entire history of furniture-making, I take this subject first and trace its development from the baluster type of the oak period to the refined work of the late 18th century and the first fifty years or so of the 19th century.

Turned legs   A point to realize about turning is that the shape must be normally contained within the square section from which it is worked. Thus in a square of, say, 2 in. no part of the turning can be of greater diameter than this 2 in. – in fact, the fullest part will be a trifle less as otherwise small flats are liable to appear on the rounded shape where the turning has not quite cut away the flat surfaces. The idea is shown in Fig. 1. This restriction has necessarily had its effect on the resulting shape. The turning must not weaken the leg, which in turn has meant that hollows could not be cut in too deeply because they would be a source of weakness. Compare (a) and (b), Fig. 1. The latter is quite impracticable because of the weakness at the narrow hollow. At (a) however the weakness is minimized by making both hollow and rounded parts of elliptical shape, and also by slanting the small squares which separate the shapes at an angle. Thus the relatively flat shapes are the outcome of practical necessity, yet, in making a virtue of necessity, the result has produced the characteristic forms which belong to professional turning. The very acceptance of a

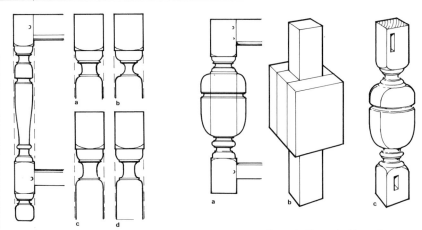

Fig. 1 Early turned leg.
a Use of elliptical shapes and sloping square members.
b Impracticable turning cutting too deeply into the wood.
c, d How sloping flat members **c** avoid cutting too deeply into the wood at the hollow member. At **d** the curvature is the same but the hollow member is necessarily deeper owing to the small flat members being vertical.

Fig. 2 Built-up bulbous leg.
a Elevation of the leg.
b Thicknessing pieces glued on.
c Appearance of completed leg.

restriction over many years of trade practice has produced grace and refinement. Yet if you gave a turner a pencil and asked him to draw the shape of a leg he would probably be quite incapable of doing so. But give him his gouge and chisel and he could turn a graceful shape almost instinctively.

Incidentally, the small squares mentioned were not always at an angle as shown, but it is clear that the slope as at (c) does give greater scope for bolder curvature because the hollow shape starts nearer the outside than if the squares were parallel (d).

Apart from the practical requirements of turning, however, an advantage of the turning in Fig. 1 was that the original square of wood could first be planed straight and square, the turning not affecting the surfaces where the joints had to occur. This point becomes more obvious in the next development in which provision had to be made for a turning of greater diameter. Most readers will be familiar with the huge bulbous turnings used on many dining tables and cupboards of the late 16th and early 17th centuries. To make such a turning out of a solid piece of wood would have several disadvantages. Firstly, it would involve using a huge piece of timber – sometimes up to 12 in. diameter, much of it to be cut away in waste. Then again the reduction at top and bottom would cut away the square surfaces where the joints occur. They would have to be cut back and planed independently in true alignment with each other, an

Fig. 3 Carved oak panel depicting a bulbous leg being turned on a pole lathe.

awkward job at best. Lastly, unless the wood were cut from a tree of great girth, it would contain the pith or heart and this invariably causes splitting as the wood dries out, as explained more fully in Chapter 3.

The Tudor turners got over the difficulty by using a main centre square of reasonable size, its section being that of the portions occupied by the joints at top and bottom and glueing on thicknessing blocks at the sides as at Fig. 2b. In this way all the drawbacks were avoided. The joints scarcely showed and in any case were made scarcely noticeable by the carving which was a common feature of these legs (see Fig. 6a).

It is only the man who has had to do it who can realize fully what turning a 12 in. piece of English oak can mean, especially using the primitive lathe in use in the late 16th and early 17th centuries. It is probable that today there is nobody left who has done such work with no more power than that supplied by the foot. A carved panel showing a 17th century joiner's shop depicts a large bulbous leg being turned on a pole lathe, see Fig. 3. The labour involved and the slow speed of the machine can be imagined. The sole purpose of the pole, a large springy sapling, was to raise the treadle (so reversing the rotation) ready for another stroke. A cord attached to this pole was fixed at the other end to the treadle, and was taken a turn around the work. Thus as the turner pressed down with his foot the wood revolved towards him. As he raised his foot the pole, by its spring, turned it backwards. Clearly the turner could use his gouge or chisel on the down stroke only.

Until only a few years ago there were 'bodgers' at work in the beech woods of Buckinghamshire using this method of turning Windsor chair parts (see Fig. 4) and amazingly quick they were at it. But such parts might be only a full inch in diameter at the thickest part. It was a quite different story turning a table leg of 10 or 12 in. diameter. Bodgers, too, had the advantage of turning their wood when it was green – that is as cut from the recently felled log, full of moisture. It was consequently much softer than dry wood. A table leg with planted-on pieces could not be turned in this way because glue does not hold over wet timber. It must, therefore, have been dried first and was necessarily much harder.

Fig. 4 One of the chair 'bodgers' at work in the Buckinghamshire woods. This photograph shows how the cord from the sapling was taken around the work down to the treadle. (University of Reading)

The treadle lathe with heavy flywheel and connecting rod giving continuous rotation in one direction does not appear to have been used in England until the 17th century, and, although it was a great improvement, it must still have been heavy going. It is probable that the treadle must have been made extra long to enable a second man or boy to help in treadling; or there may have been a device similar to that used by the wheelwright for turning large wheel hubs, a large wheel with a handle fitted to one end and connected directly with the driving chuck of the lathe. This would have been worked by an assistant whilst the turner concentrated on the actual turning, though here again there may also have been a treadle to help the drive.

This method of thicknessing the wood locally to enable a bulbous part to be turned continued right into the walnut period. The chair leg in Fig. 12 for instance was built up in this way, but the day of huge bulbous turnings largely passed with the end of the 17th century and was not revived.

Chair legs of the first half of the 17th century and up to about the restoration period were made in a variety of designs as shown in Fig. 5. Many of them were of vase shape (a); others were founded on classical columns (b); but the plain bobbin or reel-and-bead turnings were also common (c) and (d). Mostly they were in oak though after about 1660 many were turned in walnut. As shown by the dotted lines at (a) the turnings were invariably confined to the substance of the square from which they were cut. Dining-table legs, however, were frequently thicknessed up to give a bulbous shape, especially in the late 16th century and early years of the 17th century. The method of doing this has already been described. Generally the tendency as the 17th century progressed was to eliminate the full bulbous part and make the turning of no greater diameter than the size of the square from which the leg was made. Fig. 6 shows some typical patterns of dining-table legs.

As mentioned in Chapter 5, after about 1650 the habits of people began to change, and there arose the need for small tables at which anything from two to four or six folks could sit. Small side tables and gate-leg tables were the usual types. Mostly they were in oak, but walnut was used increasingly as the century progressed. Typical legs used with such tables are shown at (a) and (b), Fig. 7. There were many variations in detail but the elongated urn, bead and reel, or plain bobbin turning were common, squares being left where rails were required to join them. That turners had become highly skilled is clear from an examination of most of these

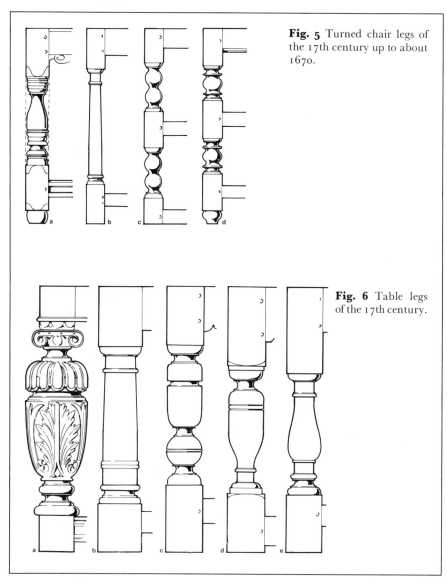

Fig. 5 Turned chair legs of the 17th century up to about 1670.

Fig. 6 Table legs of the 17th century.

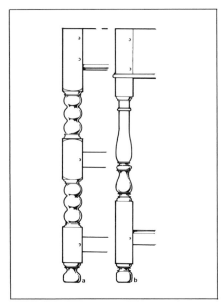

Fig. 7 Turned legs for small tables, mid 17th century and later.

Fig. 8 Twist leg in process of manufacture. The turning to the over-all shape has been completed and the spiral marked out. This is followed by the early stage of gouging the hollow between the bines.

turnings, and it was quite likely a sort of by-product of the fashion for building staircases and hand railings with turned balusters. An elaborate staircase might call for a hundred or more turnings, and in some cases there might be several different patterns in one staircase. Men engaged in such work and doing nothing else not only developed skill to a high degree but produced characteristic details which belonged peculiarly to that craft. It is often difficult to draw the shapes on paper because their subtlety of line is tied up with the fact of that they are seen from all angles, seldom square on as an elevation drawing must be.

Twist legs   A further development took place during the second half of the 17th century, that of spiral turning. This cannot be done in its entirety on the elementary lathe, though the preliminary turning to the over-shape can. Fig. 8 shows this early stage in which the square of timber has been turned to the overall shape and the spiral marked out. This is followed by hollowing out the parts between the bines with gouges as shown partly completed. Finally the bines are rounded over and the hollows completed with rasps and files followed by scraping and finally with glasspaper.

   The shapes of 17th century twist legs varied quite a lot. The simplest form, Fig. 9a, was the single bine which was rather like a screw having a single thread cut along it (the bine is the raised part). Next, and rather more interesting, is the double bine (b) in which the two bines twine one around the other. Although frequently used on chairs, it is not often found on tables, the single bine apparently being preferred. Differing in section is the fluted spiral (c), in this case a triple bine. Here the hollows are much wider in proportion compared with the bines, and in fact the adjoining hollows meet almost to a point. Lastly is the double open bine (d) used

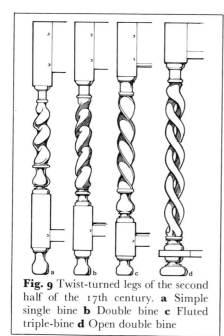

Fig. 9 Twist-turned legs of the second half of the 17th century. **a** Simple single bine **b** Double bine **c** Fluted triple-bine **d** Open double bine

Fig. 10 Photograph of various forms of twist turning.

only for light tables, never for chairs as it would not be strong enough to withstand the weight of a person sitting upon it. Each hollow is cut in so deeply that it runs into the second hollow at the back. Thus the two bines are entirely separated. The procedure in cutting this open twist is exactly the same as in the simple type but there is more work in it because the backs of the bines have to be finished as well as the fronts. Fig. 10 shows the chief types of twist.

Still more complicated is the triple open-bine because, whereas in the open double bine the file can be taken right through without hindrance, in the triple bine there is always a third bine at the back between any other two. There is nothing insuperable about it but it is certainly more costly to make.

Turned and carved legs The final evolution of the 17th century turned leg was the inverted cup type shown at (a), Fig. 11. At this period a new form of leg was being evolved, first a scrolled form, and later the cabriole leg, a type which was to remain popular for the next sixty years or so. These early scrolled legs, popular in the 1670–90 period, were usually part-turned and part-carved, and this combination appears to have suggested a means of enriching what would otherwise have been a purely turned type. For instance, that at (a) is obviously turning pure and simple, whereas at (b) carving is used not only to ornament the leg but almost as a disguise for its turned origin. Thus, except for the narrow neck and ankle, little of the turning remains. The leg is shown photographically in Fig. 12. Still more disguised is the turning at (c), Fig. 11, since, except for the neck and ankle, the entire surface is carved.

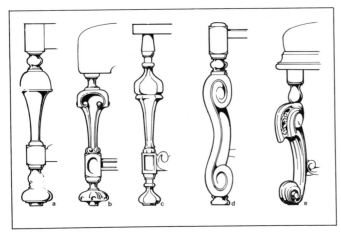

Fig. 11 Turned and carved chair legs of the second half of the 17th century.

Fig. 12 William and Mary chair leg. Although basically a turned leg, the carving largely disguises its turned origin.

Two forms of scrolled legs are shown in Fig. 11 at (d) and (e), both of which require a limited amount of turning. The method of turning these is given in Chapter 10, where the process of turning raked back legs is also described. Both types were used in the second half of the 17th century.

There were many variations of the cabriole leg and its evolution and the various types and method of making is dealt with at some length in Chapter 10. It is mentioned here only in connection with an attempt to copy it purely by lathe work. Fig. 13a shows the true cabriole leg and (b) the turned imitation, which is done by off-centring the foot. First a cylinder is turned from true centres as at (c) and the foot detail turned. The foot is then offset as at (d) and when the wood revolves a shadowy shape appears at the outside leaving a solid centre. The wood is turned down as far as this solid centre thus producing a somewhat pale imitation of the true cabriole leg.

Square legs Although the cabriole leg reached its zenith of popularity in the middle of the 18th century another type of leg was being made in increasing numbers, probably because it was much cheaper to make and was thus more suitable for less wealthy patrons. This was the plain square leg. In its simplest form it was literally little more than a square, though as a rule the inner corner was chamfered from a point a short distance below the seat rails giving a considerably lighter appearance as at (a), Fig. 14. A detail often added at the outer corner was a simple ovolo moulding (b), this adding very little to the cost but making the leg much more interesting. Yet another variation, costing rather more but not as expensive as the cabriole leg, was that moulded on two sides with what is known as a

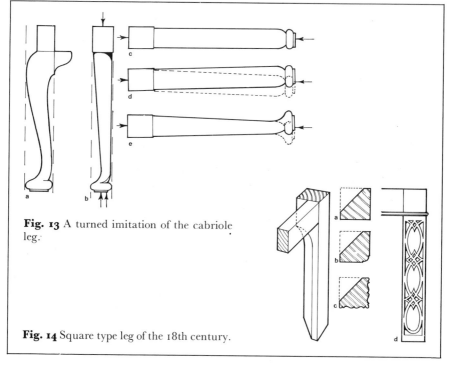

Fig. 13 A turned imitation of the cabriole leg.

Fig. 14 Square type leg of the 18th century.

toad's-back moulding as shown at (c). In some cases, particularly in the Chinese Chippendale phase, the two outer surfaces of the legs were ornamented with fretted decoration (d).

Tapered legs A natural progression from this simple square leg was the square-tapered type of which there were many variations from the entirely plain types (a) and (b), Fig. 15, to the elaborate patterns (g) and (h). It will be realized that the patterns (a) and (b) were cheap to make because the entire tapering could be done quickly with the plane from a point immediately beneath the seat rails. Where a spade foot was cut as at (c) the plane could only be used to a limited extent and quite a lot of sawing across the grain, chiselling, and spokeshave work would be needed,

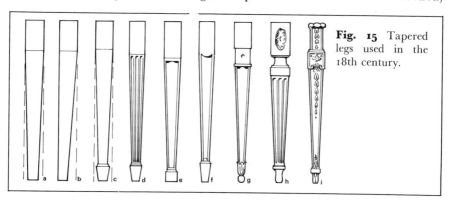

Fig. 15 Tapered legs used in the 18th century.

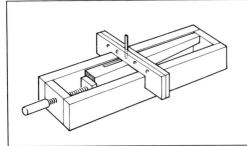

Fig. 16 The moulding box used for moulding tapered legs. It could also be used for moulding turned tapered legs.

quite apart from cutting the hollow around the foot with gouge and file. Note, however, that the entire foot was contained within the square of wood from which the leg was cut (see dotted lines). Sometimes cheap reproductions of this spade foot are made by planing a plain taper and glueing on thin pieces to all four sides, the pieces being prepared to shape in a length beforehand. This was never done in 18th century work, and if a piece is found with feet made in this way it is invariably suspect.

A still more costly development from the tapered leg with spade foot was that decorated with flutes as at (d). In some cases the flutes might be filled for part of the way with reeds. Clearly the moulding plane could not be used because both ends were stopped and the only way, short of cutting the flutes with carving tools, was to use the scratch-stock in combination with what was known as a moulding box (see Fig. 16). The leg with its taper and foot already cut was held in the box by means of a screw and could be in any position to suit the path of the scratch-stock, which was notched to fit over the sides of the box and thus worked parallel with them. In this way the middle flute could be central throughout the length and the side flutes could converge towards the bottom. In addition each flute could be made wider at the top than at the bottom by tapping the leg over to one side at the top after the full length had been worked at one setting. Furthermore, the depth could be varied if need be, deeper at the top than at the bottom. In any case the assistance of the carver to finish off the ends would be needed.

Recessed legs (f) could be worked in much the same way but sometimes, especially in the Adam period, an added complication was that a chain of husks or other ornamental detail was cut at the top. Even here the bulk of the recess could be cut as already outlined, the wood remaining untouched at the portion to be carved, leaving the wood-carver to complete his part of the work. Both legs at (h) and (i) would be costly to make in view of the shape at the necking and the foot and the detail to be cut by the carver.

Late turned legs Towards the end of the 18th century chairs with turned legs again became popular but in an altogether lighter form than during the earlier periods. Furthermore, such chairs were entirely without stretchers, so thoroughly had the craftsman learnt how to use glue to advantage in combination with well-cut joints. It is true that turnery had

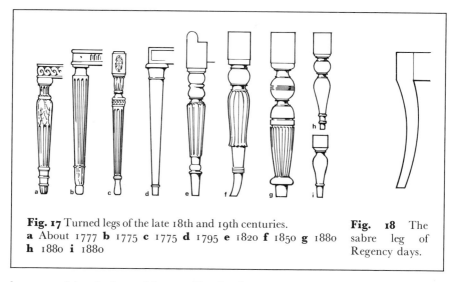

Fig. 17 Turned legs of the late 18th and 19th centuries.
a About 1777 **b** 1775 **c** 1775 **d** 1795 **e** 1820 **f** 1850 **g** 1880 **h** 1880 **i** 1880

Fig. 18 The sabre leg of Regency days.

been used in chair-making earlier in the century but this was largely in the Windsor chair type which was made almost entirely of turned spindles fitted into holes. Turned legs do not appear in Chippendale's book, nor in Ince and Mayhew, and it was not until the Hepplewhite, Adam, and later the Sheraton periods that turned legs came into popularity. An idea of the progression of turned legs from about 1780 until about a century later is shown in Fig. 17. Generally there was a coarsening of detail as the years of the 19th century passed though the actual craftsmanship remained of an extremely high order.

A type of leg that became popular in the early years of the 19th century was the sabre leg in Fig. 18. It was simple to make and used little more timber than a turned or tapered leg because, although its shape needed more width, it was usually thinner. Thus whereas the former might need 2 in. squares, the sabre leg often finished less than $1\frac{1}{2}$ in. thick. Frequently the front edge was rounded but in some examples it was moulded, usually with a combination of reeds and a centre rounded member. Since the leg invariably tapered towards the floor the entire reduction of the moulding usually took place in the centre member, the outer reeds remaining the same width throughout, enabling them to be worked with the scratch-stock. Fuller details of this procedure are given in Chapter 15.

A type of leg generally arranged in groups of three attached to a centre pillar was that shown in Fig. 19. It was usually fitted to pole screens and lighter tables, though some quite massive dining tables were made in the second half of the 18th century with tripod legs. The last named were frequently referred to as claws and were in fact so called by Shearer in his *Cabinet-maker's Book of Prices*. Round about the middle of the 18th century such tripod legs were usually of the cabriole type shown at (a), Fig. 19, and were frequently carved with claw-and-ball feet with acanthus foliage on the knees. Later, however, they became simpler with plain hollow or serpentine curves as at (b) and (c). In the Regency period (1810-20) a

189

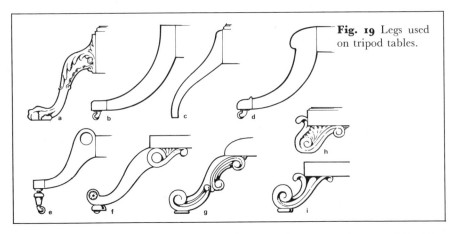

Fig. 19 Legs used on tripod tables.

rather ungainly rounded shape was frequently cut at the top (d). One sometimes wonders why some details were ever introduced. Presumably some designer felt the shape to be an improvement, or at least a change, and for some reason it became fashionable. Few people today would regard it as an.improvement compared with the dignified earlier shapes.

Incidentally it is worth noting that, since tripod legs are necessarily subjected to considerable side leverage, they should always be strengthened by a specially shaped metal plate let in beneath and screwed. In the case of a dining table this is essential. It is true that the legs were always dovetailed into the pillar in good work, but the strain is considerable and the omission of the plate almost always results in a split pillar.

Similar in general shape but generally joined to a flat base rather than to a pillar is the type shown at (e), (f), (g), and (h). That at (e) shows the pronounced hump and belongs to much the same period as that at (d). In that at (f), however, there is no hump although it is contemporary. The development in the early Victorian period is shown at (f). The examples at (h) and (i) may be classed as feet rather than legs but are similar in general form.

Whilst on the subject of legs of this kind we may mention a type of curiously unscientific form (Fig. 20) that almost invited failure. It was used on sofas and owed its origin to the classical Grecian form largely popularised by Thomas Hope. Even though the leg itself survived without splitting along the grain the joint to the rail was subjected to tremendous strain.

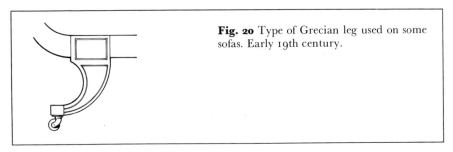

Fig. 20 Type of Grecian leg used on some sofas. Early 19th century.

Chapter 15

Furniture construction Mouldings

Since mouldings have been used in practically every piece of furniture from earliest times it is worth while considering them in detail, to see how they were affected by changing fashions, and to see how they were made. This last is of importance because methods of construction were affected by the practical work involved.

Moulding planes   When its use is practicable, the moulding plane is generally the best means of working a moulding by hand. It is the quickest method in that it removes shavings, not merely scrapes; and, unless the grain of the wood happens to run awkwardly, it gives a clean finish. As against this there are cases where it cannot be used. For instance, a moulding plane requires the moulding to be taken right through the entire length of the wood as in Fig. 1; it cannot be stopped locally because its straight sole would prevent it from reaching in at the stop (see a). Additionally, it cannot be used on a curved edge, again because of its straight sole. Furthermore, except in the case of some round and hollow planes, a separate plane is required for every section required to be worked.

It is thus apparent that in a workshop in, say, the mid-18th century, an extremely wide range of planes would be required; in fact, only a master cabinet-maker could afford to have such a range; and indeed it would not have been practicable for the journeyman to have carried such a number around with him from one job to another. Firstly there would

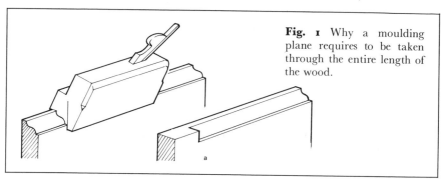

Fig. 1 Why a moulding plane requires to be taken through the entire length of the wood.

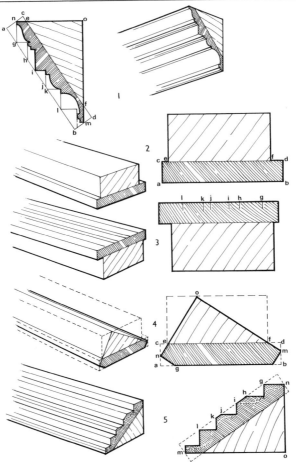

Fig. 2 Instructions for making a backed cornice moulding, based on those appearing in Sheraton's *Cabinet-maker and Upholsterer's Drawing Book*.

Prepare a full size drawing of the required section **1** and put in a sloping line **ab** to touch as near as may be the salient members. Draw another line parallel with it **cd** to give the minimum thickness of mahogany required for the facing, and at each end draw lines **ac** and **bd** at right angles. Plane true a piece of mahogany to this size **abdc**, and at the back glue on a piece of pine of width equal to **ef** and of thickness to include the entire spring of the cornice. Turn the whole upside down and draw a line in pencil square across the mahogany facing and, extending dividers from **a** to **g** prick a mark on the squared line. Make similar marks from **a** to **h, i, j, k** and **l**. From each of these marks run a gauge along the entire length of the mahogany. **3** shows this. Now set a gauge from **a** to **n** and from **b** to **m** and mark the edges of the mahogany. Set a sliding bevel with its stock against **ab** and its tongue in line with **f** and mark both ends of the wood. Plane the back of the wood to the line **mfo**. The top can then be planed square with this new surface, forming **oen**. Follow with the edge, planing away **a** square with **no** to form surface **ng**. Do the same with the other edge, planing away **b** to form a square surface. This is shown in **4**.

The wood is now fixed down on the bench on its back **mo** and a series of rebates worked along the gauge lines as in **5**. It is then a matter of using various moulding planes to form the round and hollow sections.

have been the difficulty of transporting them from shop to shop, but they would also have taken up too much space in the workshop. A medium-sized workshop might have about twenty journeymen working in it, each with his own tool chest. If to this were added twenty sets of moulding planes the space taken up would be far more than could be spared. It can therefore be taken that the employer would provide moulding planes which the workmen would use as required.

I described in Chapter 3 how, in my early days in the workshop in 1912, one of the older cabinet-makers recalled how his father laboured on Saturday afternoons on the unproductive job of sharpening moulding planes. That was in the days when only a large factory could install a machine spindle-moulder; and it is more than likely that the system was just the handing-on of a tradition from earlier days. A cabinet-maker was expected to provide his everyday tools, saws, bench planes, chisels, etc., but moulding planes, large cramps, and special apparatus were the property of the employer.

It seems that the manufacture of moulding planes developed as a separate trade early on. W. L. Goodman has records of moulding plane-makers back to the early 18th century. Indeed, except for some early specimens, it is clear that the manufacture of a moulding plane required the use of special 'mother' or reverse moulding planes. The best planes had boxwood slips inserted into grooves cut in the sole of the plane and the fitting of these would be an extremely awkward or impossible job without the use of special planes to work the grooves, which were frequently of dovetail section.

Large mouldings with several members can seldom have been worked in one operation with a single plane, though in a few isolated cases they may have been. The disadvantage was that the power required would be very great, especially in a hard wood, and such a plane could work one section of moulding only. In addition the grain in so wide a piece of wood might easily vary in direction at one side as compared with the other so that the plane would be liable to tear out the grain in parts. Cornice mouldings were therefore usually worked member by member. In fact, Sheraton in his *Cabinet-maker and Upholsterer's Drawing Book* gives exact instructions for working a wide cornice moulding which is backed with softwood. Fig. 2 gives the stages; (1) is the required section; (2) the softwood backing glued to the mahogany face; (3) gauge marks of the members marked in; (4) the bevels of back and top marked; and (5) preliminary rebating down to the gauge marks before working the final shapes with moulding planes. Similar stages are shown photographically in Fig. 3.

It will be realized that some moulding planes have to work equidistantly from an edge, and therefore have a fence (x) which bears against the edge of the wood as in Fig. 4a; also a top member which acts as a stop (y), preventing the plane from cutting too deeply. Other moulding planes, such as rounds, Fig. 4b, and hollows, have no stop because they are not always used from an edge and also may have to work shapes varying in

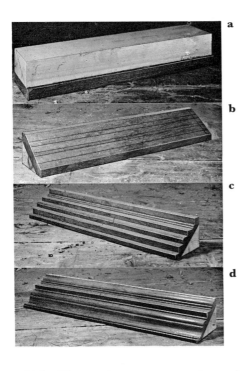

a

b

c

d

Fig. 3 Stages in working a backed cornice moulding.
a Mahogany facing backed with pine
b The triangular shape worked and the members marked
c Preliminary rebates worked
d Completed section.

width. Fig. 5 gives a group of moulding planes, and Fig. 7, page 27, shows an old plane in use working a moulding.

It will be realized that the resistance offered by a wide moulding plane can be considerable, especially when used on a hardwood. Some planes therefore had a hole near the front through which a rope could be looped, or a cross peg for the same purpose. Thus while the craftsman held the plane down on to the wood, keeping the fence up to it and guiding it generally, an assistant, usually an apprentice, pulled on the rope at the front, see Fig. 11, page 29. The trick was to pull slightly downwards and inwards so that the plane was kept up to the work. Heaven help the unhappy apprentice who pulled away from it!

Although the true mitre had been used by skilled joiners at the intersection of mouldings in the early 16th century, not all woodworkers understood how to arrange joints to enable this to be done, and even experienced men still sometimes preferred to use the mason's mitre (dealt with more fully in Chapter 8, The chest). Quite often men who made furniture used the simpler alternative of stopping the moulding just before the joint was reached. It avoided any actual intersection between two mouldings, and in fact it enabled dissimilar sections to be used on the joining members. The point about this in the present connection is that when a moulding was stopped it could not be worked with a moulding plane. It was necessary to use the scratch-stock.

The scratch-stock must have been invented and used very early on – in fact, it was the only means of working some mouldings unless they were cut with carving tools. It had the great advantage of simplicity and could

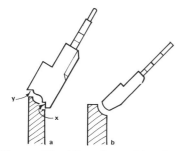

Fig. 4 a Moulding plane with a fence which bears against the side of the wood; also a stop which limits the depth to which the plane can cut into the wood.
b Round moulding plane which has neither fence nor stop.

Fig. 5 Group of moulding planes.

be adapted to suit varying sections by merely altering the shape of the cutter. The scratch-stock shown in Fig. 6 is the type that has been used by woodworkers for years and without doubt that used earlier was much the same. It is merely two pieces of hardwood fixed together with screws or bolts and notched along the underside. A cutter made from any thin piece of steel is filed to a reverse of the shape required and held between the two pieces by tightening the screws. For small sections a nail could be used. It works purely by a scratching or scraping action, the notch being kept close up to the edge of the wood It ceases to cut when the required depth is reached because the top of the notch bears down on the surface of the wood.

Another advantage of the scratch-stock was that it worked as easily around a curved edge as a straight one, and, although this may not have been of any special benefit in the early oak days, it was of tremendous value in the following walnut and mahogany periods when shapes were used widely, especially by chair-makers. A final advantage of using the scratch-stock was that it was not liable to tear out difficult grain because its action was that of scraping rather than cutting. In any case, however, it could be used equally well in either direction.

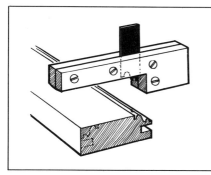

Fig. 6 The scratch-stock.

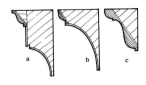
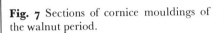
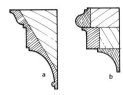

Fig. 7 Sections of cornice mouldings of the walnut period.

Fig. 8 Mid 18th century cornice mouldings. **a** Backed moulding **b** Built-up section.

While on the subject of curved mouldings it is apparent that in some cases the moulding was cut with carving tools since the sections vary appreciably in different parts of the curve, something that would not happen if the scratch-stock were used. This usually occurs when the moulding is also carved with a decorative pattern and it may be assumed that the cabinet-maker, having sawn and trimmed the shape, handed it on to the carver to cut the profile as well as the pattern. Why this should have been done is not clear, for it would have been quicker as well as more accurate to use the scratch-stock, leaving the carver to cut the pattern only.

One other point in connection with shaped mouldings was that in some cases it was possible to turn them on the lathe. Some applied mouldings in the second half of the 17th century were circular arcs and were turned. The same was true of some of the domed hoods of clock cases and some bookcases and writing cabinets during the walnut period, providing they were a circular shape. When a circular moulding had to join up with a straight part the mitre had to be curved as otherwise the members would not meet properly. It was not every craftsman who realized this, however, and they got over the difficulty by making the section slightly different in the straight part as compared with the curved. This, however, was only on large mouldings such as cornices. In small ones the discrepancy would not show.

It has already been mentioned in Chapter 4 that in the walnut period mouldings were invariably cross-grained. Some of the ways of accomplishing this around drawer fronts are given on page 158. On large cornice mouldings a similar idea was followed, the flat surfaces or large curves with fairly flat sections were veneered and the rest built up with cross-grained walnut, usually on a softwood groundwork as in Fig. 7. The thickness of the walnut was kept down to the bare minimum because it would then give appreciably in the event of shrinkage without opening unduly at the joints. When a fairly thick walnut facing was unavoidable it was usually left for as long as possible after glueing down for all shrinkage to take place. A saw was then run down any open joints and pieces of veneer glued in.

From the time when mahogany (and later satinwood) began to super-

196

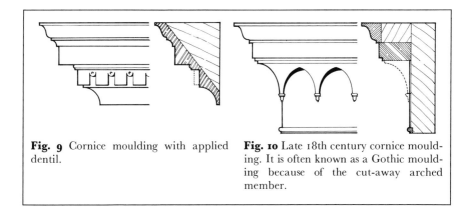

Fig. 9 Cornice moulding with applied dentil.

Fig. 10 Late 18th century cornice moulding. It is often known as a Gothic moulding because of the cut-away arched member.

sede walnut, cornice mouldings were invariably straight-grained and were usually made, either with a backing of softwood as at (a), Fig. 8, or were built up of several pieces as at (b). The method of making the former as described by Sheraton has already been given in Fig. 2. The built-up method was usually associated with larger mouldings, and had an advantage in that narrower stuff could be used up. Sometimes cornice mouldings were carved with the egg-and-tongue detail or acanthus leafage but a commoner method of enriching mouldings was that of the applied fret, usually of dentil form as in Fig. 9.

Another form used towards the end of the 18th century was the so-called Gothic moulding, in which the lower hollow member was worked separately and was fretted out in the form of a series of Gothic arches. These usually terminated at the bottom in small half-turnings, sometimes in ivory. The idea is shown in Fig. 10. As a matter of interest Shearer in his *Cabinet-maker's Book of Prices* mentions that the payment to the cabinet-maker for this was 6d extra per foot. Considering that he had to fret out the hollow moulding, clean it up, and glue it down, his reward was not exactly generous.

The reader may care to pause for a moment to consider the application of this apparently simple detail; also the dentil fret in Fig. 9. Clearly it would be difficult or impossible to polish cleanly into the interstices of the applied detail. The plan followed, therefore, was to polish first and apply the detail afterwards. But glue will not hold over polish, oil, wax, or varnish. The only way was to hold the detail in position, mark around the edges and scrape away the polish where the glue had to grip.

This, however, was not the whole problem. Obviously squeezed-out glue had to be avoided at the edges because it could not be removed cleanly afterwards and was best avoided in any case. Consider what this meant. The glue was Scotch (animal) glue which necessitated its being used hot and the work done speedily so that chilling was avoided. Therefore it could not be brushed on to the scraped away parts of the background because it could not be done quickly enough over the intricate shape, and in any case there would be danger of too much being used so that it squeezed out at the edges. For the same reasons the back of the detail could

197

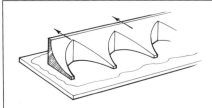

Fig. 11 How the applied arched member was glued.

not have the glue brushed on since an excess at the edges would be almost inevitable.

The method then was to warm a long, flat strip of metal and brush a coat of glue over it. The fretted detail was placed on it and drawn backwards as shown by the arrows in Fig. 11. This ensured an even coat at the back and the direction of the movement avoided any accumulation of glue at the edges. The top surface could be glued normally as it had no intricate detail or it again could be placed on the glued metal plate.

Carved mouldings The carving of mouldings has always been a common practice in all periods of furniture, and the examples given in Fig. 12 shows some of the details used. The conventional leaf forms and other details were usually the result of direct tool cuts, the carver selecting gouges of suitable shape and making cuts which enabled clean chips to be removed in two and sometimes three cuts only. This carving was done by the carver as distinct from the cabinet-maker, and the only point the latter had to watch was that the section had to allow for all carved detail. Thus in Fig. 13, although the section is really that of a cyma recta moulding as shown by the dotted line, the actual section required is that of the full line because the turned-over tip of the leaf projects forward.

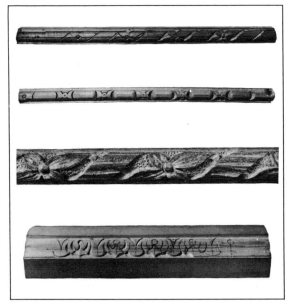

Fig. 12 Examples of carved mouldings, mid 18th century and later.

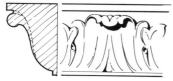

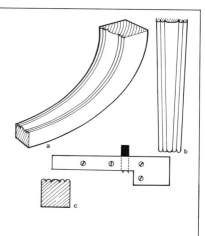

Fig. 13 Moulding carved with leafwork. Sufficient wood to enable the turn-over of the leaf tips to be carved has to be left.

Fig. 14 Moulding around a curved and tapered leg.
a The completed leg showing the two beads at each edge and the centre round.
b Plan view **c** The scratch-stock as used to work the inner beads.

The moulding of tapered members had its own special problems. It is a detail that often occurred in chair legs and similar parts. Quite often, too, the tapered moulding had to be worked around a curve as, for instance, around tripod table legs, the arms of chairs, etc. Clearly the scratch-stock was needed but, equally clearly, the cutter could not extend the full width of the moulding because the section changed progressively along the length. A typical example is given in Fig. 14. The leg is wider at the top than at the bottom and the moulding appears to become progressively wider towards the top. If it is carefully examined, however, it will be found that the beads at the edges are usually the same width throughout, all variation taking place in the centre member. This enabled the scratch-stock to be used with the same cutter from each side. This would clearly leave the centre member unfinished at one end, but the use of a narrow scraper followed by glasspaper produced a perfectly smooth member which tapered progressively. This method of confining the taper to the centre member was not invariable but it was common practice. Fig. 15 shows a curved and tapered chair back member being moulded with the scratch-stock.

The working of narrow mouldings for barred doors is dealt with in Chapter 13.

Fig. 15 Working a moulding with the scratch-stock on the face of a chair back.

Chapter 16

Veneering

Veneering is an ancient craft but it was not used in England until the second half of the 17th century, when it was introduced from Europe. It is still sometimes regarded as a cheap process in which inferior timber is concealed behind a thin sheet of good-quality wood (and it has to be admitted that this is sometimes the case). But, properly done, it is anything but a cheap process. Furthermore it is the only way in which certain decorative effects can be produced. These latter include quartered and other decorative panels, cross-banding, marquetry, etc. As an example consider the sideboard in Fig. 1. Clearly the drawer fronts and rails are veneered. If they were made of solid curl mahogany they would have no strength, and in any case would be liable to distort badly. There are snags in it for the uninitiated, however – snags which sometimes only come to light with the passing of time. In fact, it may be said that one of the tests of successful veneering is what the job looks like after about ten years, not what it appears to be when first completed.

British craftsmen probably saw the first veneered work on items imported from Holland, but the return of Charles II from the continent no doubt resulted in the immigration of workers already familiar with the craft; and later the same thing was repeated with the coming of William and Mary. The first attempts at veneering by furniture-makers in England were not always successful. A point not realized was that any blemishes in the groundwork was liable eventually to show through to the surface of the veneer. Thus any movement at joints, etc. resulted in stress marks in the veneer; and when such parts as drawers had their sides through-dovetailed to the fronts (see page 156), the slightest movement in the joints due to racking was transferred to the veneer. Many of these early pieces are witness to this defect in showing splits and stress marks in the veneer.

For the benefit of non-technical readers perhaps it is as well to explain what the craft consists of. Veneer is a thin sheet of wood, usually chosen for the quality of its grain. Until the second half of the 19th century it was always cut with the saw. Previous to the early years of that century hand sawing was the only method, and for large sheets of veneer either a frame saw must have been used or some form of two-man saw. An illustration in

Fig. 1 A semi-circular sideboard with drawer fronts finely veneered with curl mahogany. Note also the fan marquetry beneath the centre drawer. About 1785. (J. Morland Coon Ltd., Plymouth)

L'art du menuisier ebeniste, Paris, 1774, shows two men cutting veneers with a frame saw, the log held vertically in a heavy screw vice attached to a bench. Apparently the method was to make all the cuts down to a certain distance, then raise the log to enable the cuts to be taken farther down. It is reproduced in Fig. 2.

According to D. A. Wood and T. G. Linn, however, a circular saw for cutting veneers was set up at Battersea in 1805. It is not revealed by what power it was worked, but it was probably either water power or was driven by animal or human labour. Today veneers are sliced with a huge knife

Fig. 2 How veneers were cut in the 18th century. An illustration from *L'Art du menuisier ebeniste*, Paris, 1774.

and are much thinner. They are cheaper to produce because there is no waste in saw-dust. In cutting veneers with the saw as much wood is lost in dust as is used in actual veneer. Today it is practically impossible to obtain saw-cut veneer, as many a furniture restorer regretfully knows. Many early veneers were nearly $\frac{1}{8}$ in. thick and were more in the nature of thin boards.

The groundwork on which the veneer was laid was plain-grained, sound wood. It was usually pine, though occasionally oak was used. The latter is not an ideal wood to hold glue, and when quarter-cut reveals the ray figuring which is harder than the bulk of the timber and is liable to stand proud when the rest of the timber shrinks. Consequently the form of the ray figure is liable to show through to the surface of the veneer eventually. This may not be marked when the veneer is thick, but, in any case, experience has shown that glue does not hold so well over the rays because of their hard, impervious nature and, since the rays in quarter-cut oak can be really large it is clear that it is best avoided as a groundwork for veneer.

Thick veneer could only be put down in one way. Both it and the groundwork were glued and the veneer placed in position. A flat board known as a caul slightly larger than the groundwork was thoroughly heated and cramped down over the surface, the pressure applied at the centre first, the object being to liquefy the glue and drive the surplus towards the edges and bring the veneer into close contact with the ground-work. To heat the caul a shaving blaze was used, Fig. 3, shavings being piled into a brick enclosure and set alight. The same method was used sometimes even into the present century, until it became outdated by the gas- or electrically-heated press or by a thermostatically-controlled press.

When thinner veneers became practicable the craftsman used what is known as the hammer method. The veneering hammer consisted of a stock about 5 in. long with handle at one side and a strip of brass let into the edge as in Fig. 4. The veneer, having been glued and placed in position, was lightly dampened and a heated flat iron passed over the surface to liquefy the glue. The hammer was worked over the surface zigzag fashion towards the edges, the purpose being to force the veneer into close contact with the groundwork and at the same time press out surplus glue at the edges. This hammer method was used right into the present century and is still occasionally used today for odd jobs, though in production shops it has been replaced by the press method already referred to.

When a joint was necessary in veneer, as it would be for a wide surface, and the caul method was to be used, the edges were planed true on the shooting board, held together with a strip of glued paper, and the whole put down in one operation. In the hammer method, however, such joints were made during the veneering process because the damping, application of heat, and pressing down would result in distortion, making a close joint impossible. The cabinet-maker's method was to lay one sheet of veneer and put down that adjacent to it with an overlap of about $\frac{1}{2}$ in. A straight-edge was cramped down over this overlap, and a thin, keen chisel drawn along it. The waste strip of the top overlap was then peeled away. To

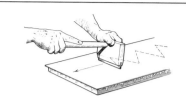

Fig. 4 How veneer is pressed down with the veneering hammer.

Fig. 3 Heating the veneering caul at a shaving blaze.

enable the lower waste to be removed, the upper veneer was raised before the glue set, revealing the overlap beneath, after which the whole was rubbed down and paper stuck over the joint to prevent it from opening as the glue dried out.

A difficulty when only one side of the groundwork had to be veneered was that it was liable to pull the groundwork hollow as the moisture dried out. This was because the dampness (partly in the glue and also in the damping of the upper surface) caused the veneer to swell. As it dried out it shrank and, since by that time the glue had exerted its grip, it pulled the panel hollow. With the exception of flush doors used in many walnut presses and writing cabinets of the walnut period, nearly all period furniture was veneered on one side only. This did not matter a great deal for carcase work and for drawer fronts which were largely held flat by other structural parts, but it will often be found that table tops have pulled hollow, and this can be disastrous on pivoted leaves which have no means of stiffening.

The much more reliable method used today in the best work is to veneer both sides. The flush doors already referred to have usually remained flat because this was done. It is doubtful, however, whether this was the original reason for veneering both sides. More likely it was because the inner sides were seen when the doors were opened. Still the lesson was there to be observed.

There are, of course, many other points to be observed in successful veneering, and the interested reader should see the text book *Practical Veneering* for the whole story.

From the above it is apparent that the veneering of a flat surface was a reasonably straightforward process; when it came to shapes it was rather more complicated. Firstly, the groundwork had to be worked to the

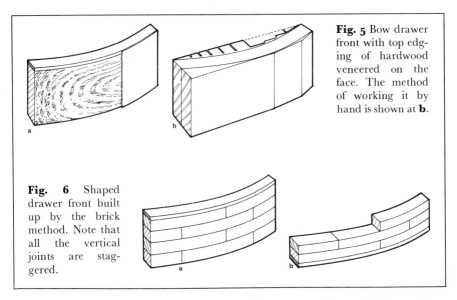

Fig. 5 Bow drawer front with top edging of hardwood veneered on the face. The method of working it by hand is shown at **b**.

Fig. 6 Shaped drawer front built up by the brick method. Note that all the vertical joints are staggered.

required contour, and the old-time craftsman set about this in various ways. Sometimes he cut the whole thing out of a solid piece of wood, a somewhat wasteful method, cutting into a lot of timber and involving a great deal of labour. Furthermore it had a drawback in that it exposed a lot of end grain, at any rate in an acute curve (it will be recalled from Chapter 9 that end grain does not hold glue well).

An example is given at (a), Fig. 5, which shows a drawer front, such as might be used in a bow-front chest-of-drawers, cut from a solid piece and partly veneered. When there was to be a cocked bead around the edges the top edge of the groundwork, which was usually of pine, was hidden. In the absence of this the usual plan was to glue a strip of mahogany (for a mahogany job) along the top edge before finally working to shape.

Some idea of the work involved in such a drawer front cut from a solid piece can be gained from (b), Fig. 5. Obviously no machine bandsaw was available in the 18th century when such chests were largely made, and it would not be possible to use the chair-maker's betty saw (see page 245)

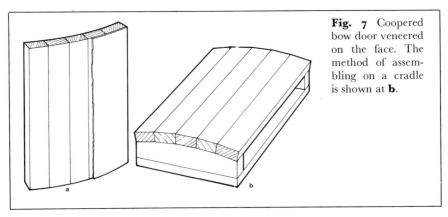

Fig. 7 Coopered bow door veneered on the face. The method of assembling on a cradle is shown at **b**.

for so deep a cut (the front might be 9-10 in. wide). The only method was to waste it away as at (b). The shape was marked out on both edges and a series of saw cuts made across the grain at the concave side. Much of the waste could then be chopped away with chisel and mallet in the direction of the grain, and the shape finally finished with a plane having its sole rounded in its length (the compass plane). The front or convex side could be partly sawn in facets as shown, reduced with the plane, and finished with rasp or file.

It was no doubt partly to avoid such laborious work and at the same time present a more suitable glueing surface that the 'brick' method was evolved, Fig. 6, details of which are given in Chapter 12, page 165. Both bow and serpentine shapes could be formed in this way.

A third method generally used for a tall item such as a bow-front door was that of coopering as in Fig. 7. Here the shape was formed by a series of strips glued together, the joints at an angle to enable the required curvature to be formed. They were assembled on a 'cradle' as at (b), shaped to the required curve, and finally veneered. The inside was hollowed to a concentric curve but was frequently given only the most elementary planing. I have an 18th century bow-front corner cupboard, the doors veneered at the outside with curl mahogany (see Fig. 5, page 226). The coopered groundwork is of oak, and the inside shows relatively coarse plane marks which, although smooth, are quite pronounced.

A much more complicated shape to make was that with compound

Fig. 8 Marquetry commode, attributed to Thomas Chippendale. Collection of Lord St. Oswald at Nostell Priory. (Faber and Faber Ltd.)

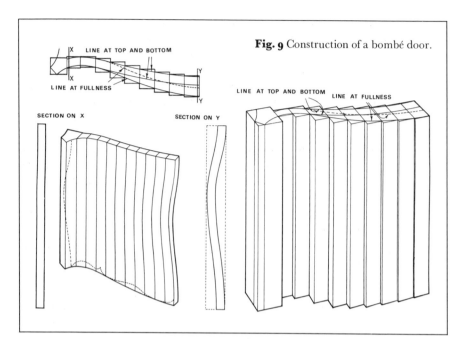

Fig. 9 Construction of a bombé door.

curvature such as is found in a bombé commode such as that in Fig. 8. It is impossible in this limited space to give in full the method adopted but, briefly, the doors (they were always made in pairs) were coopered, the pieces being of a thickness suitable to their position. This was essential because it was only by levelling them down to the joints at the centre or fulness that the two doors could be made to match. At top and bottom a plan templet was used to give the shape, Fig. 9, and another of the vertical shape at the meeting edge for the same purpose. Work on both doors would proceed in corresponding stages so that the two were alike. A series of lines drawn horizontally enabled testing templets to be used in varying positions. Finally the doors were hinged to the cupboard for the final shaping to be done. Uneven waviness could be detected by passing the hand lightly across the surface, though it would not, of course, reveal inaccuracy in shape.

Clearly a single sheet of veneer could not be used because it would crease or split – it would be like trying to wrap a sheet of paper around a football. Consequently such doors always had a built-up pattern which enabled the veneer to be tailored to the contour. Even so, a certain amount of damping and pressing the veneer with hot sandbags was essential before it could be glued down. It is another example of how practical considerations dictated design. The built-up pattern certainly looked attractive but it was a practical necessity in the first place.

For the final pressing, sandbags again were used, a special tray being made with a large flat bag of sand on top, this being thumped to approximate shape and the work then pressed into it. It is also possible that a pressing mould may have been made with a plaster of Paris mixture, this

Fig. 10 Veneered vase similar to the type used on the pedestals of the late 18th century sideboard.

Fig. 11 Ribs of the vase glued together. The interior cross-pieces are temporary, their purpose being to provide a centre for turning.

Fig. 12 The veneer laid but not yet cleaned up.

being bedded on a strong tray.

Another good example of veneering over shapes of compound curvature is that of a pair of vases such as were used on some sideboards towards the end of the 18th century. As the purpose of the vases was either to hold cutlery or a container for water they had to be hollow (though there was also a good practical reason for making them hollow apart from this). An example of such a vase is given in Fig. 10. I myself made it by the traditional method followed by cabinet-makers of the 18th century. Here again the veneer was always made up of small separate pieces arranged in decorative pattern – it had to be to enable the veneer to be tailored to shape.

The main body was built up of a series of ribs cut to shape and tapered so that all joints radiated as in Fig. 11. These joints incidentally were invaluable in the later veneering process in that they were a guide for the veneer joints. After glueing the ribs together the whole was turned to the shape, and roughened with coarse glasspaper to provide a good glueing surface. A templet in thin metal of the shape of the pieces of veneer was prepared and the strips of veneer cut out, the upper surfaces of the latter having a piece of paper glued over it to strengthen it. A certain amount of trimming to shape was inevitable, and it was here that the joint lines of the ribs were useful in that they acted as a guide. The pieces of veneer were put down with a specially shaped caul, this being heated and cramped down at each end. Fig. 12 shows the vase with the veneer strips laid but before cleaning up. The latter was done with the scraper followed by glasspaper in progressively finer grades.

Fig. 13 Late 18th century side table and pedestals with carved urns.

Chapter 17

Inlay and marquetry

Inlay

The inlaying of wood to form a decorative pattern is a very ancient craft. The Egyptians used it widely, but it does not appear to have been used in England until the second half of the 16th century and, even then, it is a much rarer means of decoration than carving. This may have been because of the early practice of painting some woodwork in bright colours, and inlay would obviously have been useless for this. Perhaps the most famous example of early inlay is that in the panelling from Sizergh Castle, Westmorland and now in the Victoria and Albert Museum, Fig. 1. This is an inlay of poplar and bog oak into oak. The inlay is about $\frac{1}{8}$ in. thick and is let into corresponding recesses chopped into the panels.

The method used would have been to draw out the whole design and make tracings which would enable repeat patterns to be made. Many of the scrolls, for instance, are identical and as many as would be needed would be cut out of thin wood with a saw having a narrow blade. These thin shapes would be held down on the panel and a pointed awl drawn

Fig. 1 Inlaid panel from Sizergh Castle, Westmorland. The inlays are about $\frac{1}{8}$ in. thick and are glued into recesses chopped in the panel. (Victoria and Albert Museum)

Fig. 2 Inlaying in the solid.

around the edge as a guide for chopping the recesses. Gouges of varying curvature would be used for the shapes of the latter, and a router used to bring them to even depth. Finally the inlays would be glued in and the surface planed level after the whole had set. Fig. 2 explains the idea.

Naturally the process had its restrictions or limitations. The inlaying of really fine intricate curved shapes would not be practicable, but these restrictions in themselves imparted an individual character to the work. It is true that long thin details could be bent to shape but elaborate scrolls with involved or acute shapes would not be possible. Thus the essential nature of this true inlay is its relative simplicity. This is in contrast with marquetry with which we now deal.

Marquetry

This began in England in about 1670 and continued until the early part of the 18th century. It was indeed a form of inlay but it was carried out in veneer and, since the entire process was done with a fine saw (no chopping out, gouging, or chiselling being needed), there was much greater scope for fine and elaborate designs. The truth of this is obvious from a comparison of Fig. 1, which is inlay in the solid, with Fig. 3, which is marquetry. There were, however, two distinct methods of cutting the latter, although in both cases the various shapes were cut in veneer and the parts interchanged.

All marquetry starts off as a 'pricking'. The design being drawn out on a sheet of paper, the outline is pricked at close intervals with a series of fine holes made with a needle point. This is the master pattern and any number of repeats can be made by placing it over other sheets of paper and dusting fine bitumen powder over it. When the master is raised the pattern is reproduced on the paper beneath in a series of fine dots. Left as it is the powder would dust off rapidly, but by heating it the bitumen melts and becomes permanent. As many copies are made as there are woods in the design, and one is stuck to the veneer to form the background, and the others cut up and stuck to the other woods, the grain in the required direction.

Since it would be awkward or impossible to handle a single sheet of veneer in this way, the practice was to cut them in packets of four or six thicknesses with a waste piece of common veneer beneath to take the rag

Fig. 3 Cabinet decorated with marquetry. Late 17th century. It is apparent that the craft of marquetry cutting gives much greater scope for elaborate effects than would be possible when inlay is in the solid. (Victoria and Albert Museum)

of the saw. It follows then that for every piece of marquetry there must have been three or five others of identical pattern. Of course, there were often corresponding marquetry veneers used in the same job, but it is extremely likely that some were also used in other pieces of furniture – quite possibly entirely different items. Some pieces may have been destroyed or lost but it is an interesting thought that for most pieces of marquetry furniture there are (or were) other items of the same pattern

Fig. 4 Table top veneered with marquetry. William and Mary period. (M. Harris and Sons, London)

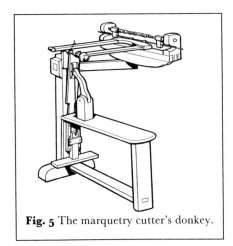

Fig. 5 The marquetry cutter's donkey.

Fig. 6 Diagram showing how two decorative patterns are produced by interchanging cut-out parts. One is the counter of the other.

marquetry cut at the same time by the same craftsman. In the table in Fig. 4, although the two sides are balanced, and apparently match, there is a difference in detail. Consequently it could not have been made by cutting two halves simultaneously, reversing one and jointing together. It is quite likely, however, that several patterns were cut in one pack, and used for other tables.

In early marquetry various coloured woods and ivory were used and, the patterns having been pasted to the background and the various packs of wood, the outline was sawn round on a device known as the marquetry cutter's donkey. This, as shown in Fig. 5, had a sort of framesaw with superfine blade running in guides. The veneer pack was held vertically in a pair of chops controlled by a pedal and the craftsman twisted the work round in whatever position was required for the direction of cut. He sat astride the seat and controlled the chops with a pedal. Any man doing a particular job over a number of years develops considerable skill, and this is certainly true of marquetry cutting, for although the parts were cut separately, they made a perfect fit, one within the other. As the parts were cut they were assembled on a flat tray and paper glued over the whole to hold them together.

Eventually the craftsman learnt another trick which could be used when only two woods were required, say walnut and sycamore. By holding together both groundwork and pattern in a single pack, both could be cut together in a single operation. This not only saved considerable time but also made a perfect fit positive, because, even if the saw strayed from the line, both groundwork and inlay would have the same defect. In practice at least four and sometimes six thicknesses were cut at a time because of the difficulty of handling less.

The method also had another result in that beside the original it produced a counter-pattern. Perhaps this is best exemplified by taking two sheets of paper, one white, the other brown, placing them one above the other and cutting a pattern, say a star, through both simultaneously. If the parts are interchanged there will be a white star on a brown back-

Fig. 7 Marquetry detail and signature from the bureau-bookcase shown on page 10. (Victoria and Albert Museum)

ground and also a brown star on a white background (see Fig. 6).

So with marquetry but, as the veneers had to be in packs of four or six veneers, there would be two (or three) original designs and two or three counter-patterns. Sometimes pairs or more could be used on the same job but the remainder and the counter-patterns would go to other entirely separate pieces of furniture. Very occasionally the original and the counter are discovered and any discrepancy found in the one is necessarily repeated in the other. The type of marquetry known as seaweed was cut in this way. It consists of finely scrolled work, light on dark or vice versa. An example of this fine work appears on the inner door of the bureau-bookcase shown on page 10. Enlarged detail from the same cabinet is shown in Fig. 7. If the letters are closely examined it will be seen that the saw has been taken continuously from one to the other. Compared with the fine marquetry in the rest of the cabinet these letters are crude, and we suspect that Samuel, having employed a professional marquetry cutter for the bulk of the work, cut in his own signature himself.

A point to realize is that in this single-cutting marquetry a balanced design was usual, the reason being that it was easy to design it in, say, four quarters so that only one quarter had to be cut in a pack of four and fit the four together to form a single whole. This would have the advantage of giving it an enhanced value since no other item would be exactly like it, except for a counter of the pattern which would certainly not be thrown away but would be used on another job, possibly on entirely different pieces of furniture. It is interesting in these balanced designs to trace any unevenness in the cutting in corresponding parts of the design.

The marquetry sheet would be put down on the groundwork with a hot caul by the method described in Chapter 16. It had to be accurately centred and the method was to draw centre lines on both marquetry and groundwork, make them coincide and drive in a couple of fine pins to prevent movement.

Some marquetry was shaded and this was done by dipping one end of the veneer into hot sand so that it became slightly scorched. Such shading was permanent and could be controlled by the time it was immersed and by the extent of veneer covered by the sand.

Parquetry

One other form of decorative veneer work remains to be mentioned, that of parquetry. It consists of a series of repeat geometrical patterns assembled to form a whole as in Fig. 8. The whole is in veneer and the method of forming the pattern is illustrated at a, b, c, and d. Strips of veneer with the grain running in the required direction were cut out (b) and (c) and were assembled side by side as at (d). Cuts were made across the whole at an angle as at (d). The separate strips thus formed were slid one against the other (e) to the extent of one diamond, thus forming the pattern at (a). Paper was stuck over the face and the veneer laid as a whole with a caul.

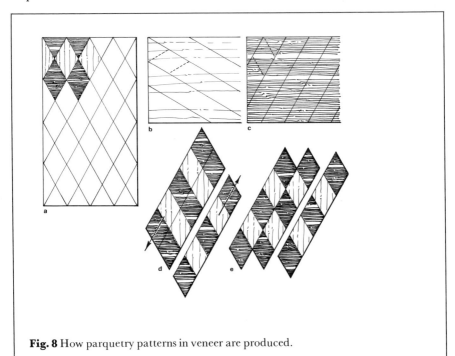

Fig. 8 How parquetry patterns in veneer are produced.

Strings and bandings

In a class by itself was the inlaying of what were known as strings and bandings. The former were simple lines or strips of inlay, either light or dark, to enable them to stand in contrast with the background into which they were inlaid. Bandings were decorative patterns prepared in long and relatively narrow strips, and both were recessed into the groundwork and glued. A group of such bandings is shown in Fig. 9.

To an extent inlays of this kind were used towards the end of the 16th century but it was not until the second half of the 17th century that they were produced in any quantity, and by then their manufacture had

Fig. 9 Group of inlay bandings.

suddenly become an independent trade, separate from both that of cabinet-making and marquetry cutting (though in some special cases the marquetry cutter had to make them).

Although these bandings were used in veneer thickness only, they were made up in quite thick blocks of solid wood and were sawn into veneer thickness. This not only enabled the bandings to be made in quantity, but simplified the process in that it was easy to handle solid wood rather than small pieces of veneer. Fig. 10 shows two blocks assembled together with a slice cut from each ready for use. The method of making bandings is shown in Figs. 11 and 12. The former is a simple cross-banding with a line at each side and it will be seen that blocks of wood with the grain running crosswise are glued together side by side, levelled and veneered at both sides. By slicing the assembly at the edge a cross-grained banding with an

Fig. 10 Inlay bandings showing the blocks and bandings sawn from them.

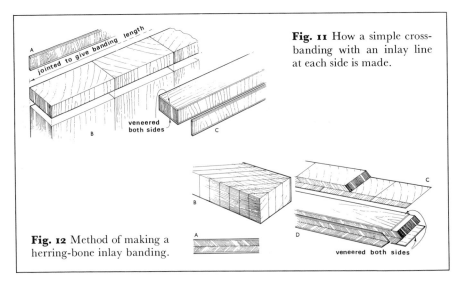

Fig. 11 How a simple cross-banding with an inlay line at each side is made.

Fig. 12 Method of making a herring-bone inlay banding.

inlaid line at each side is formed. A similar process is followed in the herring-bone banding shown in Fig. 12.

In the early periods it is possible that the cabinet-maker may have made up his bandings, especially the simpler kind, particularly in provincial and country districts. By the fourth quarter of the 18th century, however, the demand for inlays had developed so markedly that it is a reasonable assumption that there were men who made nothing but bandings. The invention that did more than anything to simplify and cheapen the production of bandings was the circular saw, however. Its advantage was

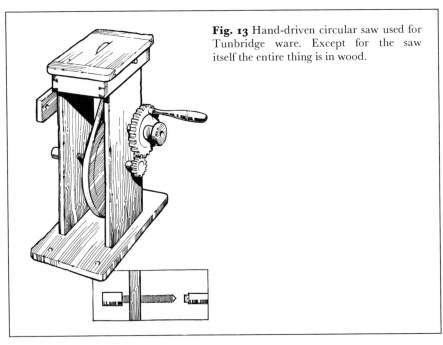

Fig. 13 Hand-driven circular saw used for Tunbridge ware. Except for the saw itself the entire thing is in wood.

that it would cut wood in parallel lengths exactly to size, making it invaluable in both the cutting up of narrow strips and in the final slicing of the built-up blocks into bandings.

There appears to be no evidence as to when a circular saw was first used for the purpose. According to P. d'A. Jones and E. N. Simons the first Englishman to master the difficulties of making the circular saw into a workshop tool was a Southampton carpenter, William Taylor, 1734–1803, although a patent for a circular saw was taken out by Samuel Miller in 1777. Whether such a saw was used for making bandings as early as this is doubtful, but the principle of the saw was certainly known by the turn of the century, and its development in the 19th century enabled the most elaborate bandings to be produced. In the museum at Tunbridge Wells is a delightful hand-powered saw that was used originally by the makers of Tunbridge ware to cut up the small pieces required by that industry (see Fig. 13). Except for the saw plate itself the machine is almost entirely of wood, including the cog wheels. It is quite likely that some such saw was used quite early in the century for the making of bandings.

Chapter 18

The finish of old furniture

It is an interesting speculation as to what old furniture looked like when it was new. Today we may see it with the mellowness of colour that time has wrought, plus the patina acquired with years of patient polishing, sometimes with the dirt of generations, the marking and damage inevitable in long service, and frequently with the attention of the french polisher in Victorian and later times. Originally it had none of these things, and was little different from a new piece emerging from a workshop today, except that it had whatever finish was in vogue at that time. It is possible that many would be disappointed if they could see it in its original state, although the design and construction, of course, would be unaltered.

Most oak furniture of the late 16th and 17th centuries appears to have been finished either with varnish or solely with wax. Some of it may have been painted originally but for the greater part it shows the natural grain of the wood. It is true, of course, that a piece may have had face-lifts with paint or lacquer at some later period in its history. There are indeed some rather dreadful examples of items which have been given a coat of varnish-stain in a misguided attempt to brighten them up, leaving a sort of dirty treacle finish which obliterates the grain and figure of the oak.

Some varnishes tend to darken with age; others become bleached; but, assuming that it was transparent originally, it does not conceal the grain, and in any case the burnishing with wax over the years has worn the varnish thin. Frequently there are little signs of varnish today, though it may have been used in the first place. Wax at all times has been the chief means of keeping furniture in condition, and its continued use over the years is largely responsible for the fine patina which is characteristic of old pieces, even though the original finish may have been varnish. The latter had one great advantage, however, it formed a film over the wood which kept out dirt. When first applied it tends to have a somewhat glittery appearance but this becomes softened with the repeated burnishing with wax.

With the increasing use of walnut in the second half of the 17th century, varnish became the chief form of finish and it appears that various types were used. In a book published in 1688, *A Treatise of Japanning, Varnishing and Guilding*, by Stalker and Parker, the authors recommend rubbing the surface of the wood with Dutch-rushes to smooth it and using 'seed-lacc' varnish in several coats, the surface being rubbed with 'Tripolee' powder to give a burnish. 'Shell-lacc' varnish is also mentioned, though in rather disparaging terms. White varnish is another type, this including 'Gum Sandrick', 'Gum Mastick', 'Venice Turpentine', 'Gum-Capal', 'Gum-Elemni', 'Gum-Benzoin', 'Gum Animae' and 'White Rosine' in its composition. Over the years such varnish has become glass-hard, and, with the constant polishing with wax for many generations, has developed a beautiful patina.

In the 18th century, varnish was still used right into the mahogany period, but was preceded by wiping over with linseed oil which brought out the beauty of the figuring of the wood and deepened its tone. In some cases, too, the oil was given a warm tint by immersing strands of bruised alkanet root in it. It is likely that the use or omission of this root is the cause of the differing shades of mahogany found in old pieces, especially in the late 18th century when the lighter Honduras mahogany rather than Cuban was used increasingly. Curiously enough Sheraton makes no mention of varnish in his *Cabinet Dictionary* but recommends the use of fine brickdust with oil rubbed on with cork. It is doubtful, however, whether this was a universal procedure. Probably varnish was still widely used.

The 19th century brought a considerable change of method due to the introduction of french polishing, a finish based on shellac. A skilled man could produce a splendid polish which could range from a high lustre to a dull shine. It owed its refined and smooth effect largely to the fact that it was applied with a rubber rather than a brush, the sheen being built up by the friction of the rubber over the semi-hard surface of preceding coats. In the best work, polish alone was used, though later on the procedure was speeded up, and therefore cheapened, by the use of a grain-filler such as plaster-of-Paris.

One disadvantage french polishing had, however, was that it was not resistant to heat marking. Items such as table tops were therefore liable to be marked badly and it seems likely that, whereas the framework of a table might be french polished, the top itself was oil-polished.

During the Victorian period polishers developed a high degree of skill as is clear from pieces which have come down to us. It is extraordinary how the rubber could be worked so cleanly and effectively into awkward corners. It is true that pieces were so made that they could be taken apart wherever practicable; panels were fitted in rebates rather than grooves, mouldings were polished first then applied and so on; but even so some awkward places to impede the movement of the rubber were inevitable.

One effect that french polishing has had is that it has frequently been used, either to brighten up an old piece, or in its repair or restoration. Its vogue lasted from the early years of the 19th century until relatively modern times – about one hundred and fifty years. In that time many old pieces must have come up for repolishing, so that many 18th century items have been subsequently french polished. Assuming that a chest-of-drawers was made in 1760, by 1860 it would have had a hundred years of use and by the standard of the time was merely old-fashioned. In an attempt to 'modernise' it the brass handles would be replaced by the then fashionable turned wood knobs, turned feet fitted in place of bracket feet, and the whole thing brightened up by being french polished. There must be hundreds of chests which have suffered this 'improvement'. Yet today the french polish of 1860 has had another hundred years of use and has become almost antique in itself. And, indeed, it is extremely difficult to detect from 'original' finish.

More reprehensible has been the fashion popular early in the present century of scraping off old polish merely because it is slightly scratched or has other blemishes. This, however, is dealt with more fully in Chapter 19.

Chapter 19

Antiques: some of the snags

We now come to some of the snags connected with the collecting of antique furniture. Feeding largely on the attraction that this latter has for many people comes the trade of the manufacturer of 'antiques'. It is all largely a question of supply and demand. So long as people are prepared to pay good money for a thing so will people be found to provide it, even though it means straining the conception of what an antique really is.

Apart from age, period furniture may be divided into various groups.

The antique, clearly genuine, in untouched condition This is an extremely rare type. Usually such a piece is in a country mansion and has never been out of it. It has been dusted and polished for years and has seldom had to face the hurly-burly of everyday use such as would occur in a piece in a small dwelling house or farmhouse where rough treatment by children or unruly adults would result in maltreatment. Apart from scarcity, or maybe because of it, such pieces are extremely high priced. An example is that in Fig. 1.

Sometimes, however, more modest items are found in excellent condition owing to the lucky chance of their always having been in a quiet household; or possibly because at one period such a piece had merely become old-fashioned and had been consigned to the garret, its place being taken by what was then a more up-to-date replacement. Such pieces are rare.

The average piece In this class is furniture which shows wear and has suffered breakages which may or may not have been repaired. Wear takes place mostly in moving parts such as drawers, and the sides of these may have so worn away that the bottoms may be scraping at the back with corresponding friction grooves worn in the runners. The extension bearers of tables may be similarly worn. Such wear has to be accepted as inevitable. Drawers packed with heavy items may have been opened and closed for a hundred years or more, and it is no reflection on either the maker or the timber that the sides have worn away.

Fig. 1 Mahogany library table supplied by Thomas Chippendale, 1767. Collection of Lord St. Oswald at Nostell Priory. (Faber and Faber Ltd.)

Frequently the piece has been repaired, this involving the fitting of packing pieces to make good the wear, and possibly the repair or replacement of runners. In later pieces of the 18th century these packing pieces beneath the drawer sides can often be seen, but in some chests of the walnut period drawers were occasionally made with the bottoms extending to the extreme width of the drawer and with slips of wood glued on beneath (see Chapter 12). Since, however, items of this age must have had at least two hundred and fifty years of use, it is more than likely that the slips have been replaced at least once, perhaps twice. This does not detract from the value because wear is inevitable.

Another form of wear is not caused by moving parts, but is due to constant handling and daily use. Thus sharp edges may be rounded, table and chair stretchers may be worn away by people having for years rested their feet on them, and table and other tops inevitably become scratched, bruised, or marked by the constant use to which they have been subjected. Unless really bad such blemishes do not militate against a piece. No item can hope to escape such marking when it has been in constant use for a long time, and it may be said to be rather like the wound of a soldier; nobody wants the wound, least of all the soldier, but there is obviously nothing about it to make him held in less esteem.

Here, however, we come across a difficulty. In my early days in the workshop there was a craze for stripping off the polish of any surface which had become scratched or marked. It was a most deplorable practice. The patina and colour acquired by a hundred years or more of daily friction polishing with wax and exposure to light was lost in an hour or so, and all for the sake of removing a few scratches. There is no special value in old wood as such. To scrape off the finish meant that the ordinary colour of the wood was exposed and its friction-polished surface lost, so that it was no different from any other piece of wood new or old. From the point of view of appearance one might just as well have had a reproduction. Furthermore the surface was then french polished, a finish it would never have had originally, at any rate in the 18th century.

Finding a table with top practically unmarked may easily mean that it has been scraped down and repolished. It will have lost the patina which only years can give and will be the poorer to that extent, but it may still be an old piece.

Breakages come under a different heading and they may be anything from the trivial to the really serious. In the former group may be included missing oddments of mouldings such as cocked beads around drawers, bruised corners, failure in joints in drawer bottoms, gaps in inlay, small bubbles in veneers, etc. All these can be made good with no depreciation of the piece. Much more serious are structural failures, especially those which have not been repaired straightaway. They can be very expensive to put right. The neglect of a breakage frequently throws extra strain on other parts and may start a train of successive failures. This is especially true of such things as chairs which have to withstand considerable racking strain. Indeed chairs in particular have been liable to suffer because so many people are not content merely to sit on them. They tilt the chair backwards, inflicting an intolerable strain on it. Other folk use them for party games, etc. Little wonder then that so many chairs have become loose at the joints or have broken legs or stretchers. Such items call for careful examination because, unless a chair is going into a museum, it has presumably to face another period of active use, and it may involve an

Fig. 2 Bow-front chest-of-drawers of about 1790. Wear in drawer sides and runners and minor damage to veneer and cocked beads is inevitable in a piece which has come in for everyday use for over one hundred and fifty years. (F. G. and C. Collins, Wheathampstead, Herts.)

expensive repair. In a really bad case it may be that the replacement of broken parts is the only answer.

In any old piece of furniture it is always possible, not to say likely, that it has at some time been repaired, and when this has been skilfully done it does not detract from it, unless the breakage has left an incurable weakness or given an unsightly blemish which cannot be corrected. In fact in some old items of unsound construction failure is almost bound to have occurred owing to movement in the wood caused by shrinkage or swelling (see Fig. 2, Chapter 1). Thus repairs have been inevitable and have to be accepted, though such pieces never have the value of really soundly-made items.

Some failures in furniture are extremely difficult to put right, and in some cases it may be that a piece is beyond repair economically. For instance, an item originally veneered with marquetry, with the latter badly broken, lifted in parts, and with many missing portions may cost so much to put right that the repair cost would be greater than the value. I have seen an 18th century bow-front sideboard, undoubtedly a genuine old piece, which had had such bad treatment that it came under the heading of a breaker. Of its six tapered legs three had broken off short in a position where the insertion of a dowel or other means of strengthening would be impossible as it would cut through other joints. At some time it had been dropped, presumably from a quite considerable height for the whole had been strained resulting in loose joints beneath broken and lifted veneer and marquetry.

In another case a piece had been left in the damp so that practically all the veneer had stripped away and most of the structural joints had failed. Unless one is prepared to make the repair a labour of love, it is better to leave such a piece alone. It is too much of a liability.

Items of doubtful ancestry These include pieces which have not come into existence happily. They still appear to carry the birth pangs with them. Usually they are not outright fakes from beginning to end but have some part which is old, the rest being added unto it. Perhaps a dealer has come across a pair of doors, maybe with traceried mouldings, and has had a carcase made to take them and possibly fitted a stand beneath. When skilfully done true to style the result can be successful as a piece of furniture but, although the doors may be genuine 18th century, it cannot be pretended that the whole represents a genuine 18th century bookcase or whatever it purports to be. As a rule such items stand out for what they are, especially when the additions are out of character with the rest.

Or take the case of Fig. 3 which shows all that is left of an early 19th century chair. If the missing parts are all replaced (the new turned and carved mid-back rail is shown on the seat) could it be claimed as a genuine piece? It is presumably a border-line case. All the new parts would be copies of the old and would be correct in style, and quite probably the intention would not be to deceive but rather to rescue something which is

Fig. 3 All that is left of an early 19th century chair. When the missing parts are replaced there will be almost as much new wood as old.

Fig. 4 Chair of about 1790 with new top rail. This can be contrasted with **Fig. 3**. Here the only replacement is the top rail and top corner of the splat.

practically a breaker. Quite likely it is a wreck which has reached the repairer's workshop from a customer who wishes it to be repaired for sentimental reasons. In a few years time it may be sold, possibly with the rest of a set of sound chairs, and, assuming the correct wood to have been used, it would be difficult to detect as being practically half-new.

Or take another case, that in Fig. 4. Here the only new part is the top back rail which presumably replaces one which was too badly smashed to be repaired or has been lost. Here is a perfectly legitimate repair. The chair would be useless without it and probably the new member would never be obvious. At what point a thing ceases to be a justifiable replacement and becomes a fake would call for the judgement of Solomon. If only the back rail of the chair in Fig. 4 had been old and the rest new it would be straining credulity to the limit to claim it as an authentic chair. Still, no cabinet-maker would ever do this; it would not be sound financially – and in the last resort the dealer-cabinet-maker is in business to earn a living – as indeed are most of us.

Mixed marriages In this class we include marriages and, oddly enough, also divorces. Maybe someone had a cabinet of some sort and by a remarkable chance found that it fitted on a stand he had or possibly on a table, so that he had only to remove the top or possibly cut it back in

Fig. 5 (left) 18th century corner cupboard on new stand. The cupboard is of curl mahogany veneered on oak. The stand was added early in the present century.

Fig. 6 Mahogany bureau with added bookcase. The two items have no connection one with the other. The bookcase happens to be the right width, but is obviously too deep.

depth to make a good fit. Both may be authentic pieces – they may have been made within a decade of each other – but they do not really belong. Or it may be that a man has a wall cupboard of some sort and finds it inconvenient to hang it on the wall. He therefore has a stand made for it. Fig. 5 is an example of this. The corner cupboard is of the 18th century but the stand was made no more than fifty years ago. Here is a case where it just does not matter. The purist could always remove it from the stand but it does no possible harm and it is certainly very convenient. Sometimes a bureau finds itself with a bookcase on top that appears unnaturally deep and projects a considerable way at the back as in Fig. 6. Clearly the two do not belong to each other.

Cases of divorce usually occur with such items as tallboy chests-of-drawers. These have good accommodation but they are not very practical. It is necessary to stand on a chair or pair of steps to reach things in the upper drawers. As a consequence the upper and lower carcases are separated. The lower one has a new top fitted to it and needs little more attention beyond general repairs. The upper one has to be mounted on a stand or fitted with bracket feet or turned bun feet, depending on period, and again a new top is generally needed because the original one, being above eye level, was usually only of pine and showed the dovetails at the ends. Thus two saleable chests are the result, commanding a better price than a single tallboy. This is illustrated on page 88.

Late copies Sometimes furniture is found whose apparent age is that of the 18th century but which may have been made in the last few decades. There has been a thriving trade in antiques this last seventy years and some of these pieces may have had fifty years of constant use and polishing and they do pose quite a problem, especially when made in the correct style, often with old wood. Such pieces were 'antiqued' in the first place and have since had the benefit of actual use for many years which has given a finish better than the original faker knew. These pieces are quite apart from genuine reproductions which are either copies of real antiques or made in the style of the period. Such reproductions were not intended to deceive and they were given a correct 'new' finish without any attempt at antiquing.

Chapter 20

Measured drawings

Mahogany bureau, about 1780

A label in the top drawer reads as follows:
Henry Kettle,
Successor to Mr Philip Bell
Upholder and Undertaker
at 23 in St Paul's Church Yard, London.

It appears that the premises at St Paul's Church Yard (*The White Swan*) were occupied by Coxed & Woster, cabinet-makers who flourished from 1690 to 1736. Henry Bell followed until his death in 1740, and was succeeded by Elizabeth and later Philip Bell. Henry Kettle again worked at the same address from 1777 till 1796. Several other pieces with labels bearing the name of the firm have been traced.

The bureau is in two completely separate carcases the joint between the two being concealed by a moulding (g).

All show parts are of solid mahogany, no veneer being used, with drawer sides, backs, and bottoms of oak. The grain of the drawer bottoms runs from side to side with a centre muntin (see o). They fit in rebates worked

The label in the top drawer of the bureau.

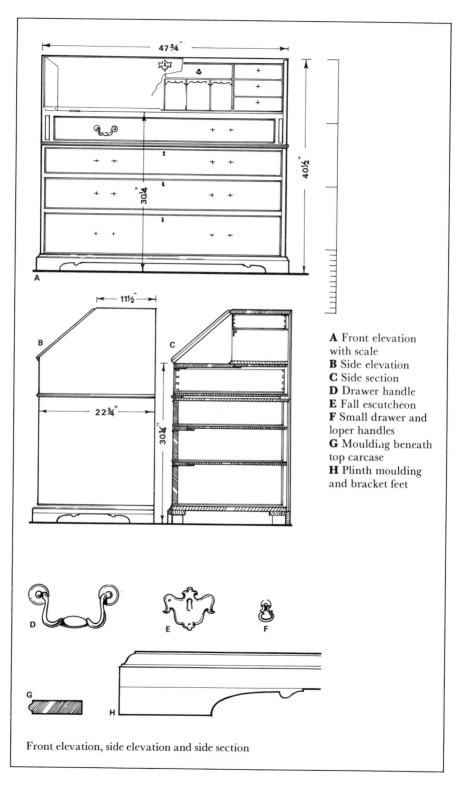

A Front elevation
with scale
B Side elevation
C Side section
D Drawer handle
E Fall escutcheon
F Small drawer and
loper handles
G Moulding beneath
top carcase
H Plinth moulding
and bracket feet

Front elevation, side elevation and side section

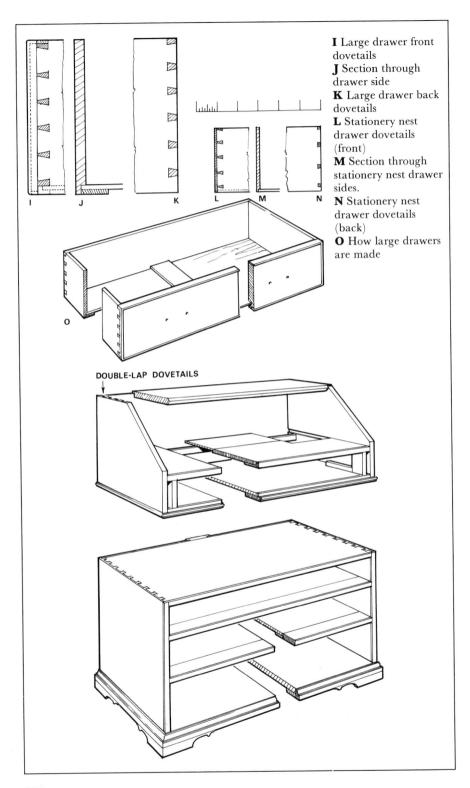

I Large drawer front dovetails
J Section through drawer side
K Large drawer back dovetails
L Stationery nest drawer dovetails (front)
M Section through stationery nest drawer sides.
N Stationery nest drawer dovetails (back)
O How large drawers are made

I   J   K   L   M   N

O

DOUBLE-LAP DOVETAILS

in sides (j) and have retaining slips beneath which also serve to widen the lower bearing surface. Fronts are cock beaded, that at the top occupying the entire thickness of the front. At the sides the beads fit in rebates which reach in as far as the laps of the dovetails. Bottom beads are also rebated in. Many concealed parts are of pine, with oak additions where wear is anticipated. Thus the divisions between the drawers are of oak about $2\frac{1}{2}$ in. wide at the front with thinner back part of pine. It is interesting to note that these divisions are jointed to the ends with plain through grooves, the whole being covered at the front with mahogany facing about $\frac{1}{8}$ in. to $\frac{3}{16}$ in. thick. Tops and bottoms are all dovetailed in, that at the top of the upper carcase being double-lap dovetailed so the joint shows as a thin line of end grain at the sides only.

The stationery nest is an independent item with mahogany drawer fronts $\frac{3}{8}$ in. thick and $\frac{1}{8}$ in. sides and back of oak. Here the bottoms (oak) fit in rebates and are flush at the bottom (l, m, and n).

Photograph of the bureau in the possession of F. G. and C. Collins, Wheathampstead.

Oak clamped chest, about 1300

From the original in the Victoria and Albert Museum.

The front and back consist each of a centre panel tenoned into heavy uprights or clamps, the joints being put together dry and held with pegs. A form of framing is used for the ends, and an interesting feature is that the framing members are so arranged that the panels slope inwards towards the top. Hingeing of the lid is by means of wood pivots, these passing through the rounded ends of the back uprights into the rear ends of the cross-members fixed beneath the top. When the lid is closed these cross-members appear as part of the end framing.

The main front panel varies in thickness but averages about 1 in. It is bare-faced tenoned into the uprights with a haunch at the top. There is no way of ascertaining the tenon length but as they are held by pegs which stand about 1 in. from the edge they must be of fair length – probably 2–2½ in. At the back a thinner panel is used and there are no shoulders to the joints – in fact the probability is that the ends of the panel form a sort of tongue.

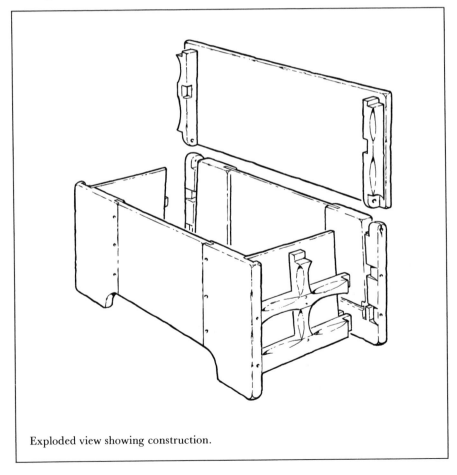

Exploded view showing construction.

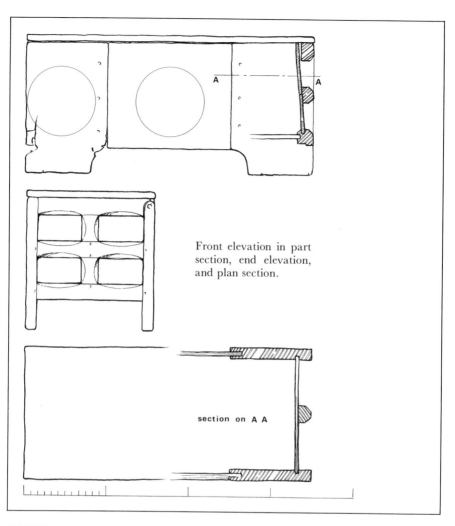

Front elevation in part section, end elevation, and plan section.

section on A A

233

Satinwood cabinet, late 18th century

The property of R. A. Salaman, Harpenden.
Height 6 ft. 5 in., width 3 ft. 1 in., depth (top carcase $9\frac{3}{8}$ in., bottom carcase $18\frac{1}{2}$ in.).

An interesting feature is the double-domed head formed by a shaped front rail rebated at the top edge, back rail straight at the bottom edge, and a thin oak filling at the top bent to shape and nailed down. The back consists of upright boards about $\frac{1}{2}$ in. thick fitting in rebates in the ends. Each door is so designed that the moulded inner edge is a semi-circle at the top, the outer edge and the cornice moulding being concentric with this. As the shoulders of the top shaped rail are vertical there is necessarily short grain running to a sharp point at the springing of the curve. Present-day practice would be to fit a sloping shoulder joint, but this was not done in the present case. The curved mouldings of the tracery are of elliptical shape, consisting of $\frac{3}{8}$ in. astragals cut in the solid and fitted over $\frac{1}{8}$ in. bars, again cut in the solid. The scratch-stock would have been used to work the mouldings. In the middle member of the cornice moulding is a dentil. Grooves to enable shelves to be fitted in various positions are cut across the upper carcase ends, and the inner front corner is moulded to give a neat finish. The bottom is lap-dovetailed in as is also the bottom of the lower carcase and the top rails. Bracket feet of ogee form are fitted, these being screwed beneath and glue-blocked in position. The lower doors consist of four pieces rub-jointed together and veneered both sides.

Mahogany chest-of-drawers, about 1790

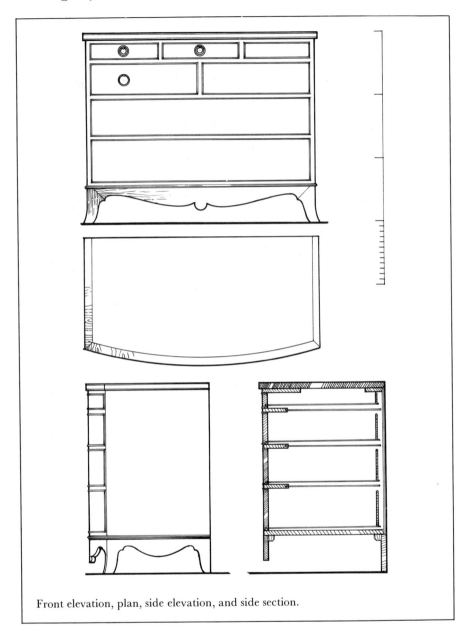

Front elevation, plan, side elevation, and side section.

Drawn from the original in the possession of F. G. & C. Collins, Wheathampstead. Height 3 ft., length 3 ft. 10 in., depth 2 ft. $\frac{1}{2}$ in.

The main carcase consists of two ends joined by a solid bottom fitting in grooves, top rails dovetailed in, and drawer rails grooved to hold dustboards. An apron piece is fitted beneath the bottom and strengthened with glue blocks at the back. To form the shaped front feet (French feet they are termed) blocks are glued into shallow recesses, the shape cut, and veneer applied. Drawer fronts are veneered on pine but sides, backs and bottoms are in oak. To support the bottoms of the large drawers a centre muntin is fitted as shown. The illustration shows the neat dovetails at the sides.

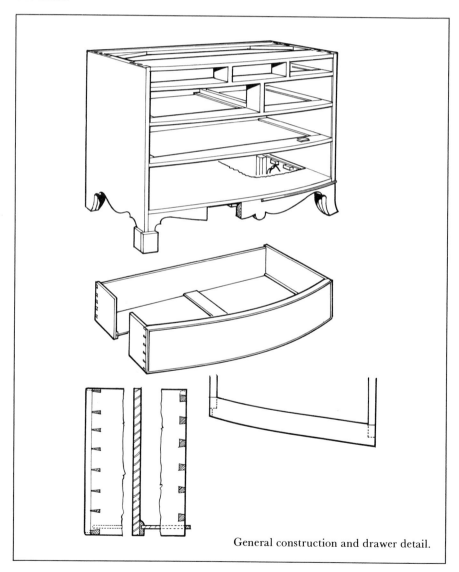

General construction and drawer detail.

Walnut chest-of-drawers, about 1700

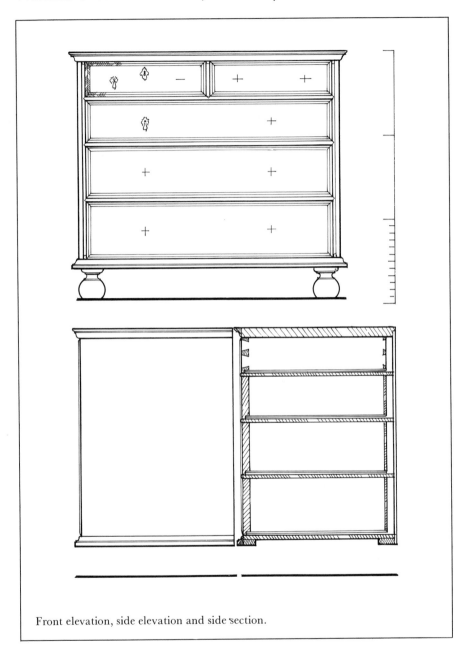

Front elevation, side elevation and side section.

Drawn from the original in the possession of F. G. & C. Collins, Wheathampstead.
Height 2 ft. 11 in., length 3 ft. 2¼ in., depth 1 ft. 10½ in. over carcase.

The entire carcase is in pine veneered with walnut. It is interesting to note that the top itself forms part of the structure, being through-dovetailed to the ends. There are no separate drawer-rails and runners but thin shelves to separate the drawers with a flat half-round moulding planted on the front edges. Drawer sides, back and bottom are in oak, the latter with the grain running from front to back. Note the rather crude through-dovetails joining the sides to the front. See photograph of the chest on page 105.

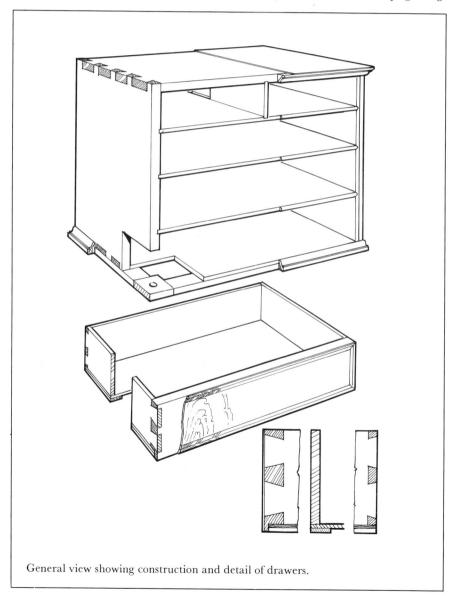

General view showing construction and detail of drawers.

Mahogany chair, 1780–90

Height 3 ft. $\frac{1}{2}$ in., width at front 1 ft. 11 in., depth about 1 ft. $6\frac{1}{2}$ in. The entire chair is in Cuban mahogany except for the loose seat framing which is not the original. The latter was probably beech. There are corner brackets at the front but these are replacements. The back legs require a width of $4\frac{1}{2}$ in. and thickness of $2\frac{5}{8}$ in. The top rail is bowed to the extent of $\frac{3}{4}$ in. Front legs are tapered on the inside only. See photograph on page 93.

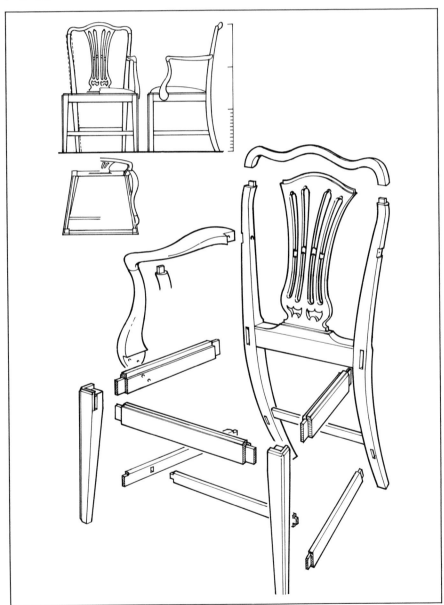

Regency chair

Measured drawing of the Regency chair shown in Fig. 48, page 143. It is in mahogany throughout except for the seat rails which are of beech. It would be somewhat expensive to make because, apart from there being quite a lot of hand work in it, it would cut into a considerable amount of timber, notably in the back legs, arms and upper back rails.

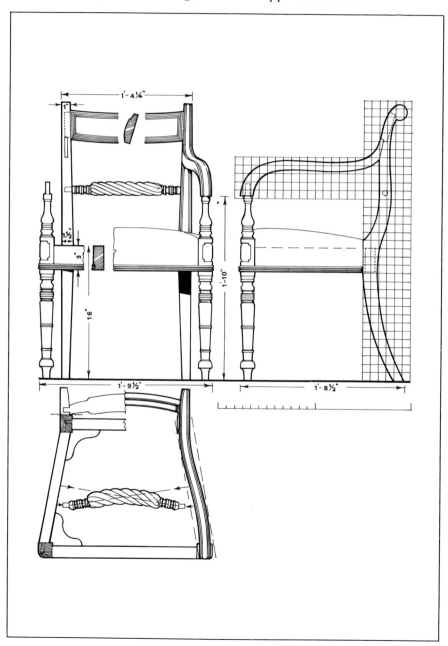

Tea table with concertina extension, about 1760

The back legs move backwards as a whole, being attached to two hinged rails. Ordinary back-flap hinges are used at two of the joints, but at the middle a special form of centre hinge with offset centres is used. To avoid accidental closing a slide about 9 in. wide runs in grooves in the side rails. The wood spring device (A) holds the legs in the closed position.

The drawing was made by the courtesy of M. Harris and Sons Ltd.

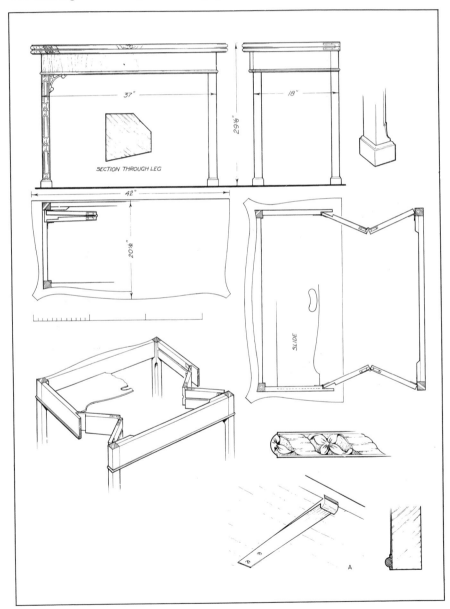

Pembroke table

Drawn from the table in possession of F. G. & C. Collins Ltd., Wheathampstead.
    Height $27\frac{3}{4}$ in., top (extended) 36 in. by $30\frac{1}{4}$ on. About 1780. Made by
Henry Kettle, St Paul's Church Yard, London. See other notes about this
cabinet-maker under Mahogany bureau, page 228.
The table is in mahogany except for the concealed structural parts which
are in oak. An interesting feature is that the bow drawer front is laminated
in three thicknesses of oak bent to shape and glued, and veneered in the
face. A $\frac{1}{16}$ in. boxwood line is inlaid at the corners of the legs and the top
and drawer front is cross-banded and also has boxwood lines.

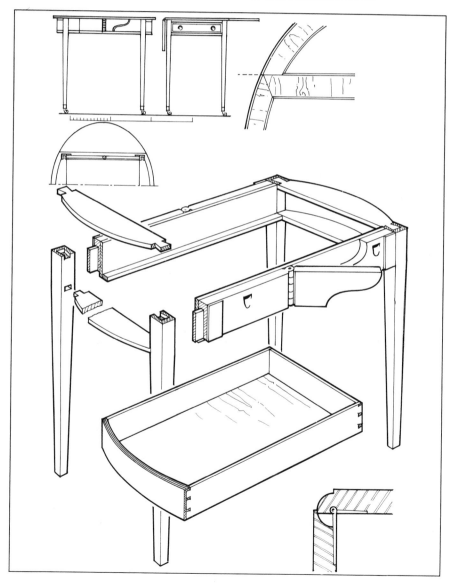

Early double-purpose reclining chair

This chair is of particular interest in that it has an early form of adjustment, the seat being hinged at the front to enable the back to be tilted backwards. It has another unusual feature, however, in that it is stamped with a registration mark (d) on the front leg at (a). This system of marking was used between the years 1842 and 1883 in an endeavour to prevent the copying of designs. This chair has the marking shown at (d), and was stamped on 8th Feb. 1843.

The back and arms are pivoted at about point (c) on specially shaped hinges which are bolted to the D-shaped frame, and are held in the reclining position by the chamfered base of the back which beds down on to the frame. In the upright position the back is held by sliding bolt (b). *The drawing was made by the courtesy of W. J. Lomas, Hepplewhite House, St. Albans.*

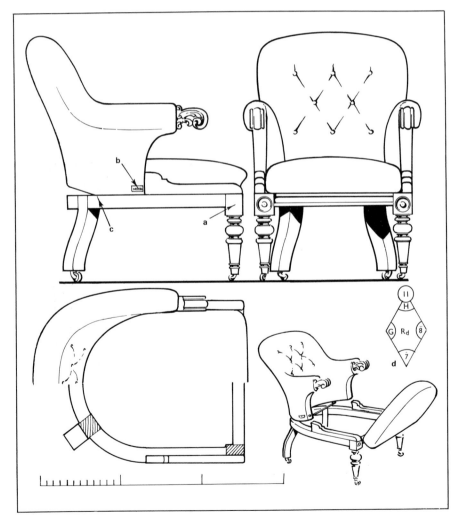

Glossary

Bare-faced tenon A tenon having a shoulder on one side only, the other side being plain. It is generally used when the tenoned piece is thinner than that with the mortise.

Betty saw A large frame saw used to cut shapes in thick wood. It was used chiefly by chair-makers and was also known as a chair-maker's saw.

Bevel An edge planed at an angle other than 90°. It occupies the entire thickness of the wood, as contrasted with a chamfer (q.v.) which extends over part of the edge only. The term is also applied to a tool for marking or testing angles other than a right angle. It consists of a stock with wood or metal tongue pivoted to it with a screw or bolt.

Bine The raised part of a spiral turning. The latter may be single, double, or triple bine. (See illustrations on page 185.)

Bolection moulding A rebated moulding which fits over the edge of a framework and thus projects from the general surface.

Bracket foot One consisting of two flat pieces cut to a decorative outline and mitred together. It was used in the late 17th century and throughout the 18th century. (See illustration on page 114.)

Bosting A wood-carving term for the main modelling of the wood with carving tools before any detail is put in.

Burr Richly figured grain, the result of a cut made across a wart-like excrescence on some trees, especially walnut. The appearance is that of closely-packed knots in wild and irregular formation. Such wood can be used in veneer form only.

Cabochon Carved decorative detail popular on mahogany furniture in the early middle years of the 18th century. It consisted of an elliptical or round raised detail,

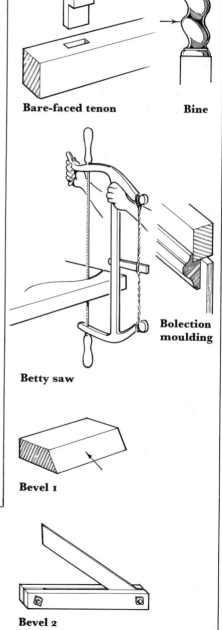

Bare-faced tenon   Bine

Betty saw

Bolection moulding

Bevel 1

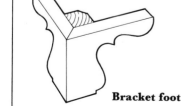

Bracket foot   Bevel 2

usually surrounded with acanthus leafage. It was frequently carved on the knees of cabriole legs.

Caul A panel of wood or of zinc backed with wood, used in the veneering process. It is heated and cramped down over the face of the veneer, its purpose being to force the veneer into close contact with the groundwork and squeeze out surplus glue.

Chamfer An angle planed at the arris of a piece of wood but not extending across the entire thickness (see also **bevel**). It is usually at 45° and may be stopped at one end or both.

Clamp One of a pair of cross pieces fitted at the ends of a panel to strengthen it across the grain. It is fixed with either tongues (q.v.) or with mortise and tenon joints. Cabinet falls, clockcase doors, etc. were frequently clamped. There is risk in the method, especially for a wide panel, unless reliable, perfectly seasoned wood is used, in that the clamps may resist shrinkage and cause a split. (See page 25.)

Club foot The bottom turned termination of a cabriole leg. It was used chiefly in the first sixty or so years of the 18th century. (See illustration under **ear piece**).

Cocked bead A small rounded moulding which projects from the surface of the work. It is usually applied to drawers and doors.

Cornice The moulding at the top of a piece of woodwork, generally above eye level. In cabinet-making, however, the term frequently includes the frieze beneath, especially in a loose or separate cornice. (See page 116.)

Curl or crotch The feather-like figure of timber cut at the junction of a branch with the main tree trunk. Owing to the wild and varied grain direction such wood can be used in veneer form only.

Dentil A small tooth-like detail used in some cornice and other mouldings. It may be either cut in the solid or applied.

Ear pieces The pieces glued at two sides of the top of a cabriole leg. They avoid an abrupt termination at the top of the leg without involving unnecessary waste in the leg itself, since they are always separate applied pieces.

Fielded panel One given a raised effect by means of a canted shallow rebate worked around the edges. It was used in the second half of the 17th century and throughout the 18th century.

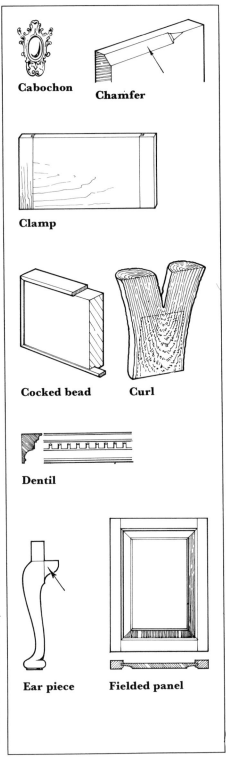

Cabochon   Chamfer

Clamp

Cocked bead   Curl

Dentil

Ear piece   Fielded panel

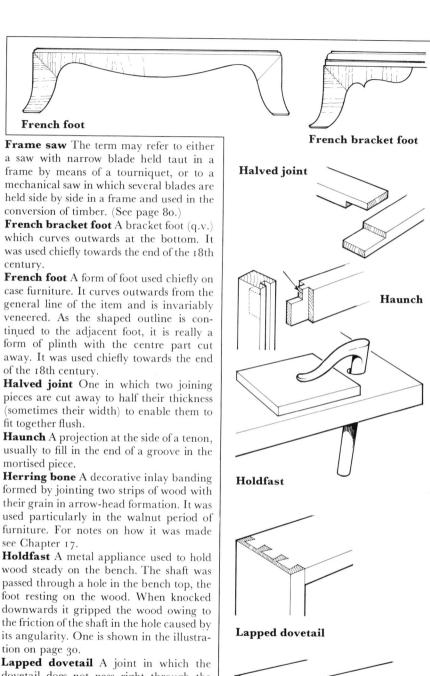

French foot

French bracket foot

Frame saw The term may refer to either a saw with narrow blade held taut in a frame by means of a tourniquet, or to a mechanical saw in which several blades are held side by side in a frame and used in the conversion of timber. (See page 80.)

French bracket foot A bracket foot (q.v.) which curves outwards at the bottom. It was used chiefly towards the end of the 18th century.

French foot A form of foot used chiefly on case furniture. It curves outwards from the general line of the item and is invariably veneered. As the shaped outline is continued to the adjacent foot, it is really a form of plinth with the centre part cut away. It was used chiefly towards the end of the 18th century.

Halved joint One in which two joining pieces are cut away to half their thickness (sometimes their width) to enable them to fit together flush.

Haunch A projection at the side of a tenon, usually to fill in the end of a groove in the mortised piece.

Herring bone A decorative inlay banding formed by jointing two strips of wood with their grain in arrow-head formation. It was used particularly in the walnut period of furniture. For notes on how it was made see Chapter 17.

Holdfast A metal appliance used to hold wood steady on the bench. The shaft was passed through a hole in the bench top, the foot resting on the wood. When knocked downwards it gripped the wood owing to the friction of the shaft in the hole caused by its angularity. One is shown in the illustration on page 30.

Lapped dovetail A joint in which the dovetail does not pass right through the thickness of the joining piece. The joint is thus concealed at one side. It was used chiefly for case funiture thoughout the 18th and 19th centuries, and for drawers.

Lapped joint One in which one piece is rebated to receive the other **a**. Sometimes both are rebated, in which case it is known as a double-lapped joint **b**.

Halved joint

Haunch

Holdfast

Lapped dovetail

Lapped joint

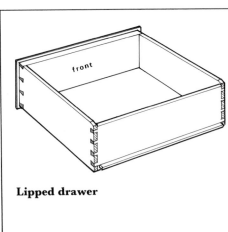

Lipped drawer

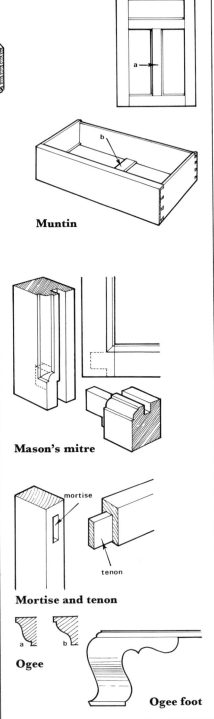

Muntin

Lipped drawer One in which the front is rebated so that it overlaps the carcase to which it is fitted. It was used chiefly in the first half of the 18th century.

Loose seat chair One having a separate seat frame which is upholstered and fits into rebates in the main chair frame.

Mason's mitre An internal mitre sometimes used in early oak woodwork. The mitre is carved in the solid wood of the mortised piece, the actual joint being square and in line with the edge of the wood. An advantage is that the mitre does not open in the event of shrinkage, but there is often unevenness at the joint itself, the result of movement in the wood.

Mortise and tenon A recess chopped in one piece of wood to receive a projection in the other (the tenon).

Muntin A vertical framing member **a** contained between two rails of a door or other framework. The term is also used for the grooved stiffening piece **b** fixed between front and back of a wide drawer to support two bottom panels. It was used when it became customary for the grain of the bottom to run from side to side rather than from front to back.

Ogee A serpentine curve. The term is usually applied to a moulding. When the hollow member is at the top it is known as a cyma recta **a**. When at the bottom it is a cyma reversa **b**.

Ogee foot A form of bracket foot (q.v.) with the outer surface curved to serpentine shape. The two sides of the foot are mitred together. It was used throughout the 18th century.

Mason's mitre

Mortise and tenon

Ogee

Ogee foot

248

Oyster shell A veneer formed by cutting a branch across the grain, either square in which case the grain is roughly circular, or at an angle when it is elliptical. Such veneers were trimmed square and placed together side by side. It was used chiefly in the walnut period. The wood might be either laburnum or walnut.

Pins Part of the dovetail joint. They are the members into which the dovetails fit. (See illustration under **through dovetail**).

Pitsaw A long two-handled saw for use on the saw pit, with one handle detachable. (See illustration on page 15.)

Plough plane A tool used to work grooves. Various widths of cutters can be fitted. (See photograph on page 27.)

Rail Almost any horizontal narrow member used in furniture, but particularly the horizontals of a door or framework. (See illustration under **stile**).

Rake The backward slope of a chair back. In early chairs the rake occurred in the upper back only, but later the back legs inclined backwards also (see page 124)

Rays Food or moisture-conducting cells which radiate from the pith of a log. In some timbers such as oak and beech they are pronounced, and when a board is cut parallel with them they appear as the typical figure or flower.

Rebate A recess worked along the edge of wood, usually to receive another part, to give clearance, or to form a joint.

Rounds and hollows Moulding planes without fence or depth stop. A round plane (see page 195) was used to work a hollow moulding, and a hollow plane for a rounded section.

Scratch-stock A tool for working mouldings, recesses for inlay bandings and strings, and sometimes for grooves. (See illustration on page 195.)

Slash sawn A method of converting timber in which parallel cuts are made through the entire log. In the case of oak only the few boards at the centre have any figure due to the rays. Also known as flat sawing.

Stile The upright member at each side of a door or other framework, as distinct from the horizontal pieces which are termed rails.

Stuff-over chair One in which the upholstery covering is taken right over the seat rails (see Fig. 35, page 137.)

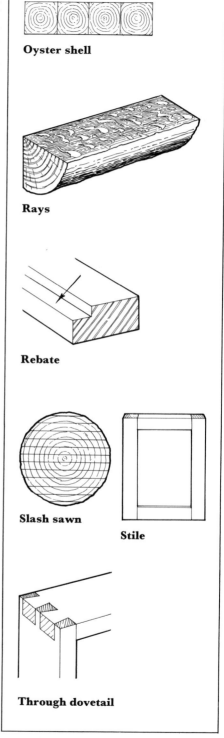

Oyster shell

Rays

Rebate

Slash sawn

Stile

Through dovetail

Tenon A projection cut at the end of wood to fit into a corresponding recess, the mortise. (See illustration under **mortise and tenon**).

Through dovetail One which passes through the entire thickness of the piece to which it is joined.

Tongue A narrow thin strip of wood used in jointing two pieces together. It may be cut in the solid, fitting into a groove in the joining piece, or it may be a separate strip, its grain running crosswise, in which case it is known as a loose tongue.

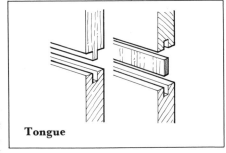

Tongue

Bibliography

Cescinsky and Gribble. *Early English Furniture and Woodwork*, 1922
Chippendale. *The Gentleman and Cabinet-maker's Director*, 1754
Edwards and Jourdain. *Georgian Cabinet-makers*, 1955
Gabriel. *Victoriana*, 1969
Gloag. *A Short Dictionary of Furniture*, 1966
Goodman, *A History of Woodworking Tools*, 1964
Goodman. *British Plane Makers from 1700*, 1968
Harris. *The Furniture of Robert Adam*, 1963
Harris & Sons. *The English Chair*, 1937
Hayward. *English Period Furniture*, 1936
Hayward. *Period Furniture Designs*, 1968
Hayward. *Practical Veneering*, 1949
Hepplewhite. *The Cabinet-maker and Upholsterer's Guide*, 1794
Ince and Mayhew. *The Universal System of Household Furniture*, 1762
Jones and Simons. *Story of the Saw*, 1961
Latham. *Timber*, 1957
Macdonald-Taylor. *English Furniture*, 1965
Negus. *Going for a Song*, 1969
Roe. *Ancient Church Chests and Chairs*, 1929
Shearer. *The Cabinet-maker's Book of Prices*, 1788
Sheraton. *Cabinet Dictionary*, 1803
Sheraton. *The Cabinet-Maker and Upholsterer's Drawing Book*, 1791
Stalker and Parker. *A Treatise of Japanning and Varnishing*, 1688
Victoria & Albert Museum. *Catalogue of English Furniture and Woodwork* (4 vols.), 1927
    Also various picture Books
Wells and Hooper. *Modern Cabinet Work*, 1922

Index